Mud, Blood, and Gold

Mud, Blood, and Gold

San Francisco in 1849

Rand Richards

Heritage House Publishers

San Francisco

Cover design by Larry B. Van Dyke.
Front cover illustrations: top, the Hounds attack; bottom, San Francisco in November 1849; photo on the left is Sam Brannan; photo on the right is John W. Geary. See Illustrations Credits, pp. 218–19 for sources. Back cover photo: Yerba Buena Cove in 1853; courtesy San Francisco Maritime National Historic Park Library.

Manufactured in the United States of America.

Heritage House Publishers
P.O. Box 194242
San Francisco, CA 94119
www.heritagehousesf.com

Library of Congress Cataloging-in-Publication Data
Richards, Rand
    Mud, blood, and gold: San Francisco in 1849 / Rand Richards. -- 1st ed.
        p. cm.
    Includes bibliographical references and index.
    ISBN 978-1-879367-06-7 (Cloth edition)
1. San Francisco (Calif.)—History—19th century.   2. San Francisco (Calif.)—Social conditions—19th century. 3. San Francisco (Calif.)– Social life and customs—19th century.   4. Frontier and pioneer life—California —San Francisco. 5. San Francicso (Calif.)—Biography. 6. California—Gold discoveries. 7. California History—1846–1850. 8. California—Biography. I. Title.
    F869.S357R535 2008
    979.4'04--dc22

                         2008011323

In loving memory of my mother

Jeanne B. Ledermann
(1928–1976)

Contents

Preface and Acknowledgments

Ask anyone who is familiar with American history to associate the year 1849 with something, and the answer is likely to be "Gold Rush." That astonishing social upheaval began with a small discovery in a remote place on January 24, 1848 when a man named James Marshall picked up a few gold nuggets from a mountain stream in the Sierra foothills in northern California. Because communication was so slow it took nearly a year for word to reach the population centers on the East Coast of the United States as well as those of other countries. But when it did, the staggeringly rich find led people from all over the world to come to California in that epic year (leading them to be tagged as "forty-niners"). All of those who came by sea, whether around Cape Horn at the southern tip of South America or through Panama, arrived at San Francisco, as many did eventually who came overland and had first gone directly to the gold region. San Francisco was ground zero for the whole avalanche of goods and cavalcade of humanity that arrived in 1849. This is the story of that time and place, and how all of the greed, lust, and violence that occurred then gave birth, in rapid fashion, to San Francisco.

The idea for this book first came to me in the mid-to-late 1990s as the 150th anniversary of Marshall's famed discovery approached. Initially I thought only of writing a magazine article, and to that end I submitted a proposal to *Smithsonian Magazine*. Six months went by before I heard anything, and when I did, it came in the form of a nice phone call from the editor I had written to saying that he liked my proposal. He expressed his regrets that the deadline had passed for their Gold Rush issue and he apologized by saying that he had been out ill for an extended period of time and had just seen my letter.

Doing the research for that proposed article planted a seed because I found myself wanting to learn more. I kept on reading about the period, and came across not only many vivid accounts but also a wealth of information that no one had previously utilized. That material had not been used because while there has been a plethora of books on the Gold Rush, this is the first that focuses solely on San Francisco in the year 1849. To that end I plumbed sources in greater depth and breadth than previous authors as I zeroed in on my topic.

Since this book paints a portrait of San Francisco as it was in the year 1849, and I wanted to use primary sources as much as possible, I naturally chose eyewitness accounts from that year. When I wasn't able to locate diaries or letters that described a representative 1849 activity, I used descriptions from other years (and in a few cases, other locales). For example, bull-versus-bear fights were held at Mission Dolores in 1849 but the only descriptions of such events that I could find were from later years. So in that case I used one from 1852. Where I have used non-1849 San Francisco accounts, I have labeled them as such.

Several of the key documents I used deserve mention. Of particular help, especially in trying to figure out the shady, self-enriching real-estate deals that leading city officials were executing in their own behalf, were the following: Alfred Wheeler's *Land Titles in San Francisco*; official city records that included the *Reports of the Alcalde, Comptroller, and Treasurer of San Francisco*; the *City Treasurer Cashbook*; and especially deed books from the period, which are in the possession of the San Francisco History Center at the San Francisco Main Library. The latter contain a mix of original, copy, and transfer deeds from the late 1840s to the early 1850s. Those large ledger-type books with crumbling leather covers contain a wealth of revealing information, such as who was selling to whom and, in some cases, the prices paid. Unfortunately, the records are not complete. It was frustrating to use the ones still extant since the handwritten records (only in 1850 did they start using printed forms) on the numbered city lots are neither in numerical nor chronological order. So it was difficult to track the chain of ownership on any specific parcel. However, by cross referencing all of the above sources with each other and with newspaper reports of the time I was able to construct enough of a picture to demonstrate just how San Francisco's alcaldes were surreptitiously converting city real estate to their own ownership.

One other source, not related to real-estate transactions, that I found especially valuable, was the House Executive Documents from the 31st Congress (1849–1850). This volume of more than 900 pages contains seemingly all of the official correspondence of the senior military officers in California in the late 1840s. It includes everything from the major proclamations of military governors Colonel Richard B. Mason and General Bennet Riley, to letters to their superiors in Washington, to missives to lesser local officials on routine matters of all kinds. The volume is a must for anyone researching the governance of the period. Also helpful, related to issues of governance and real estate, was John W. Dwinelle's *Colonial History of San Francisco*, which reprints many early official documents that no longer exist in the original.

To make the narrative as clutter free and readable as possible, I decided not to place footnote numbers in the text. I have collected all of them chapter-by-chapter in an Endnotes section at the back of the book. The endnotes are of two kinds: those that give the source of quotes; and those that I call explanatory footnotes. With the latter I repeat a sentence or phrase from the text and then provide further details.

There are many organizations and people I wish to thank for their assistance while I was bringing this book to fruition. I must start with the various libraries where I did research. I put more hours in at the San Francisco History Center on the sixth floor of the San Francisco Main Library than anywhere else. Susan Goldstein chairs that department and is ably assisted by her knowledgeable staff. Especially helpful to me was Tom Carey, who brought to my attention numerous items I might otherwise never have discovered, including some letters by John W. Geary that he had sent to his parents shortly after he arrived in San Francisco in April 1849. (How they survived and ended up in the public library is a mystery to me.) Also helpful were Jason Baxter, Mitzi Kanbara, Christina Moretta, Tami Tsuzuki, and Tim Wilson.

Second in importance for my research was the Bancroft Library at the University of California in Berkeley. Its outstanding collection contains many treasures, and the staff, operating under less than ideal conditions in temporary quarters off campus, was unfailingly cheerful and helpful.

I am very grateful to Gary F. Kurutz, Principal Librarian, Special Collections Branch, at the California State Library in Sacramento for reading the manuscript and for his enthusiasm for it. I also wish to thank Kathleen Correia and her staff in the California History Section at the California State Library for their assistance, especially in retrieving the photos and illustrations that appear herein. Other libraries and librarians I must thank include Patricia Keats and Adriane Tafoya at the Society of California Pioneers in San Francisco. I am also indebted to Mary L. Morganti, Director of the California Historical Society Library & Archives in San Francisco and her staffers Debra Kaufman and Alison Moore. Thanks also to Philip Adam, photographer at the California Historical Society.

I wished to avail myself of the great collection of Western Americana at Yale University, so I made a trip to New Haven, Connecticut and spent a productive three days at the Beinecke Library examining some choice items. I would like to thank Curator George A. Miles for the courtesies he extended, and also to thank his efficient and helpful staff. While on the East Coast I spent several days at the New York Public Library, including the Rare Book Room, where I found several useful items.

The only library containing a significant collection of Western Americana that I did not use was the Huntington Library in San Marino, California. I saved it for last, but by the time I had collected material from all of the other libraries and had done a first draft I felt that I had enough material to adequately tell the story of San Francisco in 1849. Another reason I did not visit the Huntington is that some of the best items from their collection have already been published in book form. Those include the letters of Franklin A. Buck, the memoirs of Elisha O. Crosby, and, most notably, the letters of Mary Jane Megquier, which the Huntington published in 1949 under its own imprint as *Apron Full of Gold*. So I thank the Huntington for that. I also must thank them for permission to reprint the illustration "Street in San Francisco" by Joseph Warren Revere from their collection. I am especially grateful to Peter J. Blodgett for his assistance in securing that permission and for his extra effort in arranging for a print of that image.

Individuals I need to thank include my father, Robert C. Ledermann, for his critique, Peter Browning, for copyediting the manuscript, for his loan of old newspapers and other research material, and for much useful advice in general. I also thank my friend and fellow historian Malcolm E. Barker for lending me the images from his original copy of *The Annals of San Francisco*, which are reproduced herein. And I wish to express my gratitude to Roger W. and Polly Welts Kaufman for lending me their photo of Thomas and Mary Jane Megquier.

I also want to thank Malcolm J. Rohrbough, Kevin J. Mullen, and JoAnn Levy for taking the time to read galleys and write blurbs. I thank them for their endorsements.

Other individuals I need to thank include Larry Van Dyke for his cover design, Josh Mettee of American West Books, and Steve Mettee for his advice on publishing in general, and about this book in particular. Thanks also to Linda Somma for her helpful critique, my sister Lise McGrath, Michael Hafferty, Bill Kostura, Meredith Martin, Judy Kepler of the University of New Mexico Press, and William Kooiman and the San Francisco Maritime NHP Library.

About the Author

Rand Richards is an award-winning historian. The San Francisco-based author's first two books are local bestsellers: *Historic San Francisco: A Concise History and Guide* and *Historic Walks in San Francisco: 18 Trails Through the City's Past*. He has lectured before many groups, including the California Historical Society, the San Francisco Museum and Historical Society, and the San Francisco History Association. The latter two organizations have recently honored him with awards for his contributions to knowledge of San Francisco history.

"San Francisco is an odd place; unlike any other place in creation & so it should be; for it is not created in the ordinary way, but hatched like chickens by artificial heat."

- J. K . Osgood in a letter to a friend, August 23, 1849.

Prologue

On the morning of January 24, 1848 as the first rays of the sun rose over the hills on the east side of the bay and started to lift San Francisco from the darkness, John Henry Brown was likely already up and dressed. Although not presently engaged as an innkeeper, Brown was one by trade and was used to getting up early. An Englishman, after a youth spent traveling the world (he was now 37), he had settled in San Francisco two years previously. He had just returned from Honolulu in late December, loaded with goods to sell, mainly clothing, and was staying with another innkeeper, Alfred J. Ellis, at his saloon and boarding house just a stone's throw from the water's edge. From Ellis's adobe at the north end of town he could see pretty much all of San Francisco.

The town, no more than a village really, sat on the western shore of San Francisco Bay, nestled on a crescent shaped indentation called Yerba Buena Cove. The cove was shallow near the shoreline, gradually sloping to a depth of from twelve to eighteen feet before it merged with the deeper waters of the bay. Because of this shallowness, lighterage was almost the only way that deepwater sailing vessels calling on the port could land their cargoes. Even then goods could only be rowed ashore at high tide. At low tide the receding waters left a quarter of a mile of mudflats. The cove measured about one mile in length from its northern tip at Clark's Point, just a short distance behind Ellis's house, to Rincon Point at its southern tip. The area was still so much of a wilderness that just a half a dozen years previously grizzly bears had been sighted foraging among the brush at Rincon Point.

Although the waters of Yerba Buena Cove sloped gently into the bay, the land surrounding it rose rapidly in height all around. Only a few blocks to the north was a rocky promontory nearly 300 feet high that would soon be called Telegraph Hill. To the west the land rose swiftly in height to join two nearly 400-foot-high outcroppings a half mile away: Russian Hill and Nob Hill. Surrounding the town, but especially to the south, were massive sand hills. On Market Street, and in the area of today's Union Square, some of the dunes rose to 80 feet in height, or the equivalent of an eight-story building. Vegetation was sparse. There were clumps here and there of scrub oaks, gnarly chaparral, and wind-flattened shrubbery. All in all it was not a very promising site for a city. The cove, located on the northeast corner of the San Francisco peninsula, had only been chosen as a port because the tidal currents had proved to be too swift for safety at the previous anchorage, located near the entrance to the Golden Gate. Yerba Buena Cove was the first protected anchorage ships came to after entering the bay.

Looking to the southwest from Ellis's boarding house, Brown could see, two blocks away, the public square—the Plaza, or Portsmouth Square as it was now named. Sitting on its northwest corner was the town's only government building, and one of its most impressive structures, the Custom House. It was one-and-a-half stories high, made of sun-dried adobe brick, and was capped with a Spanish tile roof. A shaded wooden veranda extended around all but the back side. The building measured 56 feet long by 22 feet wide. It contained just four rooms and had a dirt floor. In early 1848 one of those rooms served as the office of San Francisco's top official, the alcalde, a position that combined the functions of mayor, judge, and prosecutor all rolled into one.

The Custom House had been built during 1844-1845, largely with Indian labor, at the behest of the Mexican government. California had been part of Spain's empire in the Americas since the conquistadors had starting plundering Incan and Aztecan gold in the 1500s, but in 1821, with that empire crumbling, Mexico declared its independence, and California became part of the Republic of Mexico. Mexican control of California only lasted for a generation. In 1846 the United States and Mexico went to war. Most of the fighting took place in Texas, but the United States coveted California and saw the strategic importance of San Francisco Bay. To secure that asset, an American warship, the *U.S.S. Portsmouth*, under the command of Captain John B. Montgomery, arrived on July 9, 1846. Montgomery landed a squad of sailors and marines on the beach at Yerba Buena Cove. The troops met no resistance from the Mexicans, who had fled, and marched up to the Plaza where they raised the American flag on the flagpole in front of the Custom House and claimed Yerba Buena, as the town was then known, for the United

States. The Mexican Plaza was rechristened Portsmouth Square, although many residents and even newcomers would continue to refer to it as the Plaza for years afterward. (The name Yerba Buena would be changed early the following year to San Francisco to align the town with San Francisco Bay, a name starting to gain renown among seafaring men as one of the world's great harbors.)

Not far from the Custom House, trails led to two other remnants of the Spanish/Mexican era. One threaded between sand hills to the southwest and led to Mission Dolores, the Catholic mission, about two miles away. Established in 1776, the church and its supporting buildings had been largely abandoned since the California missions were secularized in the early 1830s. The Hispanic priests having departed, the only inhabitants of the complex were a few remaining Indian neophytes and some recent settlers. The other trail led three plus miles to the northwest, to the Presidio, and the site of the Spanish-era fort. It had been abandoned for about a decade by this time, and its fort, overlooking the Golden Gate, had fallen into ruin, its cannon inoperable.

A little farther up the slope from the Custom House was one of the town's other notable buildings, the Casa Grande, a one-and-a-half story adobe with dormer windows. It was erected in 1837 by William Richardson, the first resident of Yerba Buena, who had set up on the cove two years previously with nothing more for shelter than a ship's sail stretched over four posts. Richardson was an English sailor who had first arrived in 1822 and had stayed behind when his ship returned home. He had married a Mexican woman, received a grant of land on which he set up shop as a water-front trader, and dealt in hides and tallow collected from local cattle ranches to exchange for finished goods brought by ships from Boston and other far-flung ports.

The year before the Casa Grande went up, Richardson was joined by a neighbor, Jacob Leese, an American, who also married a Mexican woman, and who built a house just south of Richardson on his own grant of land. As further testament to what a wild and lonely outpost Yerba Buena was at the time, Leese recorded in his diary in 1841 that one day a mountain lion that had been prowling around for several days carried off an Indian boy who was playing in his yard.

A block down from Leese's property, just across Clay Street from the southeast corner of the Plaza, stood another large adobe, the City Hotel, which had opened in mid-1846. It was an L-shaped one-story building, with an attic punctuated by dormer windows. The long main section of the building, one hundred feet in length, which fronted on Kearny Street and faced toward the water a block away, contained a dining hall that was said to be the largest unpartitioned room in town. Besides a barroom, the structure also had a few rooms used as offices and had a billiard room with two tables that were almost constantly in use. The attic space and a few rooms on the ground floor served as bedrooms for transients, thus qualifying it as a hotel, one of only two in town.

John Henry Brown was very familiar with the City Hotel. It had originally been called Brown's Hotel because Brown had managed it until recently. But in late October 1847 he had gotten into a dispute with its owner, William A. Leidesdorff, over the lease and Brown was sent packing. After Brown's departure the name was changed to the City Hotel. Brown would soon resume managing the hotel due to unforeseen events.

From Ellis's boarding house, looking south, Brown would have seen a muddy strip along the shore dignified with the name Montgomery Street. The town's thoroughfares, no more than dirt paths surrounding the plaza and running between the buildings and lots, had recently been surveyed and named. Montgomery Street, destined from the start to be the city's main commercial artery, was named in honor of Captain John B. Montgomery of the *Portsmouth*.

At the far end of Montgomery Street, at the intersection of California Street, visible to Brown was a bungalow-style adobe house, this one belonging to William Leidesdorff, his former landlord. Leidesdorff, a sea captain and waterfront trader of partial African American descent, had been in town since 1841 and had become a prominent citizen, serving in several capacities in the fledgling city government; in early 1848 he became the town's first treasurer. Befitting his position, Leidesdorff and his common-law Russian Alaskan wife were hospitable in the Spanish/Mexican tradition and entertained frequently. Their home boasted the only flower garden in town.

Closer to Brown on Montgomery Street stood San Francisco's tallest structure at the time, the Howard & Mellus store, a two-story wood frame building painted white. Erected in 1838 by Jacob Leese, it was the first building put up on Montgomery Street. Leese had used it as a store and, although he lived up the hill, as a part-time dwelling as well. When Leese sold out in 1841 and moved to Sonoma, he sold it to the Hudson's Bay Company. When the Company's trading operation proved less profitable than anticipated, it sold the store in 1846 to Henry Mellus and William D. M. Howard, who, with a store right at the water's edge, were to profit handsomely when the throngs arrived in the wake of the gold discovery.

Just two blocks from Ellis's establishment at Jackson and Montgomery stood several other trading emporiums along the waterfront, but none as large or elaborate as the Howard & Mellus store. Scattered about town, on the blocks between Montgomery Street on the water and Kearny Street along the eastern border of Portsmouth Square, and on the surrounding slopes, were dozens of other structures—businesses and dwellings—many of them of flimsy construction.

Brown must have marveled at the growth the town had experienced just since his arrival in December 1845. Since then, with new arrivals by sea and overland, the population had doubled and then doubled again. Still, on this January morning in 1848 San Francisco's population only totaled about 800 souls.

That same morning, deep in the foothills of the Sierra Nevada, 130 miles to the east, James Marshall was inspecting the tailrace of a sawmill that was under construction. Marshall, a carpenter and millwright, had contracted to build the mill for John Sutter, a Swiss émigré and early settler who had established himself on a large land grant he called New Helvetia near the confluence of the American and Sacramento rivers in central California, halfway between the coast and the mountains. Marshall's task was to provide lumber for Sutter's growing agricultural empire, which included a fort and thousands of surrounding acres. After some searching, Marshall had located an ideal site with the right kind of trees on the South Fork of the American River next to an Indian village called Coloma. It was less than a day's horseback ride from New Helvetia.

By January 24 the mill was nearing completion. Things were satisfactory except for the tailrace, which carried the diverted water back to the river. Marshall was concerned that it was not deep enough. With the river gate closed that morning, the fast running water had ceased, giving Marshall a chance to gauge the depth of the now still water in the tailrace. Peering into the water, which was about six inches deep, Marshall saw a small, shiny object lying on the granite bedrock. Fearing he might strain his back he hesitated to reach in for it, but seeing "another glittering morsel" he plunged his hand into the icy water and pulled it out. A surge of surprise and delight rose within him: "It was a thin scale of what appeared to be pure gold." Marshall's first thought was that the gold might have been a hidden cache of some early Indian tribe, but with the discovery of other pieces he decided that the area was naturally auriferous. After collecting a few more specimens from the tailrace, Marshall went over to his workers with a smile on his face and said: "Boys, by god, I believe I have found a gold mine!" He then displayed his hat where, nestled in the crown, were the pieces of gold he had gathered.

Marshall and his workers spent the next three days scouring the riverbanks in their off hours looking for gold. More flakes and nuggets turned up. Marshall collected the lot for safekeeping and tied them up in an old rag he carried in his pocket. Excited, but little realizing the enormous impact his discovery would have, he rode off to inform Sutter.

1

Gold Fever

Marshall arrived at Sutter's Fort that same day. Sutter, surprised by Marshall's unexpected appearance in his office in an agitated state, instinctively reached for his rifle, thinking that trouble must be brewing. Marshall closed the door behind him and gestured that they were not to be disturbed. In a conspiratorial tone he told Sutter that they were both going to be rich. Just as Sutter was starting to think that his sawmill partner was a bit touched in the head, Marshall pulled the rag from his pocket and tumbled several ounces of gold on the table. Sutter was thunderstruck.

After Marshall explained the circumstances of the discovery, both men consulted an encyclopedia and decided to perform some tests to verify that the specimens were indeed gold. These included bathing them in nitric acid and weighing them on scales balanced by silver coins. The nuggets and flakes passed both tests, and the men concluded that the shining metal was pure gold. Sutter was initially as excited as Marshall by the find, but he quickly recognized that if word got out about the gold discovery it would not only jeopardize the completion of the sawmill but also his growing agricultural empire. If his employees found out, they would be sure to head for the hills to hunt for gold.

A few days later Sutter went to Coloma to see the situation first hand. Convinced of the richness of the find he asked the sawmill laborers to keep word of the gold discovery to themselves for six weeks or at least until the mill was finished. But by early February news of the discovery was starting to leak. Sutter himself broke his own command by writing to his friend and neighboring large landholder, Mariano Vallejo, to tell him about the "extraordinarily rich" gold mine he had found. And when Jacob Wittmer, a Mormon teamster in Sutter's employ returned from Coloma after running an errand there, and tried to pay for a bottle of whiskey at a store at Sutter's Fort with some gold he had brought back, Sutter confirmed to the skeptical owner, Charles Smith, that it was indeed gold.

Part of the reason Sutter asked the sawmill workers to hold off telling anyone is that he wanted to claim the land for his own before outsiders arrived. So he bought off the local Indians with payment of some goods in exchange for a lease to the surrounding land. What he really needed was the military governor's permission. To that end he sent an emissary, Charles Bennett, off to Monterey to ask for a preemption claim. Bennett, told not to tell anyone about his mission, nevertheless couldn't resist, and on the way, stopped in San Francisco where he showed a tin box of nuggets to John Henry Brown and a few others. But the gold evoked little interest. Minor amounts of gold had been used in trade in San Francisco before, so there was no reason yet to think that this was a big deal. Only a man named Isaac Humphrey, who had mined some gold in Georgia, took notice. He accompanied Bennett to Monterey.

The pair duly arrived in Monterey, at that time the capital of California, but a town with a population of only a few hundred people clustered around a handful of Mexican-era adobes near the shore of Monterey Bay. After stating that they wanted an audience with the governor *in person* they were introduced to Colonel Richard Barnes Mason. The colonel was governor of California by virtue of being the ranking military officer in charge of land forces on the West Coast. Mason came from a distinguished Virginia family: his grandfather, George Mason, was the author of the Virginia Bill of Rights. Handsome, and of straight-backed military bearing, Mason was 51 years old and near the end of his career. He was honest, conscientious, and incorruptible—no small qualities to have in a region where rampant greed, spurred by gold, would quickly come to the fore. He also was a by-the-book officer. A story told by Walter Colton, the alcalde of Monterey, was that when two convicted murderers were hanged and the knots in the ropes slipped allowing the men to wriggle free, the priest who had heard their confessions asked Mason to spare their lives as it was a sign from God. Mason replied that the men had been sentenced to hang by the neck until dead and that the appeal to God would have to wait until after the sentence was successfully carried out.

Mason's adjutant, and chief staff officer, shared many of Mason's qualities. He was Lieutenant William Tecumseh Sherman. Sherman, a graduate of West Point, had, like Mason, arrived in Monterey early in 1847 to participate in California's role in the Mexican War. Sherman would have preferred to be in Texas, where the front lines of the war were and where his comrades were earning honors and promotions. The young lieutenant would rise through the ranks and later go on to see plenty of fighting and earn great fame during the Civil War, most notably for his march through Georgia and his laying waste of the South. But as he stood in Mason's office in February 1848 he was an unknown 28-year-old junior army officer.

When presented with the nuggets from Coloma, Mason and Sherman, like Marshall and Sutter before them, performed various tests and concluded that the samples were genuine gold. Mason however turned down Sutter's request for a preemption grant. He sent a letter back to Sutter with the emissaries explaining that because California was still a province of Mexico no U. S. laws could be applied. And furthermore, he noted, even if it had been U. S. soil a survey would first have to be done. On the return trip Isaac Humphrey stopped in San Francisco and constructed a crude gold-washing device called a cradle and headed to the American River. Charles Bennett returned to New Helvetia to give Sutter the disappointing news.

Meanwhile, at Sutter's Fort, Charles Smith, who had been reluctant at first to accept gold in payment for a bottle of whiskey, was now receiving more and more in the way of raw gold in payment for his store's goods. He sent word to his partner in San Francisco, a man who was destined to play a leading role in early San Francisco: Samuel Brannan. A commanding figure with a resonant speaking voice, Brannan was just shy of six feet tall, with "large, alert brown eyes" and thick, wavy black hair. He had arrived at San Francisco (then Yerba Buena) on July 31, 1846 on the *Brooklyn*, a ship carrying 234 passengers—men, women, and children—nearly all of them Mormons, of which, despite being only 27 years old, he was the chief elder and leader. They had left New York nearly six months before, intending to settle in a virgin land far from the persecution their sect had experienced in the United States. To Brannan's dismay they arrived in California just weeks after the American conquest. The arrival of Brannan and his Mormons had instantly doubled the hamlet's population to about 400, making San Francisco for a brief time a Mormon town. Brannan and his flock adapted readily to the new reality. The Mormons were welcomed because they did not try to convert the locals to their religion, and even more because they had brought with them much needed agricultural and mechanical tools as well as three grain mills. Brannan, a journeyman printer, had also brought along a printing press. With it he established the town's first newspaper, the *California Star*, which published its first issue on January 9, 1847.

In early April 1848, in response to his partner's news, Brannan went from San Francisco to Sutter's Fort to see for himself. It is not clear exactly when Brannan first received word of the gold discovery, but both his *California Star* and the town's other newspaper, the *Californian*, had published articles the previous month giving news of the event for the first time. The *Californian* was first off the mark when it published a news article on March 15 that was headlined simply "Gold mine found." It noted that one person had collected thirty dollars worth of gold in only a short time. The brief piece concluded with the sentence "Gold has been found in every part of the country," a bit of hyperbole that would soon prove to be largely accurate. But this and several other news items over the next few weeks about increasing amounts of gold being found were greeted with skepticism. Alcalde Colton perhaps put his finger on the reason why when he wrote of the populace: "They could not conceive that such a treasure could have lain there so long undiscovered."

At Sutter's Fort, Brannan saw that plenty of gold was freely circulating in exchange for goods. He rode to Coloma for a closer look. Many of his fellow Mormons, some who were part of Marshall's original sawmill crew, were happily digging away, turning up more and more gold. Even more convinced of the richness of the find he purchased a store there to complement the one he shared with his partner at Sutter's Fort. He also filled a quinine bottle with dust and nuggets.

Brannan returned to San Francisco on May 10. After landing at the cove he strode ashore and, with a flair for the dramatic, he waved his hat and held his bottle of gold aloft and shouted "Gold! Gold! Gold from the American River," as a crowd gathered. Brannan was well positioned to profit from his announcement with his two stores stocked with shovels, pans, and other goods gold miners would need, so that was no doubt a factor in his grandiose gesture. But he also was a naturally ebullient person who might just have been carried away by his own enthusiasm. Whatever the case, from that moment on, all doubts vanished. The pendulum swung completely in the other direction and skepticism was supplanted by "gold fever."

San Franciscans lost no time in outfitting themselves for the trip to the gold region, snapping up pickaxes, hoes, vials, and brass tubes, "the latter for holding the prospective treasure." And in the first of many examples of the topsy-turvy economy that the Gold Rush would spawn in San Francisco, shovels jumped in price from one dollar to six dollars, even ten dollars or more apiece. Thus supplied, within days a good chunk of the town's population had departed. With so few bodies left in town the cost of labor rose tenfold. Real estate plummeted in value. (The thinking was that the action would move to Sacramento and the Sierra Nevada foothills.)

When the word reached Monterey a few weeks later the reaction was similar. Alcalde Colton, who had a flair for words—he called the gold mines "nature's great bank"—described the exodus this way: "... the blacksmith dropped his hammer, the carpenter his plane, the mason his trowel, the farmer his sickle, the baker his loaf and the tapster his bottle. All were off for the mines, some on horses, some on carts, and some on crutches, and one went in a litter."

In San Francisco, with virtually no readers left, the town's newspapers shut down. The first was the *Californian* on May 29. It closed with an article expressing its exasperation:

> The whole country from San Francisco to Los Angeles and from the seashore to the base of the Sierra Nevada, resounds to the sordid cry of *gold! GOLD!! GOLD!!!* while the field is left half planted, the house half-built, and everything neglected but the manufacture of shovels and pickaxes. . . .

In early June, Lieutenant Sherman convinced Governor Mason that as the leading official in California he had a duty to investigate the gold phenomenon further. Both men saddled up and departed Monterey on June 17. They arrived in San Francisco three days later and found the town almost deserted. Nearly all the male inhabitants had gone to the mines. As they proceeded on to Sutter's Fort they found "mills were lying idle, fields of wheat were open to cattle and horses, houses vacant, and farms going to waste." At Sutter's Fort however things were bustling. As the major jumping-off point to the gold region, launches were discharging passengers and cargo, merchants were doing brisk business, and a two-story hotel had just opened.

Mason and Sherman proceeded quickly to the gold camps of the American River, where they spent about a week in early July. The banks of the river were strewn with tents and rude brush shelters. Mason estimated that overall about 4,000 men were engaged in washing gold. "Even the ragged Indians are on their knees worshiping the common idol," Sherman noted with disgust. Indeed, Mason estimated that over half of the miners were Indians. Most, at least initially, were employed by whites and were paid in food and merchandise. Mason was told that two white men had employed four other whites and about 100 Indians and in only one week's time had cleared $10,000 in gold after paying off their workers. At Coloma, Mason met with gold discoverer James Marshall, who told the governor that the miners in his area were averaging from one to three ounces of gold a day, or from $16 to $48. (By way of comparison, the average wage in the U. S. at the time was about $1 to $2 a day.) Marshall's claim may have been exaggerated, or perhaps miners in his area were luckier than most, but based on these stories and many similar tales of success, Mason conservatively estimated that overall from $30,000 to $50,000, if not more, was being obtained daily by the 4,000 gold diggers currently working in the Mother Lode.

Mason left the gold country greatly impressed. In his report to his superiors in Washington describing what he had seen he estimated that "there is more gold in the country drained by the Sacramento and San Joaquin Rivers than will pay the cost of the present war with Mexico a hundred times over." And he put his finger on just why California gold would prove so alluring to individuals all over the world: "No capital is required to obtain this gold, as the laboring man wants nothing but his pick and shovel and tin pan . . . many frequently pick gold out of the crevices of rocks with their knives. . . ."

One man who needed not even a pen knife to gather much more gold than most miners was Sam Brannan. Mason stopped at Brannan's store at Sutter's Fort on his return trip to Monterey and found that the store had taken in $36,000 in gold in payment for goods from May 1 to July 10, or an average of over $500 a day. More than half of that was pure profit.

And considering profits, one thing Mason pondered during his Mother Lode visit was whether and how the U. S. Government might benefit from all the gold being plucked from its land. He wondered whether rents or fees might be imposed on the miners but he quickly rejected the idea, realizing that the small force he had under his command was inadequate to enforce any such imposition, especially over an area so vast and remote. Furthermore his troop levels were diminishing rapidly; soldiers and sailors were deserting, since they were just as susceptible to gold fever as anyone else, perhaps more so. It was tough to appeal to their sense of duty when they could make more digging for gold in a few months or even weeks than they would make in five years of military service.

Once back at Monterey, Mason prepared his report to his superiors in Washington. At the end of August he sent one of his lieutenants, Lucien Loeser, to Panama and on to the East Coast with the report. Accompanying Loeser and the report was a tea caddy filled with close to 230 ounces of gold that Mason had purchased (with government funds) at the mines.

In San Francisco another army officer, Captain Joseph L. Folsom, who had accompanied Mason and Sherman to the diggings, heard many more stories from returning miners that confirmed what he had already seen for himself. Folsom, 31 years old, and like Sherman a graduate of West Point, had arrived in town in March 1847 as quartermaster for Colonel Jonathan D. Stevenson's First Regiment of New York Volunteers. The regiment had been formed in New York the previous year to go to California to supplement regular army troops during the Mexican War. When the war ended in 1848 the regiment was disbanded in August of that year, and many of the troops, Stevenson included, decamped for the gold country. Folsom did not. He remained in San Francisco as Collector of the Port, in charge of collecting customs duties from ships that were arriving with increasing frequency at Yerba Buena Cove. Folsom daily met people who had been gone to the mines less than three months and had returned with anywhere from $200 to $5,000 in gold dust. One man told Folsom that he and four other men had dug 17 pounds of gold, avoirdupois weight, in only seven days, which meant that with gold pegged at that time at $16 an ounce, their pile was worth over $4,300. And to prove it they showed him the gold. Folsom met many others who had been making from $25 to $40 a day, and he knew of a few who had obtained as much as $800 to $1,000 of gold in a day. Writing in September to one of his many correspondents, Folsom estimated that by the three months ending September 1848 over $500,000 of gold would have left California, most of it going to foreign markets to buy goods and supplies. All the gold he saw led him to conclude: "I see no prospect of exhausting the mines."

Just as a stone thrown into the center of a pond creates ripples that spread in an ever widening arc to the shore, news of "gold in fabulous quantities . . . to be had for the mere digging . . ." started reaching other lands. Word reached Honolulu on June 17 on a ship that stopped there to pick up supplies. Since the Hawaiian Islands were a Pacific crossroads, the news spread from there to countries all around the Pacific Rim. Oregon heard of the gold discovery shortly after—from a ship that arrived there from Honolulu. Sonora, Mexico got wind of the discovery about the same time. Many Sonorans were experienced miners. They were quick to head overland. They clustered at the southern end of the Mother Lode, where they gave the gold-rush town of Sonora, California its name. South America, most notably Chile, first got the news in August from a ship that had arrived in Valparaiso from San Francisco.

Word started to reach the eastern seaboard in late summer. California Mormons had brought the news to their brethren in Salt

Lake; from there, eastbound travelers carried it on with them. The *New York Herald* was the first newspaper on the East Coast to publicize the gold discovery when it ran a small article on August 19. The *Baltimore Sun* followed on September 20. These initial reports were greeted with skepticism. Most felt that the stories were exaggerated, that it was a "humbug" designed to get people to emigrate to a distant and desolate land. On September 27 the *Herald*, in an editorial, allowed that golden dreams would excite the imaginations of many, but it cautioned:

> To all such we would say, beware of the mania of hasty money-making; beware of seeking to become rich by sudden and extraordinary means; be assured that all the gold in the world will not make you happy.

This kind of prescient self-assured moralism would not only soon be ignored but quickly swept away. Indeed, despite its own admonitions, over the next two months the *Herald*, and other papers, would continue to stoke the fires by printing stories extolling the rich finds of gold being made.

In San Francisco during the summer and fall of 1848 innkeeper John Henry Brown was one busy individual. Shortly after returning from Honolulu six months previously, to get back into the hospitality business, Brown had partnered with Robert A. Parker, a recent arrival from Boston, and the two of them started construction across from the east side of the Plaza on what would become the town's premier hotel and gambling emporium, the Parker House. The foundation, the frame, and the weather boarding were in when construction came to an abrupt halt as news of the gold discovery emptied the town. Work on it only resumed when would-be miners, who found that gold digging was harder work than they had expected, filtered back to San Francisco. But the scarcity of labor meant that they still held the whip hand: carpenters could command as much as $20 a day. Construction costs on the Parker House quickly mounted to $3,000 a week.

Brown was able to help finance these expenses because of what was for him a fortuitous event. His former lessor at the City Hotel,

William Leidesdorff, had died unexpectedly in May. After leading merchant William D. M. Howard was appointed administrator of Leidesdorff's estate, Brown was invited back to manage the City Hotel. He resumed his duties there on July 4, which coincided with a grand Independence Day celebration.

By late summer and into the fall the City Hotel was starting to do a brisk business as miners came down from the hills for supplies and new arrivals came by sea. It was all Brown could do to keep his guests supplied with food and drink. On at least one occasion he recalled giving a departing ship captain 20 pounds of gold dust in bottles to bring back food and drink from Honolulu. The scarcity of everything except for fresh beef meant high prices for meat and produce. Small roasting pigs cost from $10 to $15, eggs were $6 to $9 a dozen, potatoes 75 cents apiece, onions one dollar, fresh butter $1.50 a pound. Brown employed a local man who brought him lettuce, cabbages, carrots, and turnips from a vegetable garden near the mission at a cost of $15 to $20 a day.

The costs were high but the markups were even higher. Baskets of champagne that he purchased at from $24 to $30 he sold for $120. Patrons didn't seem to mind paying such high prices, especially for liquor, which was in great demand; by late 1848 the barroom alone of the City Hotel was bringing in $2,500 to $3,000 a day. Driving this prodigious spending in part was a peculiar psychology: gold was becoming so plentiful it started to depreciate. Although the price had been officially pegged at $16 an ounce at a town meeting in September, its price dipped as low as $6 to $8 an ounce at times. With this kind of downward spiral, traders feared that gold dust would depreciate even further, so they spent it freely instead of hanging on to it. This redounded to Brown's benefit, because while it may have been plentiful in San Francisco it was not elsewhere; gold that Brown was buying at $8 an ounce was purchasing goods in Honolulu at double that value.

Brown was making money not just from liquor sales. Rentals from gambling tables in the hotel increased his take as well. Originally he had installed a few billiard tables, but as the guests tired of billiards they clamored for some real action: gambling. Eight tables were put in. Brown collected $200 a day plus hourly charges for the use of them. Office and hotel room rentals brought in further revenue. By November the City Hotel was crowded to capacity with over 160 lodgers. There were two beds to a room and both beds were occupied night and day: gamblers slept in them during the day, others at night. With all these sources of revenue, by one estimate, the City Hotel was bringing in $4,000 to $5,000 a day.

With gold flooding the town, exuberant high spirits came to the fore. One day in late 1848 one of Brown's lodgers, Isaac Montgomery, a local merchant and auctioneer, approached the innkeeper with a request. Astride his horse, and fueled by liquor, he asked Brown how much it would cost him to ride his steed through the window into the hotel's barroom. Thinking it would dissuade him, Brown quoted the exorbitant price of $500. No sooner had the words left Brown's mouth than Montgomery threw a bag of gold dust at his feet and shouted: "Weigh out your $500, and take enough out for a basket of wine." Before Brown could reach for the bag both horse and rider came crashing through the barroom window.

At about the same time, gold fever was heating up on the East Coast. Colonel Mason had sent two couriers east with copies of his report on his findings in the Mother Lode. Only Lt. Loeser had samples of gold with him, but a second courier, sans gold but with a duplicate copy of the report, arrived in Washington, D. C. in late November, ahead of Loeser. Mason's report, with its glowing accounts, quickly leaked to the press. On December 5, lame-duck president James K. Polk delivered his last message to Congress, and with it he mentioned the California gold discovery: "The accounts of the abundance of gold in that territory are of such an extraordinary character as would scarcely command belief were they not corroborated by the authentic reports of officers in the public service." Two days later Lt. Loeser arrived, and the 230 ounces of gold he was carrying were put on display at the War Department where the public formed long lines to take a look. Polk's message, along with the gold as proof, instantly changed the talk of California gold from rumor to fact. The word spread like wildfire up and down the East Coast. Skeptics were transformed into true believers. Newspapers fanned the flames. The *New York Herald* on December 12 reported the results: "The gold mania rages with intense vigor, and is carrying off its victims hourly and daily."

One of those who caught the contagion was 22-year-old New York City resident Franklin Buck. Like many others he had heard fabulous tales: of gold diggers making $50 to $100 a day; of one man finding a nugget worth $4,000. Then he saw some of the gold himself and gold fever hit with a vengeance. Seeing others outfitting themselves to go off to California he wrote to his sister in Maine telling her about those "$4,000 lumps" he was going to pick up and send back to her. Buck no doubt echoed the thoughts of many when he confided to his sister: ". . . there is something about it—the excitement, the crossing the Isthmus, seeing new countries and the prospect of making a fortune in a few years—that takes hold of the imagination, that tells me 'Now is your chance. Strike while the iron is hot!'" By early January Buck was ready to go. As his ship pulled away from the dock a fellow passenger threw his last $5 gold piece ashore exclaiming "I am going where there is plenty more!" Buck was exuberant as well: "It beats all! I declare, this California fever."

Back in San Francisco as the year 1848 drew to a close, miners from the Sierra foothills were returning to town to wait out the winter rains. The city's population rose to about 2,000. Infrastructure and services however were practically nonexistent. The "streets" were little more than ill-defined trails between the buildings, and were turning into muddy ravines with each rainfall. There were no sewers and no sidewalks. Clean drinking water was hard to find. Decent sleeping accommodations were scarce and expensive. Rats and fleas were ubiquitous. The city's government was embryonic and feuding. The "police force" consisted of exactly one lone constable. San Francisco was totally unprepared for the hordes that were about to arrive.

2

Arrival

Once confirmation of the gold strike reached the East Coast, news of the remarkable discovery quickly spread to Europe. Untold thousands of emigrants from the British Isles would form the largest group of European sojourners to California, followed by those from the German states. French Argonauts made up the third largest contingent, but what they lacked in numbers they made up for in enthusiasm. Many French were only too eager to leave France: the country had been convulsed by revolution in 1848 and was suffering a subsequent economic depression.

On the other side of the world, countries at the far edge of the Pacific Rim had received the gold news earlier than their European brethren. Word had reached Australia late in 1848; the first ships to depart for San Francisco left in January 1849 (and arrived in early April). China had heard the news even earlier, but the Chinese were at first slow to respond. Several hundred would arrive in time to be categorized as "forty-niners," but it wouldn't be until the 1850s before the Chinese started to emigrate in large numbers to *Gam Saan* or "Gold Mountain." Only Japan remained unaffected. The country had largely been closed for two centuries: the emperor forbade Japanese citizens to emigrate.

Although the gold rush would prove to be an international event, Americans made up the bulk of the emigrants who made it to California in 1849. The exact numbers from all countries will never be known, but the estimate of total arrivals by sea ranged from a conservative 20,000 to more than 41,000, while those who came across the plains numbered anywhere from 30,000 to 50,000. Americans made up perhaps 75 percent of the combined totals.

There were three major ways for Americans to get to California in 1849: overland, typically by ox-drawn covered wagons across the central plains (although smaller numbers took the southern route through the desert southwest to southern California); by sea from East Coast ports southbound through the Atlantic Ocean and around Cape Horn or through the Strait of Magellan at the tip of South America, then north through the Pacific Ocean and up the West Coast; and thirdly by sea from Atlantic ports through the Gulf of Mexico to Panama, then by boat and horseback across the Isthmus to the west side and then by sea again up the coast to California. The latter two routes finished their journeys directly at San Francisco.

Each route had its advantages and disadvantages. The main overland route was the logical choice for those who lived closest to the primary jumping off points at Independence and St. Joseph, in western Missouri. It had an advantage in that a trail had been established for almost a decade before the gold rush began; small parties of emigrants had already made the trek to Oregon or Mexican California. This was also the shortest route in terms of physical distance traveled at about 2,000 miles, but it was not the fastest since it took four months or more to make it to the diggings in the Sierra foothills. Going overland offered other advantages: it was the cheapest way to go, since one could generally spend less than $200 to provide for all one's needs for the length of the journey. And one could take a lot of belongings. Travelers on the overland route also had more in the way of freedom of movement—they weren't confined to a small space as were the shipboard passengers.

There were numerous drawbacks to the journey by land. One was the fear of attack by Indians, although that turned out to be mostly just that, fear, since very few wagon trains were actually assaulted. (What was more of a problem was Indian thievery, especially of livestock.) A more serious concern was the disease cholera, which was prevalent on the trail in 1849. Less threatening, but debilitating nonetheless, was the reality that although virtually all the emigrant parties used wagons drawn by oxen, mules, or horses, many land travelers ended up walking most of the way to California because there wasn't much room for passengers along with the goods the wagons had to carry. And after months of monotony and fatigue crossing the plains the hardest part of the long journey came in the final weeks. The Argonauts first had to cross the alkali deserts of present-day Utah and Nevada, a grueling trek featuring heat, dust, and thirst. They then had to face the arduous climb over the Sierra Nevada to reach the gold fields on the other side. Travelers were forced to keep up the pace: many were aware of the fate of the Donner party of 1846, which had gotten caught in early snows as they scaled the Sierra summit and became trapped in the mountains until the following spring. Out of food, the survivors had resorted to cannibalism of their dead comrades to stay alive.

A sea voyage around Cape Horn proved alluring for residents of Boston, New York, and other ports on the East Coast. The main advantages were that one had guaranteed accommodations, meals were served at regular hours, and little labor was required; there was plenty of time for leisure activities. A major drawback was that it was the longest journey of all the routes at nearly 13,000 miles. It consequently took longer to get there, anywhere from four to eight months, although a few unlucky ships took almost a year before they reached San Francisco. The routine of shipboard life took its toll on passengers who had to endure an unvarying and innutritious diet, and cramped conditions, which sometimes led to flaring tempers. It was also, at times, a dangerous journey, especially in trying to navigate the treacherous waters of storm-plagued Cape Horn at the tip of South America.

The main advantage to the Isthmus of Panama route was that it was the fastest. Although it was a journey of about 5,500 miles—nearly three times the length of the overland route—travelers via Panama could make it to San Francisco in as little as six to eight weeks if there were no delays in making their connections. That wasn't always the case since there were usually lots of travelers waiting on the west coast of Panama for the ships making their infrequent runs northward. Being the fastest way to California also meant that it was, in most cases, the most expensive. But for those passengers who could afford the $350 to $400 price of a first-class ticket they could enjoy better food and sleeping quarters than those who traveled via Cape Horn. The main risks to traveling the Panama route, especially the land-based portion through Panama itself, were the oppressive jungle conditions, including encounters with snakes and voracious mosquitoes, and the chance of contracting malaria or other tropical diseases.

Whatever route the forty-niners took it proved to be a memorable adventure, something they would never forget. That is, for those who made it safely to California; untold numbers died on each of the routes, their bodies either buried in shallow graves or consigned to the watery depths.

Those who made the journey, especially those who came by Cape Horn or the Isthmus, were almost exclusively men. Few official records were being kept in 1849, but San Francisco's harbor master, Edward A. King, logged arrivals by sea and found that between April 12 and November 28, 1849, of the 25,500 people who had landed during that period, only 667, or 3 percent, were women. Single men constituted the majority, many of whom were off on a nothing-to-lose youthful adventure, but substantial numbers were married, some with children. Virtually all of the latter however were traveling without their families. One reason men didn't bring their families was practical: the journey was expensive, there was danger along the way, and they knew they would encounter primitive conditions once they got to San Francisco and the gold fields. The other major reason for leaving their wives and children at home was the prevailing mindset: they did not intend to stay. Their goal was to make their "pile" and return home with their riches.

Those arriving in 1849 may have come from different backgrounds and from all points of the globe but they shared one thing in common: they were overwhelmingly young. Most were under 30; some were in their teens. To underscore just how young they were, when pioneer merchant Nathan Spear (for whom Spear Street is named) died of heart disease in October at age 47, his obituary in a local paper, the *Alta California,* was headlined "Death of the Oldest Inhabitant of San Francisco." Despite the youthfulness of the city's population many of the new arrivals were not only men of means—after all, passage to San Francisco wasn't cheap—they were also in many cases quite accomplished. Some had abandoned successful businesses or professions back home to try their luck in California. A fair number had college degrees, a few even from Harvard and Yale, and thus were highly literate, which is fortunate for the historical record since hundreds of forty-niners kept journals and wrote letters documenting their experiences.

All throughout that landmark year, as gold fever spread world-wide, more and more people arrived in San Francisco. Descriptions of the town vary according to when exactly a person came; later arrivals found a more crowded, bustling city than earlier ones. But many general impressions were similar. For those who sailed through the Golden Gate the initial reaction was one close to euphoria. After a long voyage (especially those who had come around the Horn) passengers' spirits invariably rose as they prepared to land and get their first look at the famed El Dorado. The large, magnificent bay of San Francisco impressed nearly everyone. Off in the distance, especially on the hills to the east and the north, cattle could be seen grazing peacefully in a pastoral landscape. The view of San Francisco itself however was less appealing. Mahlon Fairchild, who arrived in July from New York, noted: "Great sand dunes were piled over the landscape from ocean to bay. . . ." They shifted their position in the stiff breeze "like snow drifts in a mountain gale." Franklin Buck, who had departed New York in January and whose ship anchored in Yerba Buena Cove in August, during the dry season, wrote: "The whole country is yellow, not a green thing to be seen and not a tree." Another observer, echoing the lack of any substantial vegetation, felt that "a large, luxuriant elm would attract more attention in San Francisco than a menagerie or circus."

Sailing ships arrived in San Francisco on virtually a daily basis throughout 1849, but the first steamship to reach port called for a special celebration. That ship was the *California*, and it cast anchor in Yerba Buena Cove on February 28. It owed its existence not to the gold rush but to California's becoming part of the United States in the wake of the Mexican War. As that conflict was winding down, but before James Marshall's fabled discovery, Congress, wishing to provide civilian transport and mail service to its newly conquered province, authorized the establishment of a seagoing transportation line on the West Coast. Six-figure subsidies were offered as an inducement. The Pacific Mail Steamship Company was formed, and three side-wheel wooden steamships were built to serve the West Coast between Panama and San Francisco: the *California*, the *Oregon*, and the *Panama*. (Other steamers provided the connection between Atlantic ports and Chagres on the east coast of Panama.)

The *California* left New York on its maiden voyage around the Horn in early October 1848. It was carrying only about a quarter of its complement of 210 passengers. By the time it reached Panama City on the West Coast in mid-January the news of the gold discovery was out. Chaos reigned as it approached the port: as many as 700 Americans were crowding the shore, clamoring for passage to San Francisco. Not only couldn't the ship accommodate nearly that many, but in stopping at Callao, Peru on the way to Panama City it had taken on 69 Peruvian gold seekers. Irate that foreigners were going to beat them to the gold—American gold—the Americans demanded that the Peruvians be put off the ship. Instead, a compromise was reached whereby the Peruvians left their cabins but were allowed to sleep on the open deck for the remainder of the voyage. Over 300 Americans clambered aboard.

One of the Americans boarding at Panama was General Persifor Smith, who was reporting for duty in California as the senior army officer for the western command. In an attempt to quell the Americans' anger he issued a written edict prohibiting non-citizens from carrying off "gold belonging to the United States in California." Smith had no legal authority to take such action nor the means to enforce it, what with troop levels dwindling due to desertions. Furthermore, his proclamation was in contradiction to Governor Mason's earlier "open door" policy, which had declared that the lands were open to everyone. What Smith's statement did do was to give an official stamp of approval to anti-foreign, nativist sentiment that was already emerging. This would lead to the driving out of Latin Americans from the Mother Lode gold camps and indirectly to a crime spree and riot in San Francisco that summer instigated by a gang of hoodlums known as the "Hounds."

With the immediate situation resolved, the *California*, now carrying roughly 400 passengers, nearly double its authorized capacity, chugged away from Panama City and northward to California. When it stopped in Monterey for refueling, Lieutenant Sherman came on board for the final leg to San Francisco. Sherman had intended to resign his army commission so that he could return to civilian life and make money like everyone else. General Smith not only convinced him to remain in service but also persuaded him to become his aide and adjutant, since Governor Mason would soon be leaving.

When the overloaded *California* sailed through the Golden Gate, the ship listed to the starboard side as its eager passengers crowded the deck to get their first glimpse of San Francisco. The town was ready to greet the first steamship on its inaugural run. As hundreds of miners in town for the winter and others gathered on the hills, several U. S. Navy vessels in port, adorned with bunting, fired a welcoming salute, the cannon booms reverberating off the hills. As a band on board the *California* struck up a lively air and passengers waved handkerchiefs, sailors on nearby ships and townspeople on Telegraph Hill let out cheers. The ship anchored, the passengers disembarked, and all the *California*'s crew, except for the captain and one crew member, deserted for the mines. It would be over two months before the vessel could secure enough of a crew for the return journey to Panama.

Once ashore, passengers from the *California* and the many other ships that were to arrive that year found themselves disoriented; it was akin to landing on another planet. One newcomer said he felt "like a countryman in London, completely bewildered." New arrivals, far from home, suddenly found themselves amongst strangers from all over the globe. Americans, especially those from small towns, were startled by the diversity. Besides Americans from all parts of the settled states, ranging from New York lawyers wearing fashionable broadcloth to backwoodsmen sporting coon- skin caps, there were Englishmen, Germans, French, Australians, Russians (some garbed in furs and sables), turbaned Turks, Kanakas—as Hawaiian Islanders were called then—Chileans, Mexicans from Sonora, their heads crowned with sombreros, and Chinese with their silk blouses and pigtails. One man saw some South Sea Islanders, their faces "tattooed all over with curious figures." Added to the mix were an occasional Indian and a sprinkling of native Californians down from their ranchos and wearing brightly colored serapes and "jingling their spurs at every step."

Adding to the exotic feel was the babel of many languages. Frenchman Ernest de Massey, who arrived in December, wrote: "Ask a question in English and your reply may be in German; if you speak in French you may perhaps be answered in Spanish, Italian,

Russian, Polish or Chinese. This would be amusing if it were not such a handicap."

But the main players in this cavalcade of humanity were the Americans. They especially dominated the mining population. When they would return to San Francisco from the Mother Lode dirty and unshaven, they could be easily identified by their own distinctive garb, almost a uniform of a kind. Although no two dressed exactly alike (this was the era before machine-made clothing) miners typically wore broad-brimmed slouch hats, red flannel shirts, and pants or leather leggings tucked into long-legged boots. Many had Colt revolvers, Bowie knives, or both, slung through the belts or sashes holding up their trousers. The carrying of firearms was almost *de rigueur*. Historian Hubert Howe Bancroft claimed: " . . . no one was supposed to be decently dressed without them." Despite their raffish, even rough looking appearance—most had let their hair grow and wore beards—a fair number of the miners were refined, intelligent, and well educated. J. D. Borthwick, an Englishman with a perceptive eye, noted: "It was the gentlemen who insisted on posing in the most picturesque attire."

If the people were eye-catching the town itself was not. Until late in the year when more substantial buildings started going up, San Francisco was chiefly composed of canvas tents, shanties made of packing crates or rough boards, and one-story frame buildings, many of which had walls and roofs of canvas. The slapdash, transitory nature of the place was captured by one American, who, after arriving in September, climbed to the top of Telegraph Hill and surveyed the scene: "But for a few old adobe houses it would have been easy to imagine that the whole city was pitched the evening before for the accommodation of a vast caravan for the night. . . . I felt that those tents might all be struck some morning, and the city suddenly leave its moorings for parts unknown." Partially because of the sprawl and the fact that goods unloaded from ships were stacked on any vacant space due to lack of storage facilities, the streets, which were "uneven, ungraded, unpaved, and unplanked" were hardly discernible. This was especially true outside of the immediate Portsmouth Square area, most notably from California Street south, where the "streets" were nothing more than invisible lines going up and over sand hills.

Many new arrivals were also less than thrilled with the climate. San Francisco rarely experiences extremes of temperature (it rarely gets above 80 degrees or below 40 degrees Fahrenheit). But having just come from the tropical warmth and humidity of Panama or the South Pacific, whether they arrived in winter, during the rainy season—generally from November to April—or during the summer, when San Francisco typically experiences raw mornings infused with fog, new residents found it tough to adjust. "This is your Italian climate," snorted one man, having been led to believe that since Italy and California were on the same latitude the climates would be comparable. "Paradise!" spat another as he shivered in his tent.

Another problem was the wind, which usually kicked up in the afternoon, swirling sand all around, making it hard to protect oneself from its effects. Wind-driven sand and dust got into boots, pants pockets, hats, into hair, even into mouths and noses. Mary Jane Megquier, one of the few women in town, wittily called San Francisco ". . . the City of dust not altogether gold dust." A writer for the *Alta California* described it more vividly: ". . . the blinding sand and choking dust with which the air is filled . . . whirls in gusts through the streets as water rushes through the sluiceway."

Lack of proper sanitation contributed to the misery. According to forty-niner Dr. Joseph Middleton, the immigrants transformed the town into "one vast garbage heap." There was no indoor plumbing. Some of the primary buildings in town had outhouses nearby, but those not zealously guarded must have been taxed to their limits early on. Tent dwellers and others that had chamber pots simply pitched the contents into the street or the bay. Those without pots likely utilized nearby sand hills to do their business. Disposal of garbage and offal—intestines and discarded parts from slaughtered cattle and other animals—was also haphazard. Animal entrails were simply tossed into the streets, onto vacant lots, or into the bay. Because shallow Yerba Buena Cove was a favorite dumping spot, when the tide was out the stench, especially on warm days, was particularly bad. City authorities were aware of the problem. In 1847, during a rare heat wave, they passed a law imposing a fine on any person killing or maiming vultures, sea-gulls, and other carrion fowl, because they performed the valuable service of scavenging the remains of dead animals. By 1849 however, with a largely ineffectual city government, and the town overrun with immigrants, little was done to alleviate sanitary woes.

If people came from all over the world to San Francisco so did another living creature—the rat. Wood rats and other rodents had co-existed with local Native Americans prior to the coming of the whites. But with the Gold Rush rats came in great numbers on vessels from New York, Boston, Valparaiso, Liverpool, Canton, and from cities everywhere. There were huge gray and black ones as well as white "China rats." The rats were ubiquitous, and although primarily nocturnal, could be seen during daylight hours as well, swimming from ship to ship in the harbor or scurrying around the port and gnawing on the piles of goods left stacked in the open.

Despite all these drawbacks, newly arrived gold-seekers kept their eyes on the prize. Immediately upon landing the first thing everyone wanted to know was: Was gold as plentiful as claimed? Chilean Argonaut Vicente Pérez Rosales got his answer when he arrived in early February and approached a few of the locals: "Wrapped in rags were nuggets as big as walnuts, and gold dust like lentils." Most residents had dust or nuggets to show. They carried the precious metal in simple leather pouches or pokes. Wild claims were made: "The goldfields could not be exhausted by 10,000 miners in fifty years." The visible presence of gold buoyed spirits and no doubt made the hardships easier to take.

Anyone in town about the time Rosales arrived, and who witnessed the following incident recorded by innkeeper John Henry Brown, would no doubt have had their spirits buoyed. Having wintered in San Francisco after much success in the Mother Lode in the summer of 1848, a miner known only as "Flaxhead" checked out of the City Hotel in preparation for returning to the mines. Since he was a drinker but not a gambler he had had trouble spending all of the twenty pounds in gold he had accumulated. After proprietor Brown had deducted his room charges and the cost of a box of claret and one of whiskey, Flaxhead still had six pounds of gold left. Convinced that he would experience bad luck if he left town with any gold, he resolved to spend it. He purchased a pair of boots, discarded one, and emptied the gold dust into the other. He poked a stick through the boot's ears, slung it over his shoulder, walked over to the Parker House, and planted himself at the bar, where it was "drinks for everyone" until all the gold was gone. When Brown admonished Flaxhead over his spendthrift ways the latter replied that there was plenty more gold at the mines.

While everyone knew that the place to find gold was in the Sierra foothills, more than one account tells of newcomers washing dirt in the streets of San Francisco and finding gold dust. (Gold is not native to San Francisco itself.) Whether miners like Flaxhead carelessly spilled some, or as one report has it, Robert A. Parker, in a fit of generosity and amusement scattered several thousand dollars worth of dust along Clay Street and watched eager crowds down on their knees washing it out, it only served to heighten the excitement of San Francisco as being the locus of the famed El Dorado.

At least one such incident of "salting" was deliberately designed to take advantage of gullible newcomers. Several locals salted Kearny Street one night with two to three ounces of gold dust. In the morning one of the conspirators rounded up 40 to 50 strangers, took them to the spot, and after washing out a pan of dirt produced nearly two ounces of gold. Excited by the find the party raced off to the closest supplier—who was in cahoots with the salter—and quickly bought all of his gold pans at two dollars each. The first miner gleaned about twenty cents worth from his washing of dirt but the rest came up empty-handed. It didn't take the crowd long to realize that they had been had.

Since it took months to cross the plains or to get from East Coast and foreign ports to San Francisco by sea, it was mid-1849 before large numbers of American and European immigrants started to arrive. Prior to that a large proportion of miners and San Francisco residents were Latinos, mainly Mexicans, Chileans, and Peruvians. They had heard the news in 1848, and with less distance to travel had reached California that same year. And they kept coming. It was no surprise therefore to Vicente Pérez Rosales when he noted in May 1849 that San Francisco was "as Spanish as Valparaiso." Harbor Master King's statistics bear that out. From April 12 to June 30 only 2,053 out of 5,677, or 36 percent, of immigrants arriving by sea were Americans. Mexicans and Chileans, at nearly 1,500 each, made up the largest contingents of foreigners.

The tide turned in July. That month 3,565 immigrants arrived by sea; about 3,000 of them, or 84 percent, were Americans. That percentage would dip a bit in the months following, but the harbor master recorded almost 20,000 arrivals from July through November, of which 77 percent were Americans. The total number of ships that arrived during that same time period has been pegged at 549, or an average of about three or four a day. Some days were far from average. On September 17 a record 21 ships arrived. By fall the cove was clogged with vessels of all kinds—steamers, ships, brigs, and schooners. Only the Pacific Mail steamships made departures; almost all the sailing vessels had been immediately abandoned by crew and passengers on arrival and stood cheek to jowl, at anchor in the bay. A few were hauled onto the shore to be used as much-needed storage facilities. Others finally found crews and departed, but most would eventually be dismantled for salvage.

Passengers who came by ship around the Horn mostly arrived in good health despite the long voyage. Some however did not. In mid-August, William Redmond Ryan, a mustered-out veteran of Colonel Stevenson's regiment, was asked to attend an inquest for a man who had died a few days after arrival by sea. Ryan trudged through the sand to Happy Valley, a rag-tag encampment south of Market Street, a half-mile from the "downtown" area surrounding Portsmouth Square. The dead man lay in a tent on a blanket stretched across several boxes. From the features still discernible Ryan could see that the deceased was young and had been a handsome man. But the now bloated corpse had turned black and was covered with ugly pustules. A partially eaten away tongue protruded through blistered lips. He was a victim of scurvy.

Scurvy, which is caused by a deficiency of ascorbic acid, or vitamin C, was not a problem in San Francisco itself, since there was always enough in the way of fruits and vegetables (good sources of vitamin C) available, especially as the year progressed. But scurvy was a problem both in the Mother Lode where miners would go months on a diet lacking in curative properties and on long sea voyages where fruits and vegetables were not readily obtainable. The unnamed man Ryan saw had come on the *Brooklyn*, which gained the reputation of a "hell ship" because scores of fellow passengers on the same voyage developed scurvy, half a dozen dying from it as a result. Surviving passengers testified that early in the voyage, which lasted seven months, the ration of beans and rice had run out and that the potatoes had spoiled and been tossed overboard. Many passengers alleged that the captain, Joseph W. Richardson, had refused their requests to put in at ports along the way such as Rio de Janeiro and Valparaiso where they could have obtained fruits and vegetables. Their diet was reduced for the final months of the voyage to salt beef, pork, hard bread, and molasses, and passengers started developing scurvy. Captain Richardson and the ship's owners were brought up on charges as a result of the affair. The jury rendered a verdict in the amount of a $2,000 fine, less than half the $5,000 that had been sought.

All throughout the year 1849 thousands of people poured into San Francisco "like bees to a swarming." Most are forgotten today. Some however left their mark. One of those was John W. Geary. Geary, for whom Geary Street/Geary Boulevard is named, would only spend three years in San Francisco, but he would loom large in the city's early history. After leaving the city for good in early 1852, he would go on to a stellar military and political career including a stint as governor of Kansas Territory, as well as leading troops as a general in the Civil War, which included seeing action at Gettysburg and Chancellorsville. He marched with Sherman to the sea. After the war he served two terms as governor of Pennsylvania. But all that was in the future.

Geary was born in western Pennsylvania in 1819. His penniless father died when he was 14, forcing young Geary to leave school to work to support his widowed mother. He worked variously as a schoolteacher and surveyor; and soon saved enough money to not only pay off his father's outstanding debts but to put himself though college, where he studied law and civil engineering. During the Mexican War, Geary served as a lieutenant colonel with the Pennsylvania militia. He was wounded twice and participated in the capture of Mexico City. As a reward for his wartime services, President Polk appointed him San Francisco's first postmaster, on January 22, 1849. After crossing the Isthmus of Panama with his pregnant wife and three-year-old son, Geary arrived in San Francisco on March 31 aboard the Pacific Mail steamer *Oregon* (the first steamer to arrive after the *California*). He carried with him ten sacks of mail containing 5,000 letters. With no government buildings worthy of the name, he rented an 8-foot by 10-foot room in a building at the corner of Washington and Montgomery streets, at the waterfront, for use as a post office. To organize the mail he chalked squares on the floor and labeled them A, B, C, etc. and sorted the letters by recipients' names. When he had finished he removed a pane of glass from a window and handed letters to eager recipients.

Like many others, Geary was dazzled by all the activity and the quick fortunes being made. He wrote to his parents (his widowed mother must have remarried) a few days after arriving and confirmed the stories of gold's abundance but noted: "Everything here costs 12 times as much as in the United States." Rather than giving up his low-paying postal job however, the duty-bound and disciplined Geary was content to bide his time and wait for other opportunities. Those would soon come in the form of political office.

If the vast majority of forty-niners was unknown and unheralded one who was not was Jessie Benton Frémont. She was a celebrity of sorts: the daughter of powerful Missouri senator Thomas Hart Benton and the wife of "The Pathfinder," John Charles Frémont, well known for his explorations of the West and his participation in the Bear Flag Revolt of 1846, in which California was briefly proclaimed a republic just before the American takeover. She came to San Francisco to rendezvous with her husband, who was coming overland to meet her. She arrived in June, disappointed to find that he was not yet there (he arrived ten days later).

She was also disappointed by the town: the chilling fog; the windswept treeless hills; the ramshackle structures; the deserted ships in the harbor, rocking back and forth with the tide. Even the seemingly simple act of getting from ship to shore was a problem. "The crews who took boats to shore were pretty sure not to come back," she wrote in a memoir published years later. Fortunately for her, since word of her arrival had preceded her, leading merchant W. D. M. Howard sent his private launch out to bring her safely ashore. Howard, as administrator of the estate of William Leidesdorff, the town's first treasurer, who had died the previous year, had taken over the latter's fine home. He moved out, and installed Mrs. Frémont in it. She was grateful to be staying in a house of relative luxury, a well-built adobe with a veranda "and a beautiful garden kept in old world order by a Scotch gardener." The house was adorned with beautiful carpets and fine furniture—there was even a piano—but it lacked such basic necessities as a house-maid and firewood for the fireplace. The latter were two things almost impossible to find because of the scarcity of women and the high cost of wood.

In August a man named Bayard Taylor arrived by sea. He was unusual in that he had come not to dig for gold or to engage in spec-ulation. He was a reporter for Horace Greeley's *New York Tribune* and he had come to cover the biggest story of his day, the California Gold Rush. Like John W. Geary a native Pennsylvanian, Taylor was 24 years old. Despite his youth, he had five years previously embarked on a two-year, 3,000-mile trek on foot through England, France, Germany, Switzerland, and Italy. His best-selling book *Views A-Foot*, based on his travels, had caught the eye of Greeley, who hired him to work at the *Tribune*. His love of travel and adven-ture made him a natural choice to go to California.

As soon as Taylor landed he got a taste of the summertime cli-mate: "A furious wind was blowing down through a gap in the hills, filling the streets with clouds of dust." He and a fellow ship-mate engaged two Mexicans to carry their trunks, and they headed toward the Plaza and the Parker House. Along the way Taylor noted the array of people from all over the world, goods stacked out in the open, and "canvas sheds, open in front, and covered with all kinds of signs, in all languages." Arriving at the Parker House, he discharged the Mexican porters after paying them two dollars each, "a sum so immense in comparison to the service rendered that there was no longer any doubt of our having actually landed in Califor-nia." The reporter only stayed in San Francisco two days during his first visit, but as the year progressed he returned several times for longer visits, each time marveling at the changes that had occurred in his absence.

A month after Bayard Taylor arrived another man named Tay-lor landed. He was William Taylor and, like his namesake, he had not come to seek his fortune. He was a Methodist street preacher and he had come around the Horn from Baltimore to save souls. Six feet tall, with penetrating eyes and a commanding, resonant voice, the stern, straight-laced William Taylor had not made himself popular with his shipmates on the way because he condemned them for working on the Sabbath even though the ship needed repairs after being damaged during a storm. The Reverend Taylor arrived in San Francisco with his wife, who was so weak from chronic diarrhea during the long journey she could barely walk. With them was their three-month-old daughter Oceana, so named because she had been born at sea during the voyage.

After settling in, Taylor preached the gospel in Portsmouth Square every Sunday. His crowds eventually grew so large that they started to block up the entrances to the gambling saloons facing the square. When the proprietors complained, Taylor exclaimed that his listeners were merely blocking up the entrance to Hell.

Although hundreds of Americans left behind journals, diaries, letters, and even whole books documenting their experiences in gold-rush San Francisco, written accounts by those from foreign countries are much less numerous. Some European visitors and a few Latinos left written descriptions. Accounts by Asian visitors, however, are almost nonexistent. But a Chinese man named Luchong did leave behind a letter for posterity (published in translation) to his cousin back in China, in which he described his impressions of San Francisco, "this infant Hercules among cities. . ."

Luchong arrived in the latter half of 1850, by which time San Francisco had grown rapidly, with substantial frame and brick buildings having replaced many of the flimsy shacks and tents of 1849. Despite his post-1849 arrival, his keen observations and unique perspective provide a rare look at gold-rush San Francisco through the eyes of an Asian man.

Luchong was from Pekin (Beijing), arrived by ship, was traveling alone, and appears to have been young. Like so many others, he had come to seek his fortune in the land of gold. As his ship sailed through the Golden Gate he was surprised that there were no battlements, no major fortifications to protect the populace from hostile nations. (The crumbling remains of the old Spanish fort, the Castillo de San Joaquin, obviously didn't impress him.) Once landed he looked in wonderment at "the grotesque collection of sights that greeted me on all sides." Western dress struck him as comical. The men's slouch hats with their dimple in the crown looked to him like inverted flowerpots. And the women's elaborate and fashionable hats seemed to him nonsensical since they failed to shield the face from the sun. He further felt that they did nothing to enhance the beauty of a woman's face.

Superficial observations aside, Luchong quickly zeroed in on the American psyche, noting that "profit is the great ruling spirit of the American mind." He was amazed and impressed by all the Yankee can-do spirit and the energy and wealth that surrounded him, but felt that the Americans, in such a pell-mell rush to transform their environment, were oblivious to the natural beauty that surrounded them. Instead of, for example, augmenting and embellishing nature by adorning the picturesque heights surrounding the town with terraces and elegant plateaus such as would have been done in his native China, the Americans were busy chopping down the hills and shoveling them into the harbor.

Luchong concluded that his countrymen were greatly superior when it came to elegance and taste. The Americans, he felt, not only lacked finer sentiments but also any sense of restraint: "These people think there is nothing that cannot be improved upon. They would gild the rays of the sun."

3

Necessities: Lodging, Food, Water—and Mail

After landing, newcomers quickly had to attend to basic needs: lodging, food, water—and mail. One could argue that mail was not a necessity, but after being gone so long, eager for news from home, many made straight for the post office as soon as they landed.

The first priority was a place to sleep, preferably with a roof over one's head. For those who could afford it, hotels were the obvious choice—when they were not fully booked. As late as mid-1849 there were really only two hotels worthy of the name, the Parker House and the City Hotel. Both were primarily saloons and gambling dens, with lodging only a secondary consideration. Rooms in the Parker House cost an expensive $10 a night, and according to one observer some paid as much as $50 for a favored room. Reporter Bayard Taylor had stopped here first after he arrived in August, but with no rooms available he hauled his trunk over to the City Hotel. He spent his first night in a garret there where his accommodations consisted of a cot, a coarse blanket, a chair, a rough table, and a looking glass (a mirror). This was a fairly luxurious accommodation for the time but the quarters were so cramped that in the morning as he sat up in bed he painfully banged his head on a rafter.

As the city rapidly developed more hotels were erected late in the year. Notable among them was the St. Francis Hotel, predecessor of today's historic hostelry on Union Square. It was made up of twelve prefabricated cottages, which were stacked on top of each other to a height of three stories. A narrow stairway led to the upper floors. Despite its stature, it was of flimsy construction. A woman guest who stayed there in June 1850 told how the hair-stuffed mattress she slept on was comfortable enough but the walls between the rooms were separated only by canvas and paper. She described how one night she had just gotten in to bed when two men started to talk to each other from their own rooms through hers; she coughed to let to let them know that someone was in the middle room. The conversation ceased but a "nasal serenade" soon commenced, making it hard for her to sleep.

At least she didn't have to endure the noise in the hotels that also catered to gambling. Sleep was difficult in these establishments because of "the perpetual racket of drinking, shouting, fiddling, clinking of coin, and the tramp, tramp, tramp, in and out, night and day." William Redmond Ryan, who had participated in the inquest of the scurvy victim, spent his first night in gold-rush San Francisco in April curled up in a corner of a gambling saloon, but got little rest due to the noisy revelers at the bar. While sleeping he "experienced the peculiar roaring sensation of deafness incidental to immersing one's head in the water. . . ." Awakened with a start, he discovered that a bar patron had poured liquor in his ear. He thought it a poor joke but laughed it off.

Some establishments that advertised themselves as "hotels" were little more than four posts driven into the ground, wrapped and covered over with a piece of canvas. Théophile de Rutté, a young Swiss who arrived in October, discovered no lack of such facilities, but thought that these joints, topped with signboards, "more pompous than reassuring."

For those that couldn't afford a bed in a hotel, there were less expensive alternatives. Some men simply slept on the bare ground; others slept in crates, or in empty boxes. Mahlon Fairchild, who arrived by sea in foggy July, spent his first two nights in a shack on Pacific Street. It was so chilly, breezy, and uncomfortable that he "yearned for the forsaken quarter of the afterdeck of a whaleship and its tropic warmth." A few men even slept in coffins: a coffin maker laid them across sawhorses and rented them out as sleeping accommodations.

For newcomers who wanted a roof over their heads—an important consideration, especially during the winter rainy season—dormitory-like lodging houses filled the need. They typically cost from

$1.00 to $1.50 per night. Some places provided straw to serve as mattresses and pillows, while in others a man had to bring his own bedding. Englishman William Shaw, who arrived from Australia in early September, described one such establishment as being a drafty building of rough wood plank about 60 feet long by 20 feet wide with no windows. Around the sides of the interior were two rows of wooden shelves used as bunks. Between 10 p.m. and midnight men would come trooping in carrying their own blankets, because the management provided no bedding. If you were early enough, he wrote in a memoir, you got to sleep on a wooden shelf, which offered some breathing room from the others. If you were too late for a shelf the proprietor pointed out a space on the ground. On a wet night, when the place was packed, people of all nationalities would find themselves crowded together on the ground, sleeping in such close proximity that during the night you might get a kick in the ribs from a restless neighbor, or you could awaken to find a boot just inches from your face. "As it was customary to sleep in one's clothes," he wrote, "abominable odours arose, and creeping things (mainly fleas and lice) abounded." By morning the heat and effluvia were so oppressive he sometimes felt nauseous.

To avoid the stuffy conditions associated with the dollar-a-night lodging houses, many chose to live in tents. (According to one estimate, by June more than half of the inhabitants were living in tents.) Campers commonly fashioned such structures from canvas sails taken from abandoned ships. Tent living offered a roof over one's head, but tents were drafty and they got wet when it rained. One windy, rainy night two forty-niners had to hold on to their tent for nearly three hours to keep it from blowing away. In the morning they found that most of the tents surrounding them had blown down.

To escape miserable conditions on land, some solved their housing problem by staying on their ships in the harbor. This was a popular option for women, especially in winter, so that they could avoid the muddy conditions on shore. Preacher William Taylor kept his wife and daughter on their ship for several weeks while he chopped wood, which he ferried over from the East Bay (the closest place with trees of any size), and used it to build a one-story frame house in San Francisco. Similarly, a woman named Anne Booth and her husband stayed on board ship for a month before buying a lot in town on which they built a house with lumber salvaged from their vessel's stateroom. They used the topgallant sail for their roof. By painting the sail they made it "impervious to rain." Some stayed onboard even longer. James R. Garniss and several of his shipmates purchased the ship they came on and lived on it through the spring of 1850. He and his mates had comfortable and spacious staterooms. They invited friends aboard for card parties, and when they needed supplies they hired lighters to take them between ship and shore.

Toward the end of 1849, as more substantive wood frame structures went up, those who had their own stores or businesses solved the where-to-bed-down problem by locking their doors after they closed and simply sleeping in their own establishments. They would stretch out on or under their counters or on cots that they kept on the premises. One shopkeeper, referring to himself and other merchants, wrote in a memoir years later: "People generally slept in their offices among their goods like cats."

With building materials and affordable housing in short supply it wasn't long before entrepreneurs elsewhere, seeing a business opportunity, started shipping prefabricated houses to San Francisco. They were made mainly of wood or iron. The price of iron had fallen in the 1840s, rendering houses made of it easily affordable. Basic models were advertised for sale for as little as $100, and a Liverpool manufacturer offered a two-room iron house (assembly required) that included "five plate glass windows, two beds, one table, one chest of drawers, two chairs, a fountain washstand, and a complete apparatus for cooking," for only $150. Close to 600 iron houses were shipped to California in 1849.

Iron houses were promoted as being more comfortable than tents and also as being fireproof. The reality was different. As for comfort, Englishman Frank Marryat, who inhabited one, said the interiors became too hot when the sun beat down, and too cold after dark. On warm days the anti-corrosive paint gave off a sickening smell, and when it rained it sounded like a shower of small shot on the roof. Their alleged fireproofing qualities also didn't stand the test. Witnesses who lived to tell the tale related how people, thinking they were safe, locked themselves inside as flames approached.

As the interiors became intensely hot the inhabitants tried to get out only to find that as the metal expanded in the heat they couldn't open the doors. Some victims literally roasted to death. Flimsier models, when they became engulfed in flames, collapsed entirely.

Wooden prefabs cost more but they had a better reputation. They were imported from various locations, but the best ones came from China. William Redmond Ryan admired the solidly constructed log houses and felt that they were "infinitely superior and more substantial than those erected by the Yankees. . . ." John and Jessie Frémont bought a Chinese import and erected it in on a lot they owned in Happy Valley. It was a two-room affair with a shingle roof, which they found to be clean and spacious.

Along with where to sleep, what and where to eat was something that had to be attended to immediately after arrival and on an ongoing basis. Everyone was tired of monotonous shipboard fare, especially those who had been months at sea coming around the Horn. San Francisco offered a variety of foods in a variety of settings. With most people focused on mining gold, local markets took time to develop. Food products such as flour, beans, dried apples, and canned oysters and sardines, among many other items, were imported throughout the year. Fresh produce could not survive long journeys but squashes and cabbages were brought from Hawaii. Other foodstuffs came from Oregon. Closer to home, especially towards fall, after the summer growing season, onions, radishes, peaches, pears, grapes, and other fruits and vegetables were brought from Sonoma, Mission Dolores, and Mission Santa Clara, where gardens had been established at the missions by the Spanish in an attempt to help them become self-supporting. As a general rule, however, produce was scarce and expensive. A walnut-sized potato cost twenty-five cents. Eggs and oranges could cost as much as a dollar apiece. Green vegetables, except for local wild lettuce, were virtually unknown. (One entrepreneurial restaurateur came upon a family with a vegetable garden. He paid ten dollars for a water bucket full of produce and made a nice profit retailing it at fifty cents a forkful.)

Much more plentiful was local game. Bears, ducks, geese, deer, rabbits, elk, quail, and fish of all kinds abounded in the Bay Area and were easily shot, trapped, or caught. One San Francisco resident saw a brown bear at a local market; it had been shot across the bay. "The fat on its back was 3" thick," he marveled. "The meat was selling rapidly at $1.00 per lb." Bear meat was also apparently very tasty. Grizzly bear steaks were a choice dish. Bayard Taylor tried one and found that: "The flesh was of a bright red color . . . its flavor was preferable to that of the best pork."

Beef was most plentiful of all. It was also relatively inexpensive due to the large herds of cattle still to be found on the ranchos all around the bay. It could be purchased cheaply enough, but some local entrepreneurs brought cattle to market at an even greater profit by rustling them. Thieves would sneak over to the Castro or Peralta ranchos in the East Bay, butcher cattle, and then ferry the carcasses across the bay to San Francisco. Beef became a staple of local markets and in restaurants. It was too much of a staple for city resident Levi Stowell, who wrote in his diary in late July: "Fried steak for breakfast, stewed steak for dinner, & warmed steak for supper & hashed steak for Sunday, Oh for change. . . ."

Although a few San Franciscans boiled coffee and cooked simple meals in their dwellings, with few homes or hotels worthy of the name, dining in restaurants, or "eating houses" as they were more commonly called, became the norm for most. Restaurants varied widely in quality and cost. Choices ranged from top-of-the-line Delmonico's, namesake of the famous New York eatery, which opened in September, and where a meal with wine could cost $10.00 or more, to the plainest greasy spoon where $1.00 would buy boiled beef, bread, and bad coffee. Cooks were generally inexperienced, and standards of cleanliness were low: "Very many devoured food of the precise character of which it was quite as well that they were kept in ignorance." The ambience in some establishments also left something to be desired. Many restaurants were housed in little more than tents. William Redmond Ryan dined in one drafty wood frame structure with a canvas roof near Happy Valley. Dubbed "Café Français," he found the food to be good, that is what he could taste of it, because as he ate, the wind swirled throughout, depositing dust and fine sand into the salt, into his coffee, and onto his beefsteak.

Those who couldn't afford leisurely dining in a Delmonico's or Café Français ended up taking their board at one of the aptly named "eating houses." William Shaw described one as being a long plank building inside of which were two rows of tables parallel to each other running the length of the building. A variety of dishes—boiled and roast meats, curries, stews, fish, rice, frijoles, and molasses, the latter a favorite with many since it was eaten with almost everything—would be placed on the tables. A dinner bell or gong would then sound and men waiting outside would make a rush for the tables. "Lucky is the man who has a quick eye and a long arm; for everyone helps himself indiscriminately, and attention is seldom paid to any request," wrote Shaw. The contents of the dishes rapidly disappeared; ten minutes or less and the meal would be over. Out would come the quids of chewing tobacco that had been temporarily stuffed in pockets—or sometimes even plopped right on the table next to the food. Others would light their pipes while servers wiped off the greasy knives in time for the next sitting.

For those seeking a change of cuisine, there were at least three Chinese restaurants in town. They were well patronized, not only because they were inexpensive at a dollar a meal but because many Americans felt that the Chinese also served the best food. (Bayard Taylor thought that their coffee and tea especially were unsurpassed.) When forty-niner James Delavan entered a Chinese restaurant for the first time he wondered if he would have to push rice around with chopsticks. He was relieved to find however that meals were served "in the American style," that is with knives, forks, and spoons. The Chinese waiters spoke no English, but after ordering, another diner, James O'Meara, noted that the server would return with a plate filled with hot food. "It was not always easy to ascertain just what he was feasting upon, but the average customer was more bent on quantity than quality," he wrote.

A final option for those seeking edibles was one of the numerous outdoor stands. They typically served hot coffee, small pies, and light bites. Just the thing for those in a hurry, which many men were as they rushed from place to place on their way to conduct business.

Besides housing and food, another critical need for every resident was clean water. Despite its sparse vegetation and abundance of sand, San Francisco did have a few springs dotting the landscape here and there. But the primary source of water for the residents of the downtown area (near Portsmouth Square) in the pre-gold-rush era was Laguna Dulce, a stream-fed freshwater pond on the water-front near Montgomery and Sacramento streets. During the Mexican era, whaling ships and other vessels filled their casks from it. Local Indians also used it as a rinse bath after sweating it out in their smoke-filled temescal a short distance away. When the lagoon was filled in in about 1844, other sources of water had to be tapped. Sausalito, on the north shore of the bay, turned out to have springs that produced abundant clean, good-tasting water, so kegs of it were barged over and vended to local residents. Still, the town could not rely solely on imported water, so wells were dug. Some produced potable water, others did not.

One of the wells that did produce acceptable water was sunk next to the Ellis boarding house and saloon at Montgomery and Jackson streets. In 1847 the 23-foot deep well became the focus of an incident that became the talk of the town. One time after a stretch of about three or four days the water from the well became very rank. It was too foul to drink, then even unfit to use for washing, so proprietor Alfred Ellis hired men to clean it out. After some of the water had been removed, hair from a man's head could be seen floating on the surface. The body attached to it proved to be that of a missing Russian sailor who was thought to have deserted from his ship. After a drunken spree on shore one stormy night he had fallen into the well and drowned. When news of this discovery circulated, a number of residents who had been to Ellis' establishment and drunk his water suddenly became sick to their stomachs.

By 1849, with the population increasing day-by-day, abundant clean water became even more of an imperative. With wells in the downtown area under strain, and some less than pure to begin with, a bad situation was made even worse when an attempt was made to bring the city's rat population under control. Rat poison was set out, but the rats, driven mad with thirst after ingesting it, dived into the wells, thus making the water totally unfit to drink. With residents now having to lug water considerable distances in buckets or pitchers from unpolluted springs farther away, some entrepreneurs spied opportunity. They began cartage services, hauling kegs of water in to town and taking it to their customers' doorsteps to be sold on a per bucket basis. This practice seems to have started as a paying business at least by 1848 when two men, tapping a well they owned on the slope of Telegraph Hill, went door-to-door selling water by the bucketful from kegs attached to two mules. In 1849, to keep up with demand, they added more mules. They were soon joined by other competitors who brought water from as far away as the Presidio, over three miles distant, where Mountain Lake and Lobos Creek were sources of abundant, clean, fresh water. Water cartage was a profitable business if one had access to a source. The costs were transport and the labor involved in getting it to one's customers. A man named Juan Miguel Aguirre, who started a water cartage business in May 1849, claimed that he sold his water for one dollar per bucketful. He purportedly made as much as $30 a day, an excellent wage for the time. Water cartage to residents did not cease until 1858, when underground pipes were finally laid.

Fresh water was also needed for washing. But with priority given to drinking water, there was precious little to spare for doing laundry. There was a pond near the town's north shore, over a mile distant from the Plaza, that by mid-1849 would be called Washerwoman's Lagoon because Mexican and Indian women were the first to set up laundry operations there. They charged from six to nine dollars for a dozen shirts, a rate so high that residents who were not in a hurry sent their clothes to Hawaii or even to China to be laundered because it was cheaper, despite the transportation costs. It also cost less, in many instances, to buy new clothes rather than wash them since frequent auctions disposed of overstock clothing at bargain prices. Some men did not bother with laundry at all, and simply wore the same garments day after day until they were too worn or foul to wear any longer and then just tossed them aside. More than one city resident reported seeing dirty shirts lying discarded on the ground.

Scarce water also meant a lack of attention to personal hygiene. Most men bathed infrequently. One described his bathing as a dive into the bay to wash off before putting on new clothes after discarding the well-worn, smelly ones he had been wearing. Later in the year ads appeared in a new local newspaper, the *Pacific News*, advertising warm or cold baths, one in a restaurant next door to the Parker House and another in front of a local hospital. Water for these probably came from nearby wells.

Oral hygiene was also less than a priority. A few dentists finally made it to San Francisco, and some forty-niners had brought toothbrushes with them. William Shaw carried a toothbrush but suffered a ribbing from others less health conscious than he because of it. Still, westerners were advanced in this regard compared to the local Californios. Shaw recalled visiting Mission San Jose, where his toothbrush was an object of great curiosity. The Mexicans there had never seen one.

San Francisco residents might have counted shelter, food, and water among their basic needs, but for many, word from loved ones in the form of mail was just as important and even more eagerly desired. After typically long waits in line for their letters at the post office (the only way to get them, for there was no delivery service in town), recipients would read them over and over. Forty-niner Josiah Savage, who had come around the Horn, sat on a board in the street after retrieving his mail "and soon became oblivious to all but the sheet before me. On raising my eyes at the end of the letter I found I was alone and had almost forgotten where I was." Thomas L. Megquier, husband of Mary Jane Megquier, wrote back to a letter received: "Dear Cousin write us every opportunity—it is better than gold to us."

Mail arrived only by Pacific Mail steamers, typically once a month. Service could be erratic. During the summer of 1849, because of a dispute at the transfer point in Panama, no mail arrived in July, August, or September. With impatient residents fuming about the lack of delivery, tempers started to flare. Finally, on October 31, the *Panama* arrived carrying all the delayed mail—37 sacks containing 45,000 letters and bushels of newspapers.

The post office had by this time moved from the temporary location established by John W. Geary to a single-story wood-frame structure on Clay Street above the Plaza. No sooner had the bags from the October delivery been hauled inside than the little 40-foot-long building was besieged by hundreds of men while postal clerks barricaded inside sorted the letters. It took nearly two days of non-stop effort to sort them all, by which time the crowd had grown feverishly impatient. Those waiting outside alternately banged on the doors and windows, issuing threats or quietly whispered promises that they wouldn't tell anyone if only they could have their letters now. Some even offered bribes. All to no avail. When the post office was finally ready to open the delivery windows, a near riot ensued. To maintain order, the crowd was forced to form into lines, which quickly stretched for blocks. One angled down through Portsmouth Square, another snaked across Sacramento Street and disappeared into the tents among the chaparral. A third, for newspapers only, rose up the hill behind the building. It took some patrons nearly six hours to reach the windows. Some would sell their places in the front of the line for as much as $25, then go back to the end and repeat the process, making a nice income out of it. Others made money by vending pies, cakes, and cups of coffee to those standing in line.

4

Carnival of Greed

The hallmark of gold-rush San Francisco was greed. With the exception of reporter Bayard Taylor and a few preachers, almost everyone was focused on making a quick buck. They all recognized that the Gold Rush provided a unique opportunity to get rich. Countless numbers were doing so. John W. Geary, shortly after landing in April, in a letter home wrote: ". . . many of those who have been here one year and upwards have realized immense fortunes, by the unprecedented rise in prosperity. Speculation is rife everywhere. . . ."

Commercial activity started before some ships' passengers even had time to catch their breath. Traders scrambled to be first on board vessels arriving in the cove. Unaware of the prices they could get onshore, passengers sold goods and possessions at what they felt were good deals only to land and discover that they could have gotten much more had they waited. One of those was New Yorker James Garniss. After his ship anchored a man came on board and offered to buy Garniss's "elegant, waterproof" boots. He at first hesitated but gave in when the man offered him three ounces of gold dust, or $48, likely more than ten-fold what they had cost him. Once ashore, he discovered that such fine boots couldn't be had for less than six ounces, if at all. Garniss quickly got into the swing of things, and not long afterward *he* boarded a vessel and bought a job lot of eggs for fifty cents a dozen and sold them ashore for $4.50 a dozen. (He later learned that those same eggs had been resold in Sacramento for $6 a dozen.)

After landing, and getting their bearings in San Francisco, the aim of most was to set off for the mines as soon as possible. Astonished at the high prices in the gold-inflated economy, some, in order to raise grubstakes, sold their possessions at auction.

Others took temporary jobs. After a stint panning gold in the Mother Lode and finding out just what tough, backbreaking labor it was, shoveling dirt and rock hour after hour or standing in icy mountain streams with the sun blistering one's back, many gave up and returned to San Francisco to look for an easier path to fortune.

Everyone, it seems, had a scheme to make money. Even Bayard Taylor, although he had come strictly as a reporter, got into the act. When he saw that a man from New York had disposed of 1,500 copies of the *Tribune* at a dollar apiece in the space of only two hours, Taylor suddenly recalled that he had about a dozen newspapers that were being used to stop up crevices in his valise. He quickly sold them for $10, a gain he excitedly wrote that gave him a profit of four thousand percent.

Taylor noted that many ships' passengers started transacting business as soon as they landed. Some had prepared in advance for it. Franklin Mead, who had come around the Horn, arrived in early October with 30 terrapin that he and friends had captured on the Galapagos Islands on the way. They quickly sold 17 of them for $1,400.

David Hawley, a native of Connecticut, also came prepared. When he arrived in early April via the steamer *Oregon*, he was carrying a bunch of guitars (probably purchased en route). After asking permission from William D. M. Howard, he set up a couple of sawhorses in front of the Howard & Mellus store on Montgomery Street. He laid boards across them to display the guitars, and rapidly sold them all, taking in Spanish doubloons by the handful as payment. His profits amounted to between 4,000 and 5,000 percent. Hawley, a true entrepreneur, used those profits to buy a few small boats, which he manned with Chileans, whom he paid five dollars a day, and then charged five dollars per person to land passengers on shore from ships arriving in the harbor. This business provided a further advantage in that it provided information as to what merchandise the ships carried, enabling him to make offers on the most desirable goods. On one cargo he gladly paid the owner a 100 percent profit, then resold the cargo at a profit of 300 to 400 percent for himself. Hawley built four lighters and commenced charging $25 a load to bring goods ashore. Using his accumulating profits from these endeavors, he bought two 20-ton schooners to deliver passengers to Sacramento and Stockton in the rapidly developing inland waterway trade. The untiring Hawley soon opened stores in San Francisco and Stockton. His Stockton location, he wrote, brought in profits of an astounding $9,000 a week.

Hawley didn't record how much he made from his schooner transport service to Sacramento, but he may have shifted his efforts to his stores when the *Senator*, a large side-wheel steamship, arrived in San Francisco in late October. She had been built in New York in 1848 and had started her career carrying passengers and goods to ports along the eastern seaboard. Two hundred and nineteen feet long, with a 400-ton cargo capacity, she was a luxurious vessel for the time. Bayard Taylor described how "her long upper saloon, with its sofas and faded carpet, seemed splendid enough for a palace."

In 1849 the *Senator* journeyed around Cape Horn to start a new career hauling men and material between San Francisco and Sacramento. Although she didn't put sailing schooners or much smaller inland steamers out of business—there was too much demand —she clearly was top-of-the-line for comfort and speed, and as such commanded premium prices. Passenger rates for the ten-hour trip to Sacramento from San Francisco ran as high as $35 for a cabin and $15 for deck space; freight rates ranged from $35 to $50 a ton. Applying those numbers and the cargo capacity to a thrice-weekly schedule yields gross revenues of $50,000 or more a week. Net profits for the ship's owners were said to be $600,000 in the first year, or an average of $50,000 a month.

Large-scale capital-intensive enterprises such as the *Senator* were the exception rather than the rule in 1849. Most forty-niners contented themselves with small-time entrepreneurial efforts. William Redmond Ryan had, at first, in typical fashion, taken a stab at placer mining. But after a not very productive experience he came to the conclusion that already by the spring of 1849 perhaps up to two-thirds of the miners in the gold country were not even making enough to cover expenses. Ryan, an artist by trade, returned to San Francisco where he rowed from ship to ship in the harbor until he found some pigments and brushes, paying $28 for supplies that would have cost about $3 in New York. Using his trunk as an easel he created a makeshift studio in his lodging house. He put a sign outside advertising his services, and soon was earning about an ounce, or $16 a day, painting portraits of miners eager for a keepsake of their California adventure. Ryan was happy because he was doing something he loved, and was likely making more, for a lot less labor, than if he had stuck to panning gold. He soon was doing so much business that he took on a partner and moved to a roomier location.

Artists of another kind also set up shop. Daguerreotype photography, in which an image was captured on a polished silver surface treated with sensitive chemicals, had been invented a decade before. Practitioners of this new art form, invented in France, had spread over the globe. Probably the first daguerreotypist to establish himself in San Francisco was Englishman Richard Carr. Carr was operating a photo studio in Guayaquil, Ecuador in October 1848 when he heard of the gold discovery. He arrived in San Francisco by ship on the last day of 1848. The following month he opened an 8-foot by 12-foot upper floor studio and placed an advertisement in the *Alta California* promoting "daguerreotype likenesses in the best manner." Other daguerreotypists opened portrait galleries after Carr, including at least one woman, a Mrs. Julia Shannon, who was advertising her services in the paper by January 1850.

Some city residents tried a variety of things, moving from one occupation to another as fortune dictated. Luther M. Schaeffer made mattresses out of common muslin and stuffed them with shavings; he peddled cigars, patent medicines, and notions. But his most profitable endeavor was playing a flute—perhaps giving him the distinction of being San Francisco's first street musician.

Another one who tried various enterprises was George Dornin. Dornin, a native New Yorker who had worked as a clerk and office boy on Wall Street since age 13, was only 18 when he arrived in San Francisco by sea in August. Although as eager to make a fortune as anyone else he decided not to try gold mining. He first established a laundry in conjunction with a woman who had come on the ship with him, but the business failed after only ten days. Dornin wasn't cut out for it, and the high cost of wood (for building fires to heat the water) was prohibitively expensive at $20 a cord. He then took up sign painting and went to work for the acting coroner painting wooden slab mortuary tablets with inscriptions such as "Sacred to the Memory of." From there he transitioned to painting signs. Since that was irregular work he became a waiter in a restaurant at Montgomery and Vallejo streets, but when his employer's lease terminated a month later he was out of a job. The enterprising Dornin then struck a partnership with a local baker. His partner baked the pies while he delivered them to tent dwellers in Happy Valley in champagne baskets modified with handles. It was a lucrative business, but it came to an end when his partner decided to go off to the mines. Dornin then opened a combination restaurant/outfitter store only to be wiped out by a fire two years later, shortly after which he moved to Nevada City, in the northern Mother Lode.

Samuel Upham from Philadelphia, who also arrived in August, tried a variety of things too. When he saw that pickles were scarce and sold at fabulous prices he scooped up all the discarded pickle jars and bottles he could find; the beach at Happy Valley was littered with them. He cleaned them up and placed them around his little shack not far from the site of his finds. When a vessel arrived from Boston he persuaded the captain to sell him a barrel of salted cucumbers and half a barrel of cider vinegar. He bottled the cucumbers, turning them in to pickles, and within a week had cleared $300 in profit. For his next venture he "cornered" the market in tobacco pipes and realized $150 in twenty-four hours. Following that he talked the editor of the *Pacific News* into hiring him to sell subscriptions. That went well, but when the position of bookkeeper opened up at $100 a week he sold his carrier route for $200, unloaded his makeshift "shebang" in Happy Valley for $125, and moved into a sleeping bunk in the *Pacific News* offices.

Henry F. Williams was a clerk in a law office in Washington, D.C. in the fall of 1848 when, before the news of the gold discovery, he decided that he wanted to go to California to better his lot. Having done some carpentry work he took his box of tools with him, which proved a wise decision because when he arrived on the steamship *California* in late February 1849 he immediately put his woodworking skills to use. He constructed a number of houses around town at a good profit, but then discerned another opportunity in the need for local bay and river transport. In three weeks, and for an expenditure of $2,000 for labor and materials, he built a barge that he leased for $150 a day until it had nearly paid for itself. He then sold it for $4,000.

Bayard Taylor, after witnessing numerous examples of very profitable business deals, felt that a man became more daring, more of a risk-taker after arriving in California. He applauded the enterprise and independent action that he saw all around him and felt that it was contagious. He also concluded that, at least initially, "the rashest speculators were the most fortunate." A good example of that is seen in the following story by William F. White, in a memoir he wrote under the pen name of William Grey (here spelled Gray). White arrived in July and had barely got his bearings when he ran into a man he had known in New York only by the first name of Tony:

"How long are you here, Gray?" said Tony.

"Nearly two days."

"What have you done since you came? How much have you made?"

"Not a dollar so far."

"No? Why I have made $7,000; but then I have been here ten days."

When White asked Tony how he had made that sum, Tony told him he had gone up Sacramento Street and had seen eight lots for sale. He bought them all on credit with not a dollar down and was to pay the owner at 4 p.m. that day. To raise the money he quickly "flipped" five of the lots, selling them for the price he had paid for eight. A few days later he sold the other three, netting a pure profit of $7,000.

While the majority of fortune seekers in San Francisco were honest and above board in their dealings, the get-rich-quick climate naturally attracted some dishonest and unscrupulous individuals. William Tecumseh Sherman described how a man named Baron Steinberger, "a splendid looking fellow," who boasted that he had helped break the Second Bank of the United States by defaulting on $5 million he owed it, talked the senior military authorities into lending him a boat and supplies to bring cattle over from Don Timeteo Murphy's vast ranch in Marin. He promised them the best cuts of beef in return. Steinberger made out well. He set up a butcher shop on the waterfront and soon had a profitable business selling beef at 25 to 50 cents a pound. It was profitable because he never paid Murphy for the cattle. Steinberger bilked others in similar fashion and quickly became wealthy.

Another colorful scoundrel who arrived in 1849 was the Marquis of Pendray, a man fellow Frenchman Ernest de Massey recognized as being wanted in France for counterfeiting notes of the Bank of France. Massey vividly described Pendray as "a weather-beaten man of fine build and regular features, muscles like iron, and the fascinating look of a bird of prey" who was "haughty . . . a dangerous bully always ready with his sword or pistols." Fluent in English and Spanish, Pendray could at turns be witty and ingratiating or cold and cruel. An excellent shot, he hunted game, often returning to San Francisco dressed in heavy boots, fawn-colored trousers, and wearing a wide brimmed hat. With deer horns hanging from his neck, a rifle slung over his shoulder, and rabbits and ducks dangling from his belt along with his revolver and sword, he would parade up and down the streets. On occasion he could be seen pulling a dead bear on a cart behind him. The marquis supplemented his earnings as a hunter by fleecing local Mexican rancheros at cards after charming his way into their homes. Armed with several hundred dollars in winnings he would then return to San Francisco with his money and his game trophies.

While many freelanced and took whatever work came their way, others established businesses or professions that had fixed locations. John W. Geary was one such. Geary's stint as postmaster came to an end in July when word reached him that Zachary Taylor, who had been inaugurated as president a few months earlier, had replaced Geary with his own appointee. Geary had already formed a partnership with two men who had come on the *Oregon* with him, O. P. Sutton and William Van Voorhies. They established an auction and commission merchant business in a 40-foot by 60-foot tent on Montgomery Street near Jackson that was so close to the waterfront they had to fill in part of the bay to make room for it. They pooled $1,500 to get started but almost went broke, having spent all but $300 of it when a ship captain they knew arrived and offered to let them keep as commission everything above the prices he wanted for his cargo. The partnership cleared close to $7,000 in one month, putting them in business. After seven months they had made over $70,000.

James Garniss, who would spend the winter living aboard the ship he came on, rented a small storefront on Sacramento Street and opened up a dry goods store. Using an empty box for a desk and a keg of nails for a seat, he sold his inventory at retail after buying bulk packages wholesale and breaking them up. Not content with the income from that he started a second business. Using the broken-up dry-goods boxes he fashioned four bunks and "kept them full of sick people, one after another. . . ." He kept them comfortable and had food brought in. As soon as one man recovered another sick man would take his place. Garniss earned $20,000 from this in only three months.

Garniss had a storekeeper friend across the way named Hamilton who put out for sale various household utensils for which there was virtually no market in New York, but which fetched good prices in San Francisco. One item was a common crockery bedpan. A man came along one day, saw it and exclaimed "Holloa, that's just what I want. I have got a sick friend and that is just the thing for him. What will you take for it?" Hamilton replied: "I think I ought to have a pretty good price for it." The buyer offered six ounces of gold dust ($96), which was accepted. He weighed out the dust and walked off with his prize. The bedpan had cost just 50 cents in New York.

Professional men also came to seek their fortunes. Few dentists arrived, but a good number of doctors and lawyers made it to California. John W. Palmer, who would become San Francisco's first city physician, arrived in summer with three ounces of dust in his pocket, virtually all the money he had—received as payment for a debt—and parlayed that into 24 ounces playing monte (a card game) at the tables in the Parker House. Palmer used the stake to open a medical practice in an adobe on Sacramento Street where he soon was making $75 to $100 a day.

Lawyer John Dwinelle, who would be instrumental as a legislator in creating the University of California and who would serve as one of its regents for many years, arrived in early October. A few days after recovering from diarrhea he established a law practice in a bankers office, and not a moment too soon, because he had just six dollars in his pocket. He received $50 for his first legal work, which took not more than three quarters of an hour. "Satisfactory," he wrote in his diary.

Although not your typical business, the town's two newspapers, the *Alta California* and the *Pacific News*, sold lots of papers to local residents and new arrivals hungry for the latest news. They also did tremendous business with their "steamer editions." "Steamer Day" was the day the Pacific Mail steamships made their departure for Panama, whence the mail was carried across the Isthmus and on to the East Coast via ships. Starting in November, Steamer Day became a regularly scheduled twice-monthly routine, and on those days men crowded the offices before departure to purchase special extra editions for friends and businesses on the East Coast. The slow hand-presses worked overtime trying to keep up with the demand. Bayard Taylor, a close observer, reckoned that both papers earned annual profit of $75,000.

In 1849 with no native industries or manufactures yet developed (except for gold mining), most everything city residents consumed had to be imported. Goods of all conceivable types were thus brought by sea to San Francisco to be sold by merchants eager to make a profit. Advertisements offering goods for sale that appeared in the two local papers during that summer give a sampling, by no means complete, of the broad array of things that ships unloaded: soda water; cheese; Seidlitz powders; brushes; American, Chilean, and Singapore lumber; crowbars; hatchets and axes; shot tin plates; candles; window glass; iron safes; pistols; nails; fireproof money chests; gold scales and balances; gin, rum, and whiskey; lanterns; patent lard lamps; ships' and pocket compasses; crucifixes and rosaries; tents; Mexican and Spanish saddles; German silverware; fur and wool Mexican hats; gunpowder in pound canisters; crucibles for melting gold; Colgate's soap; letter paper; stone jugs; wooden bowls; tinware; dice and dice cups; card counters; music boxes; wagons and buggies; chocolate; champagne; port; brown stout; French brandy; dried apples; blankets; mattresses; cots; Chinese fancy goods; bread baskets; tea caddies; vinegar; rice; coffee and cocoa; boots and shoes; window shades;

chessmen; blue, red, and black ink; brass lamps; and Virginia tobacco, just to name some.

In shipping such goods, merchants in New York, Boston, Liverpool, Sydney, or wherever, were plagued by a lack of knowledge as to what the current supply and demand situation was in San Francisco for any particular product. Furthermore, they had no idea what other vendors were sending. Some San Francisco merchandisers did correspond with agents or exporters, telling them what products were in demand and which were not, but since it took months for goods to arrive, that intelligence could easily be old news. Macondray & Company, an established importer, wrote to one of their agents in Boston: "It is perfectly idle for us to quote prices for anything and we refuse to do so, for the greatest irregularities exist in the market. Everything must depend upon the amount of goods coming here. . . ."

It was not uncommon for several ships to arrive at the same time carrying similar goods, creating an instant oversupply, causing prices to plummet. Likewise, if some scarce commodity arrived that no else had the price could skyrocket. The net result was that some San Francisco importers made large profits while others, holding surplus goods, took losses. Seasonal variation also played a role to some degree on price levels. The prices of many goods in 1849 fell in the spring and summer and subsequently rose later in the year as the population increased with more new arrivals and as miners laden with gold returned to San Francisco at the onset of winter rains. The combination of increased demand for such necessities as food and shelter, along with more gold in circulation, meant higher prices.

Prices for merchandise of all sorts changed rapidly. Examples abound. A man named Charles Huse wrote in late October: "Two weeks ago . . . Flour could be bought for $9.00 the sack of 200 lbs; today you cannot touch it short of $22.00. Barley then was worth $7.00 the bag; today $12.00. Three days ago lumber was selling for $275.00 per thousand board feet. Yesterday, at $400.00. Last night it rained and today it will probably go up $50.00 more." Another observer that same month noted that in June merchants could hardly give away flour, but by then it went for $40 a barrel.

Molasses, which had gone for $4.00 a gallon, plummeted to 65 cents when a new shipment arrived.

Mary Jane Megquier, a native of Maine who arrived in June with her husband, Thomas, and who wrote a series of letters to family back home documenting her experiences, noted that when she arrived pork sold for $6 a barrel. By early November it was $65; sugar which earlier had sold for three cents a pound, rose to 50 cents per pound. Conversely, earlier in the year especially, prices decreased just as rapidly. Dr. Victor J. Fourgeaud, a South Carolinian of French descent who had arrived in 1847, recorded that hams, which had sold for more than one dollar per pound in January 1849, had by March declined to 27 cents a pound. Brandy, which had commanded $8 a gallon, had dropped to only $2 a gallon. Blankets, which had cost a dear $50 a pair in December 1848 sold for only $5 the following April.

Prefabricated houses provide a good example of how a market could become saturated when too much of a given product arrived. Franklin Buck was one entrepreneur who took a chance and brought some with him rather than waiting until he got to San Francisco to see what the need really was. He and some partners carried on their ship four 14-foot by 28-foot frame houses that they had purchased in New York for $147 each. Upon debarking in San Francisco they sold the lot for $4,000. Buck bought a two-quart tin pail for one dollar and delightedly spooned the gold dust used as payment into it. He and his companions were fortunate because when they arrived in August there still was strong demand and a limited supply of pre-fab houses. By late in the year, however, many more had arrived and there was a glut on the market. Daniel Knower of Albany, New York had twelve knocked-down wood frame houses sent out, but because they were delayed and didn't arrive until the market was tanking, he was lucky to break even—the freight charges and selling price equaled his cost. Some even less fortunate shippers turned their houses over to anyone willing to have them brought ashore, since the additional cost of lighterage would have resulted in a loss.

Imbalances in supply and demand led to a strange anomaly in the price of watercraft. James O'Meara, who arrived in September, wrote: "A sailboat which carried eight tons was one day sold for

$4,000; while the offer of a good seaworthy bark of 250 tons at $5,000 found no takers." The reason ocean-going vessels like ships, barks, and brigs went begging for buyers was twofold. First, there was a huge glut on the market. Dozens and later hundreds of them sat idle in the cove, it being almost impossible to hire a crew for the return journey. Second, deepwater vessels were unfit for navigating the shallower inland waterways that led to Sacramento and Stockton, the two major embarkation points for the gold fields. As the story involving carpenter Henry F. Williams cited earlier illustrates, demand was high for boats and other small craft for this lucrative traffic. Sea captain George Coffin of England, who managed to sell his ship for $13,500 (in late January 1850 after the market had temporarily improved) recognized the trend and went into the lighterage business. He bought a scow of 20 tons capacity for $1,300, "an extravagant price," then two other small boats, at a total cost of $3,600, for which he might have paid $1,000 in Boston.

There were some products that were almost always in high demand and short supply. Foremost among these was lumber, which should be no surprise in a city undergoing a building boom, especially as the year progressed. San Francisco itself, having no forests, had to rely on surrounding areas with their primitive and costly to operate sawmills, or on imports from foreign countries, to bring lumber to town. Labor and transportation costs made either option expensive. Prices for sawn lumber typically ranged from $350 to $500 per thousand board feet, a cost so dear that it initially was only used for construction that would pay a high return, such as for gambling emporiums or hotels. Using wood for ordinary campfires was prohibitively expensive. Jessie Frémont found that out when she moved into the Leidesdorff adobe and had to settle for using broken-up boxes and brushwood in her fireplace to keep her warm. To further illustrate how valuable wood was, a local undertaker made a lot of money by recycling pine coffins. He would charge $100 for one, and when the service was over his thrifty attendants would slide the body into the grave and return the coffin to be used again and again.

All throughout 1849 there were three other items for which there was continuing strong demand but no lack of supply. These were liquor, tobacco, and firearms. San Francisco was a boisterous, hard-drinking town, and liquor and wine merchants on the East Coast and in Europe delivered a steady stream of spirits and liquors to California. France especially was good about providing wine and Champagne for thirsty forty-niners. Virginia tobacco made its way to San Francisco in such great quantity that at times it was in such oversupply that boxes of it were thrown into the muddy streets during the rainy season in an attempt to provide solid footing. Several city residents even claimed that crates of it were used as foundations for buildings. Revolvers and pistols were also in plentiful supply. So plentiful, one man wrote (in January 1850), that firearms cost less in San Francisco than in Philadelphia.

Prices of services also went up and down, but were less volatile than those for goods and changed less rapidly. They tended to remain on the high side, since labor in San Francisco was in demand—more men preferred digging gold in the foothills. Skilled craftsmen such as carpenters, painters, and tinsmiths, who would make $1.50 for a 12-hour day elsewhere in the United States, were paid from $12 to $20 a day in San Francisco at peak times in 1849. The inflated prices paid for labor led to a reversal of the normal dominance of capital over labor. As one forty-niner wrote: "Labor is unshackled and unoppressed; it receives its full recompense." More than full recompense according to some. That same writer, in a letter that was published in a Washington, D. C. newspaper in May, wrote: "A cook or a house steward commands in this country a higher salary than the Governor of New York." General Persifor Smith grumped that a good carpenter made more than a major general in the U. S. Army.

The high labor costs served to inflate the cost not only of services but goods as well, since those costs were built into the selling prices. Thus it cost 50 cents to wash a shirt, but a new one could be purchased for as little as 25 cents. Women in town could buy calico at three to six cents a yard, but it cost $25 to have it made into a dress. Good beef could be purchased for 12 cents a pound, but a slice of roast beef in a restaurant cost $1.50. With this kind of leverage, laborers clearly had the upper hand. On December 1, 1849 a "Meeting of Carpenter and Joiners" was held at the City Hotel for the purposes of fixing their services at $16 a day. It was, in effect, what appears to be the city's first labor union.

While wage earners were certainly well paid, the flip side of the coin was that they needed to be because their own living costs were so high. A lawyer from Ohio, Robert P. Effinger, who arrived in early December, put things in perspective: "In this country no one can form a just estimate of what one is making. A man may receive $10,000 per month, but if it takes all this sum to pay his monthly expenses I would like to know how much he is making." John W. Geary certainly felt the pinch, at least initially. While his $800 per annum salary as postmaster would have been adequate back home, it wasn't close to a living wage in gold rush San Francisco. Shortly after he arrived, Geary, in a draft of a letter to his superiors in Washington, D. C. that appears not to have been sent, wrote that he had with great difficulty found lodging for $125 a month, which, he didn't need to spell out, was twice his monthly salary. (As noted, Geary went into business with two partners and thereby alleviated his financial straits.) The high prices of virtually everything led to some perverse boasting. The *Alta California* told of fresh salmon from the Sacramento River brought to market for one dollar a pound. "Think of this ye Eastern epicures," it gloated, "a single fish in California sold for forty-five dollars."

For those trying to make a living in San Francisco the developing marketplace led to some unexpected role changes. Lawyers, doctors, and other professionals without clients sometimes had to wait tables, wash dishes, or black boots to make ends meet. New Yorker John McGlynn became one of the first to start a draying business; there was a great need to haul goods around once they were unloaded from the ships. In a letter home to his mother he bragged that he had hired a lawyer as a teamster to drive a mule team: "That is all the use lawyers are out here." No occupation was considered demeaning according to Bayard Taylor. "A graduate of Yale considers it no disgrace to sell peanuts on the Plaza," wrote another observer.

This democratic leveling and classless society especially impressed foreigners. Frenchman Ernest de Massey saw gentlemen from Paris, London, and New York carrying trunks for people that previously they wouldn't even have had as servants. Chilean Vicente Pérez Rosales watched as some of his high-society countrymen worked as common laborers. He wrote letters home that told of this "remarkable breakdown in social classes." The sense of equality was a breath of fresh air for many, regardless of nationality. It heightened the zest for new enterprise based on the perception that everyone had a fair and equal chance. A man here was judged not by where he had come from or his prior station in life, but by what he could do.

That mindset, combined with the prevailing get-rich-quick mentality, led to an intense focus on business activities. Reporter Bayard Taylor felt it as an almost tangible presence: "The very air is pregnant with the magnetism of bold, spirited, unwearied action, and he who but ventures into the outer circle of the whirlpool is spinning, ere he has the time for thought, in its dizzy vortex." "Time is Money" was never truer than in San Francisco in 1849. "People had no time to stop and talk . . . everybody acted as though they had but a few hours only to attend to a year's business," wrote one resident. One man was so lost in thought on a business deal he was contemplating that as he was walking along he bumped into another man in the street. The first man's hat was knocked off but he didn't even notice as he kept on going. Jessie Frémont, holding court at the Leidesdorff adobe shortly after her arrival, was flattered when prominent businessmen came to call in the daytime. She was even more flattered when she was told that "'time was worth fifty dollars a minute,' and that I must hold as a great compliment the brief visits which were made to me constantly through the day by busy men."

For those purchasing goods at retail there was little shopping around and no haggling. Part of the reason was that it was hard to comparison shop. Few merchants specialized in particular products. Vendors sold whatever they could get their hands on that they thought they could re-sell. Customers paid what was asked, and moved on. Some newcomers, shocked at the high prices, did shop around only to discover that prices had increased while they were dithering, leaving them to pay even more later. Those negotiating business deals did so in most cases on the basis of a handshake. Debts were paid punctually. Business was conducted seven days a week, a situation that discomfited some who would have preferred that Sundays, as back East, would be a day off to honor the Sabbath, with shops closed. Even holidays were not sacrosanct. Margaret De Witt, who had come out with her husband, wrote to her mother in late November to complain that business went on pretty much as normal even on Thanksgiving: ". . . very few of the stores were closed—all are so intent on making money that they have time for nothing else."

A number of other factors contributed to the velocity of trade and the rapid turnover of goods. One, of course, was the fear that another ship would arrive with a cargo of merchandise similar to what was already being offered, thus driving down the price, which provided the incentive to sell everything quickly. Another reason was that storage space was scarce and expensive. Storage costs could consume all one's profits in a matter of months. Other expenses such as commissions—for those who used brokers to sell their goods—unloading charges, which were hefty, and interest rates on borrowed money, which could run from 2 percent to 10 percent a month or more, all impelled a fast turnover of merchandise. The absence of trustworthy insurance—"three quarters of the insurance here is not worth a straw," wrote one—also contributed to the fast pace of business, because no one wanted to be holding uninsured goods if a fire swept through. (There was no fire department until the end of the year.) Abundant gold dust also helped speed the velocity of transactions. When, on occasion, gold dust became so plentiful that it started to depreciate from its normal $16 an ounce to as little as $10, the incentive was great to spend it rather than hold it. Auctions, with their gavel-down fast pace, were a favored method of quickly disposing of goods for which there was marginal demand, thus further accelerating business activity.

The frenzied business climate of 1849 was a far cry from the San Francisco of only a short time previously. In sleepy Spanish and Mexican California trade and commerce had not amounted to much. Transactions between mission fathers, local rancheros, and the foreign ships that came to trade were occasionally done with gold doubloons or pieces of silver, but coin was so scarce that most exchange was by barter. The locals primarily used cow hides, which were so accepted that they came to be known as "California banknotes." Hides were used as payment in San Francisco as late as the beginning of 1848. The discovery of gold, however, instantly transformed the economy from one of barter to a gold exchange, cash-based one.

Most of the transactions were conducted in the medium of exchange that was rapidly flooding the town: gold dust. "Gold dust is abundant in the shops. One sees it standing on the counter, in tin pails as one would oats or beans at home," wrote one. (Gold *dust* is really a misnomer since it was comprised more of grains, kernels and flakes rather than powder.) Most retail merchandise was paid for with it. The dust was "turned out carelessly from dirty buckskin bags" into merchants scales. Many observers noted that in keeping with the fast pace of business in San Francisco, few attempts were made to assay dust or to estimate its purity. Merchants who suspected that a customer had adulterated his dust would take it only at a discount. But trust was generally the order of the day. To facilitate transactions, gold dust was sometimes wrapped in brown paper bags and marked on the outside with the value—$50, $100, etc.

Gold dust had obvious disadvantages compared to coins as a way of facilitating transactions. It was bulky, shapeless, had to be carried in bags or other receptacles, and, as noted, there was no ready way to determine its purity without assaying it. And as anyone who has seen the movie *The Treasure of the Sierra Madre* knows, gold dust, in its finest state, is also in danger of blowing away in a strong wind, no small consideration in frequently windy San Francisco.

Coins or paper currency certainly would have been preferable. There would be no national "legal tender" paper money however until the 1860s, so until then the country had to rely heavily on banks in individual states to issue paper money, with all the disadvantages that entailed. The primary problem for San Franciscans was that all the states in 1849 were at least two thousand miles away, and banks' paper money could really only be used within the state of issue or redeemed for coin by presenting it to the banks themselves, a difficult proposition at best for anyone in California. That left specie as the only real alternative. But coinage was scarce. The United States issued gold coins in the amount of $2.50 and

$5.00, but only sporadically from 1805 to 1834. U. S. silver dollars also were minted irregularly, and there was a stretch from 1806 to 1840 when none had been produced at all. To compound the problem, many coins left the country to pay for imports or to be melted down, the latter applying especially to silver dollars.

As an example of just how scarce, and valued, coins were in San Francisco, Thomas O. Larkin (one of the shrewder businessmen of the time) ran into Sam Brannan one morning in October 1848 as both were walking along Montgomery Street. Larkin told Brannan that he had a lot at the corner of Montgomery and Washington that he wanted to sell. Asked how much, Larkin replied that he would take $10,000 in gold dust or $5,000 in silver dollars. Given a right of refusal only until 2 p.m., Brannan, not having that much of either kind of money readily available, walked down Montgomery a couple of blocks to see his friend William D. M. Howard about a loan. Howard had only about a thousand silver dollars but he had plenty of gold dust packed in glass bottles sitting on shelves in the back of his store. Bottle after bottle was emptied until the requisite $10,000 was reached.

Another reason that coins were in such short supply in San Francisco was because of Custom House regulations. In the summer of 1848, as gold dust began to flow into the town, Governor Mason, under pressure from local merchants who lacked specie and needed it to pay for imported goods, instructed the Collector of the Port, whose job it was to assess and collect duties on foreign imports, to accept gold dust at the going rate of $16 an ounce. Mason quickly had to reverse his position when he learned that this was a violation of U. S. tariff laws, which specified that only gold or silver coin (or Treasury notes, which were non-existent on the West Coast) were acceptable as payment for customs duties. So Mason revoked his order, but in view of the difficulties merchants were having obtaining coin, he allowed them to temporarily deposit gold dust at the Custom House at the rate of $10 an ounce with the stipulation that they redeem it in coin within 60 days. Merchants, with few options for obtaining enough coin in that time span, pressured Mason to extend the deadline, so he stretched it to half payment in 90 days, the other half in 180 days. By the December deadline the

Custom House's gold dust had been redeemed for an average price of a little over $10 an ounce.

To help fill the gap created by a lack of U. S. coinage, foreign coins were used. Their use as legal tender goes back to the early days of the republic when Treasury Secretary Alexander Hamilton recommended that Congress legalize foreign coins to aid the domestic money supply until the U. S. mint could meet domestic demand. It took the mint decades to reach that goal, so periodically throughout the first half of the 19th century Congress re-confirmed the legal tender standing of designated foreign coins. Newspapers from time to time published tables showing the official exchange rates for the various approved foreign issue. It wouldn't be until 1857 that Congress would revoke that approval and make U. S. coins the sole legal tender.

In San Francisco, with U. S. coin scarce and with the arrival of people from countries all over the globe, it wasn't long before a dizzying array of foreign coinage made its appearance in local transactions. Gold coins found in circulation in San Francisco in 1849 included German thalers (said to be the origin of the word "dollar") and ducats, Belgian and French francs, and British sovereigns. Among silver coins, doubloons (worth an ounce of gold, or $16), dollars, half-dollars, and quarters from Mexico and South American countries predominated, but also to be found were German crowns, florin, and gulden, and British half-crowns and shillings. Some silver coins in circulation, such as the French five-franc piece, were intrinsically worth only about 93 cents but they passed for the equivalent of a dollar, so desperate were vendors for coins instead of dust. Likewise, Spanish pesetas and single French francs were worth only about 20 cents but they passed as the equivalent of quarters. Fractional money, worth even less than 20 cents, included such exotic pieces as Austrian zwanzigers and Spanish *reales*. (Eight-*real* coins were sometimes cut up into "bits" as a way to make smaller change. Two bits equaled 25 cents.) American dimes were the smallest coins to be found in circulation. Copper pennies were non-existent, because with the inflated prices of everything there were very few items that could be purchased for less than 25 cents.

The difference between the intrinsic value and the accepted value of some of the foreign coins such as the French franc led to arbitrage profits for those lucky enough to have those coins. But arbitrage on gold dust was more common because it was much more plentiful. Arbitrage only works, of course, when the disparity between what a commodity can be bought for in one place and sold for in another is great enough to cover one's costs and leave enough left over for profit. According to an article in the *Alta California* in March 1849 gold dust purchased at $16.00 an ounce in San Francisco could fetch $18.05 an ounce at the mint in Philadelphia. With freight, insurance, and other charges totaling 92 cents that left a profit of $1.13, or 7 percent, not a bad return for a relatively effortless transaction. Some wheeler-dealers made substantially more. Speculators who had coin and redeemed unclaimed gold dust at the Custom House at $10 an ounce during Mason's extension reaped great profits. Those who made the trek to the Mother Lode mining camps sometimes did even better. Miners, loaded with bags of gold, sometimes sold their dust for as little as $3 to $8 an ounce. Most of these large discrepancies occurred in 1848. Things changed in 1849, as forty-niner Daniel Coit found out. He arrived in San Francisco in April with the intention of bringing in Mexican gold and silver coins to use to purchase gold dust. By then, however, gold was trading near par, so Coit mostly bided his time. It was only in 1850 that he started to profit in a big way, investing over half a million dollars as gold dust once again flooded the town, driving down the price.

Another solution to the lack of coins in circulation came in the form of private mints, run by individuals or partnerships for profit. (Nothing in the Constitution barred private coinage, and Congress didn't ban such activity until 1864.) Because it took months to ship the necessary heavy machinery by sea, the first private mints in San Francisco only became operational in the summer of 1849. They soon were cranking out five- and ten-dollar gold pieces. By the end of the year at least nine private mints were in operation.

The best known and most reputable of these was the firm of Moffat & Company. To give their coins an aura of legitimacy they closely modeled their designs on that of official U. S. gold coins, using a bust of Liberty on the front and an eagle and shield on the back. The main difference between the federal coins and the Moffat issue was that the latter stamped the words "California Gold" on them. They also stamped the initials "S.M.V." on them, which stood for "Standard Mint Value." This was meant to reassure users that the coins contained the stated amount of gold. In Moffat's case they came very close, being an average of only about one percent short of the actual amount.

Other private minters turned out coins that were more debased. The poster boy for these was the firm of Kohler & Company. Frederick D. Kohler was a New York City fireman, politician, and part-time assayer who arrived in San Francisco by sea in mid-1849. Upon arrival he was contacted by Col. Jonathan D. Stevenson, whom he had known in New York. Stevenson proposed the idea of a private mint to Kohler, who agreed to it, and then to David C. Broderick, a fellow New York fireman colleague of Kohler's, who arrived in town shortly after Kohler. The three formed a partnership. Stevenson, who had made a lot of money digging gold and in other endeavors, acted as a financial backer and silent partner. Kohler served as engraver and assayer, while Broderick did the heavy manual labor of pouring melted dust into bars, weighing the ingots, and using a sledgehammer to pound out the coins sandwiched between the dies. From their office in the City Hotel they cranked out coins bearing the imprint of various banks that had hired the firm to produce their coins.

Early histories claim that Kohler & Company gold coins contained only 80 percent of their stated value, but more recent research indicates that the coins were debased more on the order of only three to four percent rather than 20 percent. Whatever the amount, using gold reportedly purchased at $14 an ounce, their built-in margin of perhaps four percent, probably combined with a coining fee, made the partners enough money that they were able to buy a lot of real estate. Broderick cashed out his share of the partnership at the end of the year just before independent assay tests started to show the short weight nature of the coins of virtually every private minter in town with the exception of Moffat & Company. (When that news hit, local merchants started accepting the debased coins only at a discount which, in the hysteria following the findings, ranged in excess of the actual amount of debasement, providing them with an advantage.) David Broderick used his profits from the coining business and from real estate deals to launch a career in politics. Elected U. S. Senator from California in 1857, after

serving in lesser offices, Broderick's political career—and life
—ended two years later when he was mortally wounded in a
famous duel with Chief Justice David Terry of the California
Supreme Court.

Debased or not, private gold coins helped steady the value of
gold, facilitated commerce, and improved the local economy.
Merchants generally preferred coins to gold dust, although dust
continued to be accepted. Indeed, those who sent their dust to the
mint in Philadelphia favored that approach due to the extra margin
they received on the arbitrage. Privately minted gold coins were not
acceptable at the Custom House as payment for duties, which was
ironic. California gold, the source of all the wealth, and the reason
the Custom House was doing land-office business in the first place,
was turned away by clerks who were instructed not to take locally
minted coins. The reason was simple: they were not on the government's approved list of what constituted acceptable specie.

Also helping to stabilize and improve the economy was the
emergence of banks. They developed out of the need of miners who
wanted someplace to store their gold while in town. Miners would
leave gold with merchants or bankers who would give them
receipts, or notes, which served as primitive paper money,
although they did not circulate as such. That left banks only one
step removed from making loans on the gold deposited with them.
Paper money would have been handy for such transactions, but
there was one big sticking point, namely the fear paper money
engendered. That fear dated as far back as the American Revolution
when "Continentals," paper currency issued to finance the war,
became virtually worthless, as it became known that far too many
were circulating backed by too few hard assets, namely gold and
silver. Since the Revolution there had been periodic economic busts
occasioned by similar promiscuous issuance of currency, with
banks going out of business and leaving depositors holding the bag.
The most recent instance had occurred in 1837 when, in the wake of
President Andrew Jackson's refusal to re-charter the Second Bank
of the United States, state banks, which had taken up the slack,
caused an inflationary boom, then economic bust, by printing far
too many notes. When Californians got serious late in 1849 about

forming a state government, and a Constitutional Convention was held, the debacle of 1837 was still within recent memory, so the issue of whether to allow banks at all was hotly contested. After much debate, it was decided to allow "associations" that could take gold and silver on deposit, but they were forbidden from issuing paper notes that could circulate as money. (Part of the thinking also was that with so much gold floating about, paper money wouldn't be necessary.) The associations could and did issue checks, especially after 1849, which were made payable in coin or gold dust.

Banks first sprang up in San Francisco beginning in early 1849. They facilitated transactions for miners who wanted to remit funds to their families back home and for importers who needed to pay for goods brought from the East Coast. Local merchants seeking to pay for imports from New York, for example, would deposit gold with a San Francisco bank, which in turn would ship it to a correspondent New York bank. A supplier there could then present a draft, sent from San Francisco, for an invoice in a specified amount for payment at the New York bank. Banks in San Francisco also made local loans, but adequate collateral was required and interest rates were exorbitant compared to the rest of the country, running as high as 15 percent a month, depending on the borrower's credit worthiness. Interest rates were so high because many loans were high risk. In fast-moving, transient San Francisco a borrower could be here today and gone tomorrow. There were also times when shortages of capital became acute (such as Steamer Day when a lot of money left town), leaving lenders at risk. Real estate was commonly used as collateral, but with rampant speculation and land titles uncertain, loans based on ownership of lots were considered less than a sure thing. All of these factors kept interest rates high.

The biggest and seemingly most profitable of banks established in San Francisco in 1849 was started by Thomas G. Wells. A native of New Hampshire, Wells (not related to Wells of Wells Fargo) arrived in May as part of a company of nine men who had pledged to split evenly the profits of all their endeavors. While his colleagues went off to the mines, Wells stayed in San Francisco, and by August had started a banking business. He began by sending miners' remittances home in exchange for a commission. He quickly added another service by importing specie from Mexico with which to buy gold dust. Wells wrote to his wife: "The first shipment of $40,000 I received by the last steamer, and am now purchasing gold with it, for which I charge a handsome commission. . . ." The gold dust he purchased he shipped to the London office of the premier European bankers of the time, the Rothschilds.

In September, Wells moved his operation to a new, larger space at the corner of Clay and Montgomery streets and hired a clerk to help him. The two of them had enough business to keep them busy from 5:30 a.m. to 9:00 p.m. At night they slept in the office in berths behind a screen partition. Such accommodations, the banker noted, were very comfortable for San Francisco.

In November, the rainy season having commenced, Wells's dispirited partners returned from the Mother Lode with little to show for their efforts. Rather than continue to share with them the enormous profits he was making he bought them out for $3,000 apiece to release him from their compact. "No division of profits by nine," he noted. By the end of December, Wells had accumulated $132,000 in deposits and considered himself to be the top banker in San Francisco.

The story of Thomas Wells and so many others who arrived in 1849 to make their fortunes at the bustling town by the bay serves to illustrate how much choice and opportunity awaited those who would seize it. Some achieved success beyond imagining. Most did not. Regardless of the outcome, many found their San Francisco experience a liberating one. Far from home, untethered from family ties and the need to conform to accepted standards of behavior, able to do as they pleased, many men gave into temptation and indulged in vice, namely gambling and prostitution.

5

Gambler's Paradise

Many commentators, in their journals or in letters home, wrote about the great extent to which gambling was carried on in gold-rush San Francisco. One couldn't avoid it. By the end of 1849 there were dozens, perhaps hundreds, of gambling houses, most with saloons attached. The north, south, and east sides of Portsmouth Square were given over to a large degree to buildings housing gaming establishments. Side streets radiating out from the Plaza in all directions contained many more. Gambling went on 24 hours a day, 7 days a week. Although gambling houses had to pay license fees starting in the fall of 1849 as a way for the city to raise revenue, they were not regulated and there were no restrictions as to who could operate one or how much players could wager.

Gambling was the perfect metaphor for the Gold Rush because gold mining and games of chance were both roll-the-dice propositions. In placer mining a miner on one section of a stream might uncover a rich cache of nuggets while his neighbor just yards away might come up empty handed, and so it was in gambling where a turn of a card might lead to fabulous wealth for one individual or to destitution for another.

Gambling was attractive foremost of course for the chance it offered of instant riches. But the gambling halls offered other attractions. Why stay in a cold, damp tent when the gambling saloons[1] were warm, well lighted, and sometimes featured those rare creatures, women. They were also the main social centers of the town. Gold-rush San Francisco was intense and competitive; gambling

---

1. The word casino, in its meaning as a room where gambling was conducted, did not come into use until 1851.

and drinking relieved stress and provided diversion. It is no wonder then that *The Annals of San Francisco*, published in 1855, declared
that gambling was "the life and soul of the place."

While the Gold Rush brought gambling to full flower, its existence in San Francisco was hardly unknown before then. In February 1840, under Mexican rule, a Victor Prudon was fined 10 reales
for permitting gambling in his house. The Americans would soon
take a more lenient view, but initially they too viewed it as a vice
that should be suppressed. In late 1847 the *California Star* editorialized against the gambling dens in town on the grounds that they
provided shelter for "escaped fugitives from justice." In January
1848, two weeks before the discovery of gold, the city council
passed stringent regulations against gambling. There were to be
heavy fines levied on players, and any money found on gaming
tables was to be confiscated. But at the council meeting the following week, apparently as a result of pressure applied by gambling
interests, all the previous resolutions were repealed. Even if they
hadn't been, it is unlikely that they could have been enforced. Once
the gold-rush hordes arrived, gambling houses proliferated un-
checked like mushrooms in a spring rain.

Once in San Francisco, many forty-niners needed little encour-
agement to take part in the action. Some, however, still imbued with
the morals and values with which they had been raised, hesitated.
Dr. John W. Palmer described his reaction when he first entered a
gambling saloon: "At first you loiter innocently, a philosophic and
observant looker-on; then you take your inevitable part in the
wicked hurly-burly."

To encourage those hesitant souls, and in view of the competition from dozens of other houses, gambling emporiums did what
they could to attract customers. Larger establishments employed
musicians to create noise and excitement; others adorned their
walls with "flash pictures"—drawings of naked women—to lure
men in through their portals. Once one was inside the smoke-filled
rooms there was the blare of the bands, "the incessant clink of the
coin, and the continuous calls of the gamblers in playing, together
with the endless din of drinking and talking, the unceasing tramp
and shuffle of the multitudes in passing in and out, or about the
tables, or to and from the bar." Dealers would call out: "Come

gentlemen, here's the spot to raise your funds—walk up." After bets were placed, eager eyes would watch as the roulette ball rolled or the cards were turned over. When the results were known the jingling of coins would be heard as the winners were paid and the losers had their bets raked in by the croupier. If the dealer was profiting nicely—usually the case—he would typically treat the players at his table to drinks from the bar. He'd ring a little bell and a waiter would come and take orders. Freshly supplied, the gamblers would continue hour after hour.

The gaming tables were visual showcases. Typically covered with cloth, most often green, they would be piled high with stacks of gold coins, silver dollars, bags of dust, and gold nuggets of all sizes. On one table they formed a rampart around "a lacquered box into which the gold dust of the losers was dumped." The glittering display was not just to tempt the gazer. Large amounts of money on the table—anywhere from $20,000 to $40,000—were meant to discourage players from "tapping," that is, trying to break the bank. Although bets typically ranged from as little as 25 cents up to $5,000, occasionally a well-heeled player would wager against all the money displayed. A crowd would form, and observers would unconsciously hold their breath as the game unfolded. Twenty thousand dollars or more could change hands on the turn of a single card. One witness to a game at the City Hotel saw a man lose $56,000 (more than one million dollars today) "in *one bet*" and noted that he walked away from the table "as coolly as if he were only losing fifty cents."

The effect of such astonishing amounts of money being bandied back and forth seems to have changed the mind-set of some forty-niners. The same observer who witnessed the loss of $56,000 at one swoop marveled that men who, back home, would "have hardly risked a dollar at any game of chance, gamble away thousands." Colonel J. D. Stevenson speculated that the reason miners were so free with their money is that—at least in the early days—they felt that they could easily recoup their losses by returning to the gold fields where the attitude was there was plenty more where that came from. Such instant riches, so readily obtained, were no doubt intoxicating. Perhaps also contributing to the "easy come, easy go" psychology was the feeling that wealth easily obtained is not valued as much as that achieved through "honest" labor. The unreality of the magnitude and extent of gambling in San Francisco no doubt contributed to such irrational behavior.

Single bets in five figures were the exception to the rule, however. Many contented themselves with smaller wagers. Even so, gambling fever took its toll. One man started with $100 and within 15 minutes had won $1,700. He soon lost it all. The next day he was seen running from friend-to-friend begging to borrow $50. Another player harvested $23,500 in gold at the mines in four months. After five nights at the gambling tables in San Francisco he was without a cent. Chastened by his experience he landed a job, and after saving $1,400, he resolved to "put it where the devil could not get it." Some did know when to quit. One lawyer borrowed ten dollars, and by playing cards one night and part of the next day parlayed it into $7,000. He swore he would never play again, and he returned home on the next steamer.

The gambling halls were only too eager to take anyone's money. They were open to all. Not surprisingly, therefore, the diversity of San Francisco could be found within their walls. One French visitor told of the different races, the strange costumes, and "the babel of foreign tongues" he encountered in one establishment. All classes of people seemed to gamble as well. One patron noted that men ranged in dress from glossy broadcloth to "well-worn linsey." Usually the best-dressed men were those who bankrolled and ran the games. The Reverend William Taylor wrote: ". . . the gamblers (the bankers and dealers) were the aristocracy of the land; gambling being the most profitable, hence the most respectable business a man could follow." Some of those who ran the tables and had adopted gambling as a profession were men who had been doctors, lawyers, or who had come from privileged backgrounds. A few spectators even claimed to have seen former clergymen dealing cards. One observer, with a note of disapproval, wrote: "I have known dozens of young men, whose fathers stand among the proudest in the land in the United States, dealing Monte to a lot of dirty drunken Mexicans. . . ." While few in San Francisco looked down on those who had chosen gambling as a profession, none of those who ran games wanted it known to family and friends back home that they were making a living in such a manner. They viewed their stint in this sinful occupation as temporary. They would tell no one at home about it, and would revert later to being upstanding citizens.

With all welcome in the gambling saloons, one class that was especially welcome was women. They kept busy both as croupiers and as players, although they were few in number since women remained scarce in San Francisco throughout the year. Dr. Joseph Middleton, who arrived in December, visited one house in which "I saw one [woman] dealing the cards while a man attended to the money. At another table the man dealt while his señora attended to the cash." Latin women were also just as likely, if not more so, to be seen making wagers as raking them in. One visitor saw a group of Spanish-speaking women staking large sums at the gaming tables. They were smoking cigars, drinking, and swearing like men. Prostitutes occasionally spent their gains at the tables. One forty-niner recorded a vivid description of one such woman:

> Abandoned women visit these places openly. I saw one the other evening sitting quietly at the monte-table, dressed in white pants, blue coat, and cloth cap, curls dangling over her cheeks, cigar in her mouth and a glass of punch at her side. She handled a pile of doubloons with her blue kid gloved hands, and bet most boldly.

While it's clear that people of all kinds tried their luck, what can't be said with any certainty is what percentage of the population gambled. We can only guess. If you believe the authors of *The Annals of San Francisco*, a book that celebrated the rowdier aspects of the early days, everybody from preachers and city officials on down gambled. At the other extreme, forty-niner William F. White disparaged the sensationalism of the *Annals* and estimated that no more than 10 percent of the population gambled, and that same 10 percent consisted of idlers, loungers, and no-goods who devoted most of their waking hours to gambling.

A good number of city residents were hardworking merchants who likely calculated the slender odds of coming out consistent winners at the gaming tables and realized that a surer way to make money was to establish a business that provided in-demand goods and services. Many shopkeepers worked long hours, typically starting at daybreak, and kept their businesses open until nine or ten o'clock at night. Hours like those allowed no time for idle pursuits such as gambling.

One interesting aspect of first-hand accounts of visits to the gambling houses is that in almost none of them do the writers actually admit to participating in the games. They all clothe themselves in the guise of interested observer. This is understandable when one realizes that many men were writing accounts either in letters home or in diaries that they knew would be read by family members. They did not want to be seen as indulging in vice and, just as important, they wanted to depict themselves as responsible individuals. Many had left mothers, wives, and children at home and they needed to show that they were not risking money on chancy and frivolous pursuits.

But with the throngs crowding the gambling saloons and the large sums of money being wagered daily it is clear that substantial numbers of people were gambling. So with the *Annals* at one extreme claiming that *everybody* gambled, and William F. White on the other claiming that idlers and lowlifes were the bulk of the gambling population, where does the truth lie? Probably somewhere in between. Perhaps as accurate an estimate as any can be found in the following comment from forty-niner Henry Hiram Ellis in a letter he wrote in late November: "There are several churches here but more go to see the card dealer than the parson."

A wide variety of games was played, some still recognizable today such as roulette, keno, and twenty-one (now called blackjack). Others, many with colorful names such as lansquenet, tub-and-ball, thimble rig, and stop-and-pin, are obscure today. Card games predominated. Poker was played but not widely. It was considered too slow and too complex. The two most popular games were card games not found in American casinos today: monte and faro. They provided lots of action and a quick result, two things that appealed to forty-niners with their preference for instant gratification.

Monte had come to San Francisco from Mexico and had become a favorite of American players, some of whom had encountered it during the Mexican War. In four-card monte—there also was a two-card version—a 40-card deck was used (the tens, nines, and eights were removed). Four cards would be dealt face up on a cloth that would be divided into four sections by means of a chalk line or a braid. Two cards would be winning, and two losing. Players could place their bets on any of the four cards. The dealer/banker would then four draw cards from the remaining deck one at a time. The first and third cards drawn were winning, the second and fourth, losing. As an example, if the four cards placed on the table were a seven, a queen, an ace, and a five, the "winning" cards would be the seven and the ace. If a bettor had placed his money on the seven and the first card drawn was also a seven he would be a winner. If however, the first card drawn were, say, a four and the second—the "losing" card—was a seven he would lose his bet. After each four-card draw the winners had their bets paid—a ten-dollar bet earned ten dollars—and losers had their money swept into the banker's pile. Bettors could change their bets after each round if they chose.

Faro was even more popular. Faro had originated in 17th-century France where it was initially called Pharaoh, allegedly because early cards depicted the face of an Egyptian ruler. Like monte, faro also operated on the principle of turning over winning and losing cards, but it was more complex and offered more variations on betting. Faro required a larger table since a full suit of cards, ace through king, usually spades, would be fixed to or painted on an oilcloth spread on a table. A fifty-two-card deck was used and an abacus as well, since a dealer's partner would keep track of the cards played. Players could lay their money on any card on the table, but only winning cards were paid. The dealer would draw two cards, one at a time; the first card drawn was always the losing card, the second the winning. If both cards drawn were the same, say two kings or two fives, the dealer took half of the money staked on them. At the end of the deck, when only three cards remained (the first card, called a soda, was always discarded before play started leaving an odd number of cards at the end), players could obtain four-to-one odds by guessing in which order those three cards would come up. Faro was a fast game; with only two cards pulled each time, players could wager twice a minute or more.

Given the fact that the games were totally unsupervised or unregulated there were no doubt opportunities for cheating. But cheating appears to have been rare. The reason, no doubt, was that with most men visibly armed, the penalties for getting caught would have been instantaneous and severe. Still, with large sums of money at stake, tensions would mount and suspicions would sometimes boil to the fore. Dr. John W. Palmer, who spent enough time gambling to turn three ounces of gold, or $48, into 24 ounces, or $384—enough to open an office for his medical practice—witnessed a tense exchange of suspected cheating between a player and a dealer at a monte table at the Parker Hotel that went like this:

"A moment if you please," a clean-shaven young man quietly remarked. Covering his pile with a firm hand, he fixed a cold eye on a burly monte dealer. "You can stop there."

"Well sir?"

"Well—excuse me, but I think you drew *two* cards." (Cards were to be drawn only one at a time.)

"I believe not. I'll take your pile, if you please; the kervaiyo[2] takes it."

"Two cards!"

"Your money!"

Both men then drew back clothing to show that they had revolvers. A space quickly cleared around the table.

"Well sir?"

"Well!"

"Your money!"

"Your cards!"

At that point an unflappable veteran player intervened.

"Gentlemen," he said, "try arbitration first."

The two disputants glanced at each other. Neither spoke but their expressions said "Agreed." Both pushed back in their chairs from the table to await the result. The cards were counted out as two other dealers looked on in the role of umpires. Each card of the deck was slowly counted out, a process that took three minutes.

---

2. Kervaiyo was a card with a picture of a horse and was peculiar to monte.

"You are wrong, my friend," said the arbitrator; "no double card was drawn here. Mistakes will happen to the most careful gentlemen." Hands easing off their pistols, the two men shook hands. Drinks were called for and paid for by the challenger and the game resumed.

Disputes sometimes did escalate into fatal stabbings or shootings. But in the crowded halls most violence was nipped in the bud: "Many a knife and revolver were drawn by infuriated victims, though, as a rule, they were overpowered before blood flowed." When shots were fired the crowd would scatter, sometimes upending tables piled with gold and silver. But order would quickly be restored, the music would start once again, and the play would continue. Always keeping their cool in such instances were those who ran the games. They typically remained impassive during such furors, all the while keeping a close watch on their banks. One observer recorded the sangfroid of one: "When a banker hears a pistol shot in the room he cries out, 'Silence, down there; you damned rascals make too much noise."

Players reacted in different ways to winning and losing. Winners of course exulted in their good fortune, although some betrayed no emotion. Latin players were especially noted for their calm demeanor, even in the face of large losses. One visitor from Switzerland watched as a Mexican player increased his stake tenfold and then lost the whole pot on one turn of a card. He calmly lit a cigarette and asked the croupier for a dollar "to buy his daily ration of bread." Americans, especially novices, were less likely to bear their losses with equanimity. Cursing their fate through clenched teeth, many drowned their sorrows in alcohol. Some, crushed by their losses, impulsively put guns to their heads and ended their lives.

One question that will forever remain unanswered is how profitable gambling was to the operators of the games. No taxes were levied on gambling income in 1849 and no written records of takings seem to exist, but the simple answer to the question of how profitable is *very*. The mushrooming of competition with the huge proliferation of gaming establishments was one indicator of big profits. Another was the large sums being paid by professional gamblers to rent rooms and tables to carry on their operations. The ground floor of the town's premier resort, the Parker House, which contained three faro tables, two monte tables, a roulette wheel, and a reserve table for other card games, leased for $10,000 a month. Three separate rooms on the second floor, one of which housed a high stakes poker game, rented for $3,500 a month each. To cover such expenses gaming operators clearly had to be raking in much more. One Frenchman ran into a compatriot, a banker/dealer who volunteered the information that his profits that evening had amounted to $20,000, and he said it in a tone of complaint "for $20,000 in a night is a poor affair in this country." The dealer may have been exaggerating to impress his friend, but even if the true figure was a fraction of that, gambling obviously was an enormously profitable enterprise.

Although gambling was front and center of leisure-time activities in 1849 there were other diversions. Foremost among them were bull-versus-bear fights held at Mission Dolores. A circular ring, with tiers of wooden benches surrounding it, stood directly across from the church. Almost every Sunday gory contests between bulls and bears were held as patrons cheered and shouted while the animals attacked each other.

Bull-versus-bear fights had been held in San Francisco as early as 1816. They were rooted in Spanish tradition as part of fiestas and religious holidays, which explains the proximity of bullrings to mission churches. But it took the arrival of the gold-rush hordes to more fully exploit the commercial prospects of these events by advertising and promoting them in advance, and by charging admission. Ticket prices ranged from about $3.00 up to $25.00 for premium seats. With attendance sometimes ranging in the thousands, these affairs must have been quite profitable for their promoters. Spectators also no doubt placed bets among themselves, further heightening interest in these spectacles.

The dynamics of these contests were such that if the bull won it was usually early in the fight, because once his strength was sapped it was hard for him to generate enough of a charge to plunge his horns fully into the bear's body. Also, if from fatigue and thirst the bull's tongue protruded from his mouth, the bear would seize it with his paws and claw it to shreds.

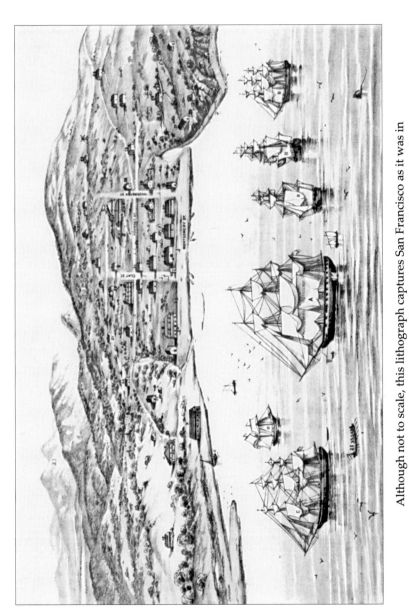

Although not to scale, this lithograph captures San Francisco as it was in March 1847, before the discovery of gold. The view is looking west from Yerba Buena Cove. The beach in the center of the picture is Montgomery Street.

Jasper O'Farrell's 1847 plan for San Francisco showing the original shoreline with proposed water lots to be offered for sale.

Portsmouth Square is labeled in the center of the image. Telegraph Hill occupies the unnumbered blocks to the north. Happy Valley was located just south of Market Street (which bisects the two grids) at the water's edge. The knob of land at the south end of Yerba Buena Cove is Rincon Point.

San Francisco in November 1848.

The view is looking east toward Yerba Buena Cove and the bay.

San Francisco one year later, in November 1849.

The *P.M.S.S. California.*

The first steamship to arrive at San Francisco, February 28, 1849.

The port of San Francisco. Depicted as it was on June 1, 1849.

Portsmouth Square in 1849.

The alcalde's office is at center top. The Custom House is center right.

Although taken in 1851 as part of a panorama of the harbor, this picture illustrates how clogged Yerba Buena Cove had become by late 1849.

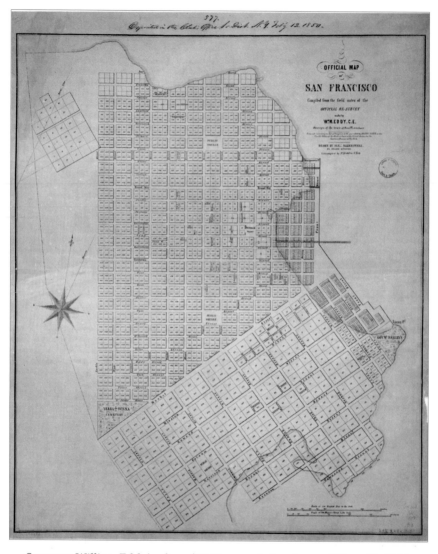

Surveyor William Eddy's plan of 1849 expanded on Jasper O'Farrell's 1847 survey, providing city officials with more lots to sell.

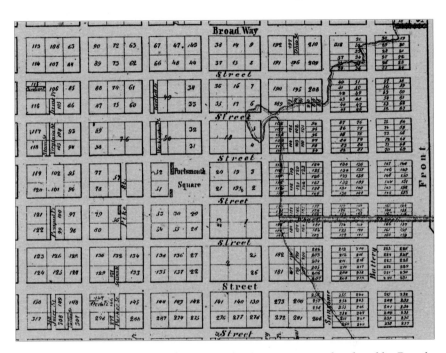

Detail of the Eddy plan of 1849 showing the downtown area bordered by Broadway on the north, Powell Street on the west, Pine Street to the south, and Front Street (underwater) on the east. The numbered lots surround Portsmouth Square. The ragged line is the original shoreline. To the east of it are the "water lots" that were sold in preparation to their being filled in.

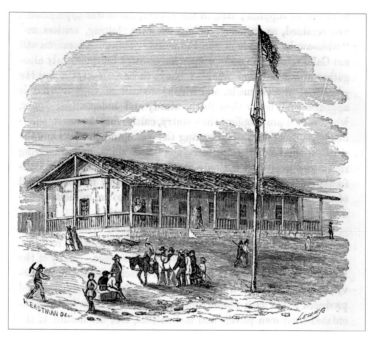

The Custom House on the Plaza.

The old schoolhouse. It stood on the southwest corner of the Plaza across from the Custom House.

The Alcalde's office, west side of Portsmouth Square.

Long lines formed at the post office whenever mail arrived by steamer.

The St. Francis Hotel, corner of Clay and Dupont streets.

The City Hotel, corner of Clay and Kearny streets, across from the Plaza.

The Parker House.

The First Presbyterian Church.

This charming drawing, done as a watercolor by Lt. Joseph Warren Revere (grandson of patriot Paul Revere) in 1849, illustrates three things that characterized San Francisco that year: tent living; the multi–ethnic makeup of the population with the black man sharing a camp with three white men; and the makeshift nature of eating arrangements with the outdoor campfire. Note the Chinese restaurant in the background.

A restaurant fashioned from a ship's galley.

PORTABLE IRON HOUSES,

RUST PROOF.

THE GALVANIZED IRON HOUSES

CONSTRUCTED BY ME FOR CALIFORNIA,

Having met with so much approval, I am thus induced to call the attention of those going to California to an examination of them. The iron is grooved in such a manner that all parts of the house, roof, and sides, slide together, and a house 20 × 15 can be put up in less than a day. They are far cheaper than wood, are fire-proof, and much more comfortable than tents. A house of the above size can be shipped in two boxes, 9 feet long, 1 foot deep, and 2 feet wide, the freight on which would be about $18 to San Francisco. There will also be no trouble in removing from one part of the country to another, as the house can in a few hours be taken down and put up. They require no paint, *and will not rust;* while the surface being bright, the rays of the sun are reflected, so that they are much cooler than either tents or painted iron-houses. They can be made of any size that may be desired, varying in price, according to size and finish, from *One Hundred Dollars* and upwards.

Although more particularly calling the attention of parties going to California to these Houses, I would also bring them to the notice of those either residing in or trading with

SOUTH AMERICA AND THE WEST INDIES,

As being equally suitable to those climates. A specimen House of the above description can be seen by calling upon

PETER NAYLOR,
13 Stone Street, N.Y.

Over 600 iron houses were shipped to San Francisco in 1849 in an attempt to alleviate the housing shortage.

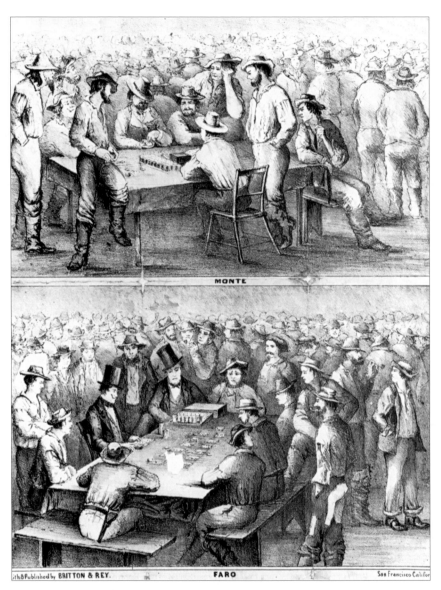

Monte and faro were the two most popular card games in the gambling saloons.

The Hounds attacked Chiletown on July 15, 1849.

The circus came to town in 1849.

An eyewitness to one such skirmish held at Mission Dolores in 1852 left a vivid account of it. One Sunday afternoon, hearing the blare of a band, he looked out his window and saw a huge grizzly bear being drawn through the streets in a cage by four horses. Attached to the sides were large posters that advertised a match that afternoon between a bull named "Hercules" and a bear named "Trojan," in which they were to fight to the death. Out at the mission, the man paid a $3 admission at the ticket office. He estimated that at least 3,500 people were present which, at $3 a head, meant a take of over $10,000 for its promoters that afternoon.

Hercules was brought into the arena first. As the gate was raised from his cage the wild bull charged around the ring, pawed the ground, and bellowed. Two Mexican picadors on horseback entered and expertly lassoed the bull by the horns. They fastened a metal log chain to his right hind leg. Trojan, the bear, was then wheeled in in a cage. The 1,400-pound animal let out a ferocious growl as he was released. To keep the two antagonists close together—and also to prevent the bear from leaping the fence to attack the spectators—the grizzly's left fore leg was chained to the right hind leg of the bull. Being chained to one another only served to inflame the two animals.

The bull attacked first by charging the bear and knocking it down. But the bear quickly got up and wrapped the bull about the neck with its large paws. As he gripped the bull tightly however the bear howled as Hercules's horns—specially sharpened for this occasion—pierced the grizzly's hide. The bear retaliated by clamping his teeth onto the bull's snout. Using his powerful jaws he crushed the bull's facial bones with such force the audience could hear them cracking.

Although usually in such contests one animal "won"—more often than not the bear—in this case the battle ended in a draw as both disengaged and drew back exhausted, wounded, and bleeding. The promoters however goaded the animals back into combat by poking them with spears until they reengaged. The bull this time shattered the bear's jaw, ". . . we could see the shivered bones dangling from their bloody recesses!" the witness wrote. Eventually neither the bull nor the bear could stand any longer; their limbs could no longer support their bodies. Their strength sapped, they just lay there in agony. Their chain was removed, horses were hitched to them, and they were dragged from the arena where they were shot to put them out of their misery.

Entertainments that were non-violent and much more civilized also took place, especially as the year progressed. The first theatrical performance in San Francisco occurred on June 22, 1849 when Stephen C. Massett, "a roly-poly little Englishman," gave a one-man performance at the schoolhouse on the Plaza. Known as Jeems Pipes of Pipesville, Massett was an itinerant jack-of-all-trades who had worked variously as an auctioneer and newspaper correspondent. He sang songs of his own composition and was a gifted mimic who turned his rich baritone into falsetto while performing seven different roles in a burlesque of a New England town meeting. The audience roared at "his imitation of a German girl and an elderly spinster trying out for a spot in a Massachusetts choir."

The circus also came to town in 1849. In mid-October, Joseph Rowe and a troupe of accomplished performers arrived in San Francisco. Rowe was a North Carolinian who had joined a circus at age 10 and had spent his youth and early adulthood performing as an equestrian with various circuses on the East Coast, in the Caribbean, and in South America. He was in Peru in 1849 when he heard of the gold discovery. Only two weeks after arriving he had cleared space for an amphitheater along Kearny Street two blocks from the Plaza. "Rowe's Olympic Circus" opened on October 29. Rowe and his wife performed gymnastics on the backs of galloping horses. Other acts included clowns, "rope dancers," and stunts with cannonballs. This totally different kind of entertainment was most welcome to the town's residents. The full houses of up to 1,500 persons at $3 a head greeted the performances with frequent bursts of loud applause. Rowe closed his show in early December and then opened with new acts in February 1850. He spent the rest of the decade touring in Australia before returning to California to perform in Mother Lode mining towns.

There were other live performances but they tended to be of shorter duration. A group of "Ethiopian Serenaders" — white actors in blackface — performed briefly at the Bella Union; they left town quickly when one of their members was stabbed to death during an argument. And for a brief spell an organ grinder with a monkey popped up in hotels around town. They were a smash success at first. The monkey scampered from pillar to post, all the while grinning as he received treats in the form of fruit or biscuits. The miners loved it and showered the duo with pieces of silver. But the novelty wore off, and the organ grinder and his monkey disappeared from the scene. They were followed by a troupe of Spanish singers, but the Italian opera pieces they performed were apparently too highbrow for the rough-and-tumble populace, and they soon left town. It wouldn't be until early 1850 that the first legitimate theater dramatic performances would be held in San Francisco.

One diversion that was popular at all times was bowling. Tenpin alleys could be found in the major hotels. Reporter Bayard Taylor noted that the owners of a tenpin alley in the Ward House prepaid their rent of $5,000 a month. The El Dorado, after it was converted from a tent to a wood-frame structure, installed four bowling alleys in its basement. All saw regular use.

With all of the constant change and never ending visual stimulation, some city residents did manage to find time for a quieter pursuit: reading. A significant percentage of those who had come to California to find their fortunes were literate and educated. They hungered especially for newspapers to keep up to date on doings in the States. And as for so many other goods in San Francisco, forty-niners paid well when they wanted something. As mentioned previously, Bayard Taylor, after arriving in August, found that out when he quickly sold those dozen newspapers he had crammed into his valise as packing material to a news dealer. Papers that originally had cost him pennies apiece in New York were snapped up at nearly a dollar each.

Books also were imported. They had been almost nonexistent in California before the Gold Rush. Official Spanish regulations had banned the importation of "unorthodox" books—that is those that the Catholic clergy viewed as having "liberal tendencies." When military officer Mariano Vallejo was serving as commandant of the Presidio in 1831 he had imported several boxes of books that included such frowned upon authors as Voltaire and Rousseau. Forbidden to bring in such material again, he secretly arranged with Thomas Larkin of Monterey to smuggle in books from New York, printed in English and French as well as Spanish.

The first real cargo of books to arrive in San Francisco came from South America early in 1849. But it was a small shipment. Only in the fall did regular batches of books start to arrive. There were books of poems by Milton, Pope, Byron, and Burns, along with novels by Scott and Cooper as well as bibles, Spanish grammar books, and other textbooks. At first, stores that sold newspapers such as the *Alta California* sold books along with their papers, periodicals, and stationery. By the fall, two bookstores had opened on streets fronting the Plaza. One, called the Pioneer Bookstore, inhabited a 20-foot by 11-foot storefront in the City Hotel. Books sold for as little as 25 cents or as much as $30. A second hand Webster's dictionary, for example, sold for $25.

6

Goddesses and Whores

If supply and demand changed almost daily for many goods and services in San Francisco in 1849, one kind of coveted "goods" that remained in low supply, and consequent high demand, was women. Women were so scarce and such a novelty that when one appeared in public men clustered about and simply stared. "Doorways filled instantly, and little islands in the street were thronged with men who seemed to gather in a moment, and who remained immovable till the spectacle passed from their incredulous gaze," wrote one woman who was there.

One petite Frenchwoman, who had come from Paris with her husband, got the royal treatment. A musician at the El Dorado gambling saloon, she owned a Stradivarius violin and played it so well that her pay was two ounces of gold a day. Everyday between two and three p.m. she crossed the Plaza from the El Dorado to her abode a short distance away. She always drew a crowd of admirers that watched her every step. One day in the rainy season she lost one of her boots in the mud. A brawny miner quickly retrieved it, kissed it, and returned it to her. Another man carried her to a doorway, where she put her boot back on. And she didn't need to worry about being molested. "It would have cost the wretch his life at the hands of that chivalrous crowd, coarsely dressed and wild in appearance as they were," wrote one man.

One Sunday in April an event featuring two women brought the town to a virtual standstill. Rev. Albert Williams asked John W. Geary, who had recently arrived with his wife and family, if he would organize a choir to sing hymns after the church service, which was being held in the schoolhouse on the Plaza. Geary readily agreed, and recruited the wife of another man to join the choir along with his spouse. When the singing started a crowd quickly gathered. The sound of women's voices raised in song was so unusual and so startling that something equally unusual happened: gamblers in the vicinity of Portsmouth Square ceased playing, exited the saloons, and crowded around the already full schoolhouse just to listen. Even Robert A. Parker, proprietor of his namesake Parker House, came out to see what was happening. Several days later when Geary, his wife, and Mrs. Simmons, the other woman in the choir, were out for a stroll a crowd of admirers followed them around. Only a few months later, much to the regret of the local populace, Geary sent his wife and family home to Pennsylvania. All the attention may have had something to do with it, but the high cost of living in San Francisco was cited as the main reason.

Young children were an even more rare sight and received just as much attention as the few women in town. When a judge, his wife, and their small children landed late in the year, men crowded around and asked the parents permission if they could kiss the little ones and shake their hands. Rough-looking miners, their eyes aglow, reached into their leather pokes and gave pinches of gold dust or small nuggets to them as gifts.

With women in such short supply one woman got it into to her head to do something about it. Eliza Farnham's husband, Tom, had gone to California from Massachusetts in 1846. He planned to send for his family when he got established, but he died in San Francisco in 1848 before that occurred. Eliza had to take ship to the West Coast to settle his affairs. She decided that she could do good—and perhaps make a profit as well—by bringing single females of good character to San Francisco as a civilizing influence. So in February 1849 she circulated a flyer in the East advertising for between 100 and 130 unmarried women of good character, 25 years and older, to make the journey to San Francisco.

The response was disappointing. Women feared that they would be rudely treated, or worse. Friends and family ridiculed the endeavor. And the trip was expensive; each woman was to pony up $250. So when the ship *Angelique* left New York on May 19, 1849 she carried only 22 women passengers. In the meantime word had reached San Francisco about the large boatload of women that would be bringing over 100 single females to town. The ship landed at Valparaiso on the way, where Farnham got into a dispute with the captain, who sailed away before she had a chance to re-board. When the news hit San Francisco of Farnham being put off at Valparaiso, San Franciscans assumed this meant that the venture had failed entirely. Frustration boiled over, and that night there was "more drunkenness, more gambling, and more fighting" than ever before. The *Angelique* finally arrived in San Francisco in late December. Its precious cargo of 22 women all quickly received offers of employment for between $75 and $100 a month. Organizer Farnham claimed that if 500 women had come they could have found employment on similar terms.

For women brave enough to make the journey, their scarcity guaranteed them special attention. One woman, whose husband died shortly after she arrived to join him, received three proposals of marriage within a week of his death. Another married a man she had met aboard ship. After only ten days on shore, however, the marriage fell apart. The husband came home one evening to find that his wife had left his home to consort with a man who had a wife in the States. After her husband beat her she complained to the alcalde; the matter went to court. A witness to the proceedings wrote of the judge as he watched the woman make her case: "One glance of the voluptuous woman's eye was of more force than a marriage contract. . . ." The judge annulled the marriage, gave her all the couple's money, and made the husband pay all the court's costs. To add insult to injury, he had the sheriff seize the man's horse and cart, the means of his livelihood.

Although women were revered, it didn't mean that they didn't have to work hard. Many worked just as hard as the men, albeit in more traditional "women's occupations" such as cooking, cleaning, ironing, and washing. One popular occupation for women was that of boarding house operator. Jerusha Merrill, who had come to San Francisco in 1847, apparently with her husband, had by early 1849 established a two-story lodging house that was thriving. Her eleven rooms on the first floor and nine rooms on the second housed approximately 60 boarders (or about three to a room) "...transients not mentioned, with hourly applications for more," as she noted in a letter to her sister back east in March. Her boarders were American, English, French, Polish, Chilean, and some were seemingly "from no country attoll [sic]." Despite the wide variety of customers and the frequent comings and goings, the men were orderly and well behaved. She charged $18 a week for board and lodging, which at an average of 60 boarders means she was taking in close to $1,100 a week. In that same letter home in March she noted: "Never was there a better field for making money than now presents itself in this place at this time. . . ." Yet she also saw what was becoming increasingly evident: ". . . yet many leave with less than they bring." Still, women's prospects were bright. "Female labour is above everything else, many get an ounce a day."

Mary Jane Megquier was another woman who established a boarding house. Her husband, Thomas, a physician, set up a medical practice and drug store while she ran the boarding house. Rather than subjecting their young children to the rigors of the journey and the hurly-burly of gold rush San Francisco, they left them behind in Maine. It was a painful decision to separate like that, especially for Mary Jane. They periodically sent gold back to their children's guardian to pay for their upkeep and education while they set about the business of making money. Thomas was earning up to $50 a day in his medical practice while Mary Jane tended to the lodgers. She made the beds, washed, and ironed. She purchased all the food, and every day baked six loaves of bread and four pies and prepared all the meals. In addition, she had a side business bottling and selling pickles that she bought wholesale. It was hard work. "If I had not the constitution of six horses, I should have been dead long ago," she wrote in a letter home. As with the male forty-niners, the feverish business climate infected her too: "The ladies have called on me but I do not care for society as I intend to go home when I get my pile."

While the women of San Francisco were finding a certain degree of independence through hard work and making their "piles" like the men, many of the male residents continued to view women through the prism of what they viewed as women's traditional roles in the 19th century, namely that of wives and helpmates who would clean up after them. Levi Stowell was probably typical of many when he wrote in his diary in July: "Oh for a woman, no clean clothes, ragged shirts, no buttons, O! the inconveniences of keeping old Bach. . . ." A month later he moaned, "Wish I had a wife . . . 3

months now keeping old Bach & not had my bed made up yet have to do it myself before long. It's getting rather hard & the sand only about 2 inches thick in it. . . ."

Women of course would have provided companionship in addition to performing domestic chores. To ward off loneliness in the absence of wives and family, some men kept pets. Dogs, and especially cats, were rare sights in 1849, so barnyard animals or even wilder beasts were used as substitutes. One forty-niner's "family," that went with him wherever he went, consisted of a horse, two dogs, two sheep, and two goats. Others kept pet raccoons, wildcats, or caged mountain lions. The Reverend William Taylor noted that a group of men near his home on Jackson Street kept a couple of grizzly bears tethered in their yard.

Besides housekeeping and companionship, men also had other needs, the kind that could be satisfied by practitioners of the "world's oldest profession." These practitioners were sometimes called "abandoned women," but in gold-rush San Francisco they were anything but abandoned. As with other women entrepreneurs in town, prostitutes were in short supply and consequently in high demand.

Prostitutes started to arrive in San Francisco as early as 1848, but the real influx didn't start until the following year. Some were camp followers of U.S. troops who had migrated north following the end of hostilities in the Mexican War. Many of the earliest arrivals had come from south of the border as word reached Latin America of the gold discoveries in California. One of the first Latinas to arrive by ship, in February 1849, was a buxom and flamboyant woman named Rosa who had come from Chile. During the voyage she serviced practically every male on the ship. When she landed in San Francisco she was wearing her finest silk dress and was carrying a parasol. She attracted immediate attention and was quickly surrounded by admirers who carried her ashore.

The first steamship to arrive from Panama had two prostitutes aboard. Their arrival naturally attracted a crowd. Perhaps given advance notice, hundreds of men were waiting on the shore when the ship docked. The two women were to pay their passage upon landing. When they argued with ship's officials about it, out of the impatient crowd burst two men who clambered aboard, and throwing a bag of gold dust at the feet of the purser, they brought the girls off the ship to the cheers of the crowd.

But before too many harlots had arrived at least one man came up with a novel idea for making money on the hunger for women. A café owner, he realized that the crudely drawn pictures of naked women on his walls (a common feature of saloons in town) couldn't compete with the real thing, so he hired women to pose nude in his dining hall. "Tableaux vivants" were set up on platforms on the sides of rooms where totally naked women were placed in "indecent poses." At eight p.m., gold dust having been paid as admission at the front door, eager men streamed through, all the while being rapidly pushed toward the exit by the men behind them. "They came tumbling out the door, cursing like fiends," according to one witness. Demand quickly slackened for this kind of display when more "abandoned women" started to arrive and hard-core sexual services took center stage.

Some ships' captains, to keep profits up and help pay the cost of the voyage, deliberately recruited women who could not pay for their passage. Upon arrival they were auctioned off to the highest bidder. The captain would keep as profit whatever he took in above his costs for the women's passage. Upon landing, the women would be assembled on the poop deck, and in one telling, the auctioneer, after praising the woman's figure, youth, and beauty called out in a loud voice, "Gentlemen, what are you willing to pay, any one of you, right now to have this pretty dame, fresh from New York, pay you a very special visit?"

In any other city in America at this time a public "slave auction" of white women would have been unthinkable. (Black slaves in the South were another matter.) This was, after all, the Victorian era, a time so straight-laced that it was considered beyond the pale to even mention in public such relatively innocuous things as a woman being pregnant. But San Francisco was far from the rest of America, not just in terms of physical distance but morally as well.

By one estimate the town's prostitutes at the end of 1849 numbered about 700 (out of a total population in the range of 20,000 to 25,000). "The fair but frail," as women of easy virtue were sometimes known, likely formed the bulk of the total female population.

Because there were so few of them, women of all kinds were venerated, prostitutes included. "Women were so scarce that men would take off their hats to the lewd women of the town . . ." wrote one observer.

Prostitutes plied their trade in various venues. Many worked as "waiter girls" in the gambling saloons where they were paid good wages to serve food and drink, or merely to stand by customers as they gambled. Some acted as dealers or croupiers although, surprisingly, considering what a draw women were, that didn't become commonplace until 1850. Women were free to solicit business with their customers once their shifts were over. Proprietors would even rent them rooms in their establishments where they could complete their assignations.

While some women freelanced in the saloons, others operated out of parlor houses under the protection of a madam or a pimp. Some of these houses functioned discreetly, others were well known among the populace. Ship captain George Coffin happened upon one of the former one day. Returning to his ship he came upon a finished house with a flower garden in front. On the piazza were two fashionably dressed women and a gentleman who were engaged in earnest conversation. As he passed the house he overheard the three become embroiled in a loud argument. He turned to see the man coming out of the gate, and the women, who had turned into "she-devils incarnate," were swearing at the man in a vulgar and obscene manner. It suddenly dawned on him: "The most genteel looking house in San Francisco was a brothel."

One day in early 1850, a town resident climbed one of the hills to the west of downtown to take in the view of the city below. In a letter to a friend he told of seeing a distinctive building not far from the Custom House that housed "a notorious house of ill fame." He no doubt was referring to the most upscale and famous brothel in town, run by a woman known only as "The Countess."

"The Countess" had come from New Orleans in 1849 and, given her savoir-faire, was probably a professional madam. By late in the year she inhabited a solid, two-story frame house on Washington Street across from the Plaza that was furnished as handsomely as any house in San Francisco could be at the time. On at least one occasion, probably her "grand opening," she held a soiree and sent

engraved invitations to the "most prominent men in San Francisco," which included businessmen, lawyers, judges, politicians,
even members of the local clergy.

After being received at the front door the men admitted were
introduced to the girls, who numbered from six to eight. There was
music, dancing, and conversation. A lavish supper, which consisted
of the best comestibles that the city could supply, followed; champagne was bountiful. Those who chose to leave after the meal were
expected to leave not less than an ounce of gold as a gratuity. Some
chose to stay. Elisha Crosby, a lawyer from New York, whose
recording of the details of one of these soirees was such that it suggests he was one of the invitees, coyly wrote: "To the best of my
belief there were a number who remained for private enjoyment of
a different character." That enjoyment did not come cheap. Tariffs
for staying till morning could range from $200 to $400 a man. (A
Parisian streetwalker of the time made $2 per trick.) It's not known
what the split between the madam and her girls was, but both
surely made out well. One male diarist of the time, not necessarily
referring to the residents at the Countess's house, wrote: "One celebrated character of this kind said she had made $50,000 and regret-
ted that she had not double the capacity for increasing her gains . . ."

The harlots in the Countess's house were undoubtedly white,
likely either American or French. But white prostitutes were in the
minority in San Francisco, especially early in the year. Most were
from Mexico and Central and South America. That isn't surprising,
since word of the gold discovery had reached those countries
months before spreading to the U.S. East Coast and Europe. Many
white forty-niners viewed women through the prism of the racist
attitudes of the time. White prostitutes were mostly held in high
esteem, but "tawny visaged" Latin prostitutes were seen as being
"generally of the lowest and most degraded character."

Latin harlots had their own house, called Washington Hall,
although it seemingly laid no claim to any of the luxuries that
would define it as a "parlor house." It housed mostly Chilean
women and stood just a few doors down from its upscale sister, the
"Countess's" dwelling. Dr. John W. Palmer described it as "a stew
of cheap prostitution." It gained a bit of notoriety when one of its
residents, a woman named Mariquita, shot and wounded another

resident, Camille La Reine. Six weeks later Camille retaliated by having Mariquita's throat cut with a Bowie knife. Despite the lower esteem Latin women were held in, Mariquita's death was lamented by the male populace because women were so scarce.

It's impossible to say what percentage of the "working girls" operated under the protection of a male backer, or pimp, and what percentage freelanced. Houses with full-time residents were most probably backed by a well-financed male. One diarist writing in his journal in October noted that "a man named Cris Lilly keeps a house of prostitution and makes a great deal of money at it." Perhaps even "The Countess" had a male backer.

One woman who was decidedly a freelancer was one of the most distinctive and well-known characters of early San Francisco, the Chinese courtesan Ah Toy. She was about 20 years old when she arrived by sea from China in either late 1848 or early 1849. By all accounts she was a great beauty. One observer, (writing decades later) who described her as tall and well built, said, "She was the finest-looking Chinese woman I have ever seen."

She combined her beauty with her exoticism—she was one of only a handful of Chinese women resident in San Francisco through all of the year 1849—to make her fortune. She initially set up shop in a little shanty off Clay Street near Portsmouth Square, and started with a kind of peep show in which she charged miners and others an ounce of gold merely to gaze at "her countenance." She even kept a pair of scales to make sure that she was getting correct weight. It wasn't long, however, before some customers tried to cheat her by using brass filings instead of gold. Not at all the retiring sort and unafraid of using American courts to address the wrongs done to her, she sued several men who had tried this dodge. In court, when the judge asked her to produce the evidence, she brought forth a huge basin filled with brass filings. This brought "a great shout of laughter from the spectators. . . ." Ah Toy did not receive justice in this case, because the judge sided with the defendants who claimed that Ah Toy had known the "dust" was really brass when she accepted it.

Ah Toy went on to outright prostitution, and by the early 1850s had become a madam in her own right, having hired several Chinese women. She made the newspapers from time to time (whose

reporters sometimes spelled her name Atoy, Achoi, or other vari-
ants), usually in conjunction with being hauled into court for
keeping a "disorderly house." Once she filed a criminal complaint
against a man who had stolen a valuable breast pin from her. (The
pin was later recovered, having been thrown away by the thief.) By
the early 1850s Ah Toy had discarded, for a time anyway, her native
clothing and paraded through the street dressed in "the most flashing European or American style. . . ." Beautiful, tenacious, determined, entrepreneurial, fiercely independent—no wonder she was
a favorite in gold-rush San Francisco.

The scarcity of women in San Francisco in 1849 is well documented, but the flip side of the coin of course is that the population
was overwhelmingly male. The men were also mostly under thirty
years of age and thus in their sexual prime. One has to wonder,
given the lack of available women (primarily prostitutes who could
command premium pay for their services, thus putting them out of
reach for those with modest resources), whether any sexual activity
between men occurred. No accounts of explicit sex between men
appear to have been recorded in gold-rush San Francisco, but there
are a few hints of such activity occurring in the mining communities
during the 1850s. A rare documented record is found in an 1856
Calaveras County divorce proceeding in which a wife divorced
her husband because he brought men home for "the purposes of
buggery."

It is certainly possible that sexual contact took place. Temporary
homosexual activity has, after all, not been unknown in largely
same-sex environments such as military camps, prisons, and boarding schools. Their inhibitions loosened by alcohol, and sleeping in
cramped tents or boarding houses in close proximity to one another
(sometimes even sharing a bed), a few forty-niners may have
engaged in some fleeting sexual activity. Just how close in some
cases they slept together can be seen in this observation from a
German immigrant who shared a small frame house with some
other men: "There we lay peacefully together, like herrings,
warmed on each side by a neighbor."

That lust existed there can be no doubt. Captain George Coffin,
who had stumbled upon the "nicest house in town" that turned out

to be a brothel, recorded an occurrence he witnessed in a gambling saloon on a trip to Marysville in 1850. In an incident he called "Kissing a Boy" he told how, as he entered the saloon, he saw sitting at one of the tables a "very pretty boy." The young man, who was dealing cards while the banker sat next to him, was dressed in a blue frock coat with a buff vest thrown open in the front. His shirt collar was rolled down, exposing a beautiful smooth neck upon which rested a profusion of chestnut curls cascading down from his head. Suddenly, a player impulsively leaned in and kissed the boy on the lips. The banker swiftly knocked the man to the ground, a fight immediately erupted, punches were thrown, shots were fired, and a general melee ensued. When the dust settled it turned out that the boy was actually a girl about 16 years old. (The girl had run away with the banker and apparently was in disguise to avoid her mother, who was searching for her.) Whether the kisser knew that "the boy" was a girl is not known. In any event, he couldn't control himself.

7

Crime Wave: The Hounds

Crime has a long and storied history in San Francisco, but in the early days things could not have been more peaceful. During the Mexican era California was sparsely settled; the population was small, spread over a wide area, mainly on vast cattle ranches, and there were no real urban centers. So it's not surprising that from 1819 to 1846 there were only six murders recorded among non-Indians in all of California. Historian Hubert Howe Bancroft noted of the period ". . . a log cabin could hold all the criminals in the country." As such there was little need for a police force. The alcaldes incorporated police functions as part of their duties, but they relied upon the army for enforcement.

After the American takeover in 1846 the policing functions were initially transferred to U.S. military forces. Navy Lt. Henry B. Watson, from the *Portsmouth,* set up a command post in the Custom House and from there controlled a detachment of 24 marines, which acted as a local police force for San Francisco. When active hostilities in the war with Mexico came to an end in California in early 1847, military control of civilian law enforcement in San Francisco ceased. E. Ward Pell, a Mormon who had come on the *Brooklyn* with Sam Brannan, was appointed sheriff, but rather than having the powers of arrest his duties seem to have been limited to acting as a bailiff in the alcalde's court.

In September 1847 the town's first elected council passed an ordinance calling for the hiring of two constables as the town's police force. Two men were duly appointed, but in December they were let go and were replaced by a single constable, Thomas Kittleman, a protégé of Sam Brannan, who likely had some influence in his selection. Kittleman was paid a salary of $50 a month, but he did little to earn it since things were so quiet that, except for the collaring of the occasional drunk, Kittleman had time to moonlight as a construction worker. Even with his powers of arrest, constable Kittleman's functions were less in the nature of patrolling streets and preventing crime than in chasing down the occasional runaway sailor and carrying out writs issued by the alcalde. This was an age when citizens were still expected to rely upon their own initiative in settling disputes; government responsibility for preserving the peace was an idea still in its infancy. When Kittleman was appointed, a further ordinance of the town council decreed that he had the power to call upon any citizen to help him carry out his duties; anyone refusing could be fined from $5 to $50.

If the town's pre-gold-rush "police force" was scanty, the jail facilities were almost laughable. Indeed, from San Francisco's founding in 1776 until about 1846 there was no jail. When a murderer named Galindo was apprehended in the jurisdiction in 1839 he had to be sent to San Jose where there was a jail, because San Francisco had none. At about the time of the American takeover a log structure was built at Clay and Stockton streets and was soon thereafter used by the alcalde as a calaboose, or jail. It was hardly an ideal place of confinement. Its flimsy nature was illustrated in a comic scene in which the first prisoner housed there—incarcerated for cutting off the tails of five horses—showed up in the alcalde's office one morning with the jail's door strapped to his back, saying that he would take his leave if his breakfast was not brought up posthaste.

After the discovery of gold in early 1848 the lazy times and small-town flavor of pre-gold-rush San Francisco quickly changed. Men from all over the world, many carrying guns and knives, poured into town. On the face of it, a society consisting primarily of heavily armed young bachelors, who sometimes drank to excess and were in an environment offering wide open gambling and prostitution, would appear to offer ideal conditions for the proliferation of crime and violence. But surprisingly, crime was mostly confined to petty theft, and that was not common because perpetrators were deterred by the swift punishment sure to follow. Thieves were either whipped or had their ears cropped. There was an increase in mayhem but not as much as one might expect. Premeditated or first-degree murder seems to have been rare. Most of the violence that occurred in 1848 and 1849 was of a spontaneous kind, such as shootings and stabbings that happened in the heat of an argument. City residents who avoided the gambling saloons—where most of these incidents took place—had little to fear.

The lack of any real law enforcement, however, opened the door to the formation of a gang of bullies called the Hounds. Their rise was little noticed at first, because in the mad scramble to make money most city residents were focused on their own business dealings and not on community matters. As long as they were not interfered with, San Franciscans were only too glad to stay out of civic affairs.

The Hounds organization had started benignly enough in late 1848 when leading businessmen and officials such as William D. M. Howard and Joseph L. Folsom paid a few waterfront idlers $25 a head to return runaway sailors to their ships. (Merchants wanted to keep ships' masters happy in port, and allowing deserting sailors to escape was bad for business.) But it wasn't long before these waterfront toughs coalesced into a larger gang, numbering dozens, perhaps as many as a hundred, that attracted Australian ex-convicts and disbanded veterans from Colonel Stevenson's regiment, some of the latter having been recruited from New York street gangs, including the infamous Bowery Boys. They dubbed their headquarters, which was a large tent on Kearny Street across from the City Hotel, "Tammany Hall." Their leader was an illiterate boatman named Sam Roberts. A self-styled lieutenant, Roberts wore a uniform and enforced a kind of military discipline within the group.

The gang employed classic bullying tactics of intimidation through threats of physical harm to extort goods and services from local shopkeepers. With their large numbers they operated in the open, since they had nothing to fear from city authorities and the virtually non-existent police force. In a typical example of their *modus operandi*, one morning a gang of about 35 to 40 Hounds trooped into a restaurant on Kearny Street opposite the Plaza for breakfast. Pounding the tables, they called out unceasingly in loud voices, "Waiter!" "Waiter!" hurrying the sole attendant "until he was half dead with fatigue and fright." When they had finished eating the leaders had their men assemble military style: "Fall in! Right about face!" One of them called out to the café's owner asking how much they owed. When the owner replied "Two dollars each," one of the Hounds replied "Charge it to the Hounds." He barked "Left face! Forward, march!" and with that they marched out the door without paying for their meals.

The Hounds took a childish delight in parading around town on most Sundays. Gaudily dressed in richly colored serapes and with hats adorned with feathers and flowers, they marched with banners flying. They were frequently accompanied by their paramours, Latin and Native American prostitutes. To announce their arrival, their processions were usually preceded by music: a fife and drum, a banjo, sometimes horns or violins, and occasionally "several pairs of rib-bones." They insulted spectators as they went. People would retreat into their homes as they approached. The Hounds at one point even threatened to hang Alcalde Thaddeus Leavenworth. Innkeeper John Henry Brown, hearing of the plot in advance, managed to hide Leavenworth in a back room at his City Hotel until the threat blew over.

The Hounds were useful in some respects. As Hubert Howe Bancroft sarcastically noted: "They were useful at the polls on election day, voting early and often themselves, preventing others from voting, and at sunset guarding the ballot-box while it was being stuffed. If you wanted a house fired, a man beaten, or a murder done, they were always at hand for a consideration."

As the Hounds grew in numbers, and saw in their forays around town that no one was challenging them or attempting to stop their depredations, they became emboldened. They changed their name to the nobler sounding San Francisco Society of Regulators, in a bid perhaps to shed the dog-like connotations of the word hound and to give themselves more legitimacy. They saw themselves as enforcers of the laws and as addressers of wrongs. The chief wrong in their view was that there were foreigners on American soil. (The Hounds' self-righteous xenophobia had been jump-started by General Persifor Smith's declaration banning foreigners from taking California gold.)

The main targets of the Hounds' anti-foreign ire were Latin Americans, especially Chileans. (This hatred apparently did not extend to the Latin prostitutes with whom Sam Roberts and other

Hounds consorted.) Chileans were reviled because they were Spanish speaking—a reminder of the recent war with Mexico—and because many of them had used peons, or virtual slaves, to help them mine gold. This unfair advantage had not sat well with American miners, who, already imbued with nativist sentiment stirred up by Persifor Smith's edict, ended up driving Hispanics from the mines. By the summer of 1849 Chileans and other Latinos, routed from the gold country, had become numerous in San Francisco. They set up a largely tent encampment at the base of Telegraph Hill, a few blocks from Portsmouth Square, in an area that came to be called "Chiletown." A number of them became successful boatmen, ferrying goods and passengers from ship to shore.

The first concerted attack by the Hounds on the Chileans occurred on June 26, 1849. That day twelve members of the gang invaded an inn run by a Chilean man, a Mr. Alegria. They ransacked his establishment, and as they set fire to it and to several nearby tents they shouted "Death to the Chileans!" That night the same twelve men marched down city streets blowing trumpets and shouting "Death to all the foreigners!" This turned out to be a prelude to a rampage that would galvanize the town and precipitate San Francisco's first civic crisis.

On Sunday, July 15, Hounds leader Sam Roberts, after returning from an outing in Contra Costa on the other side of the bay, rode up to Washington Hall, "the stew of cheap prostitution," on the Plaza to visit his new mistress, a Chilean harlot named Felice Alvarez. Roberts had taken ten ounces of gold from her not long after her arrival the previous month. She later testified that she was afraid of him. When he entered her room that day he became enraged when he found her sitting on her bed next to a German man named Leopold Bleckschmidt. Roberts hauled Bleckschmidt outside and beat him senseless with a wood plank. He then took off one of his spurs and raked it across the man's face, carving bloody streaks into it. A crowd had gathered and someone yelled out: "For shame! That is not manly!" Roberts growled that he would kill the fellow if he caught him again with his woman.

At dinner that evening in a restaurant, still in a foul mood, Roberts kicked over a table and shattered some glasses. He and a squad of fellow Hounds then went from saloon to saloon, and if not served right away, they would go behind the bar and serve themselves, all the while smashing bottles and decanters. At about 9:30 p.m. they arrived at a tent saloon at Clark's Point in Chiletown belonging to a Domingo Cruz. They ordered 20 Chileno customers to vacate at gunpoint. After helping themselves to liquor, they broke the bottles and shot up the place. Fanning out into the area they approached one tent after another. If the occupant was an American or spoke unaccented English they would move on. But if they were greeted with Spanish they used clubs on the occupants, stole their valuables, and tore down their tents. Soon, a near full-scale riot was in progress. With Roberts in the lead, bellowing through a speaking trumpet, dozens of drunken, frenzied Hounds went on a rampage, firing shots indiscriminately and kicking and beating any Latino they came across. This went on until the wee hours as screaming Chileans either fought back or mostly tried to escape. As the victims tried to flee, several Hounds mounted horses and chased them up Telegraph Hill, firing on them as they ran.

In the morning, city residents surveyed the scene: wrecked tents, broken furniture, and maimed Chilenos, their gold and silver stolen. Additionally, their boats—the means of livelihood for many—had had their timbers stove in or were otherwise destroyed. Sam Roberts, a competitor in the lighterage business, had seen to that.

Amazingly, for all the mayhem, reported casualties were few. One American was killed and one wounded. On the other side, two Chilenos were hit by gunfire; one later died. It was a remarkably light total. Perhaps with all the liquor consumed the Hounds were too drunk to have their shots hit their targets. Or perhaps they were more intent on terrorizing their victims than in killing them.

Outrage over what had happened quickly boiled to the fore. Sam Brannan lost no time in rousing the public to action. Never shy when it came to addressing an audience, he mounted a barrel at Clay and Montgomery streets to rally the citizenry. When the crowd grew too large, he and his listeners marched up Clay Street to Portsmouth Square. Brannan climbed to the roof of the alcalde's office across from the Plaza and, waving a revolver in his hand for emphasis, continued his oration. He called for justice for the Chileans saying that California "... depended on Chile for flour, on her skilled artisans for laying bricks, on her bakers for bread." Brannan neglected to mention that he had profited handsomely from selling some Chileans a leaky old boat that nearly sank when they launched it in the bay. A subscription list was opened for contributions for the Chileans' relief.

While Brannan was speaking, rumors started circulating through the crowd that Hounds were in the audience and were threatening to burn his house down. "Pale with anger and excitement" Brannan hurled even more invective when he heard about it. When a few shots were fired in the air, in a theatrical gesture, Brannan bared his chest and dared the Hounds to fire at him. One listener found Brannan's fiery appeal so stirring that ". . . I thought it fortunate for the Community that he was not a hound."

But even more important than helping the Chileans was self-preservation. "It was very evident to all that immediate steps must be taken to put a stop to this gang, or every one's life and property would be endangered," wrote one resident. Before the gathering broke up, 230 citizens were enrolled in a volunteer militia. It was in effect a vigilante group. The men, armed with muskets donated by a local gun dealer, fanned out in search of the perpetrators. Some had already fled, but 19 were captured, including Sam Roberts, who was caught trying to escape on a schooner bound for Stockton. With no jail big enough to hold them, the prisoners were confined on the *U.S.S. Warren*, an American warship in the harbor.

Two days after the rampage a grand jury of 24 was impaneled, and the captured men were indicted on four counts: conspiracy, riot, robbery, and assault with intent to kill. Included in the first count was the allegation that the Hounds intended "to commit riot, rape, and murder. . . ." The mention of the word rape suggests that some Chilenas may have been raped. But none came forward, and no Hound was ever convicted of that specific charge. Proscutors were appointed, as were counsel for the defendants.

In fast-moving San Francisco people were used to instant results. They also wanted instant justice. A jury was chosen on Wednesday, the day after the indictments were issued. The trial began the following morning. It was held in the much-used schoolhouse on the Plaza. Sam Roberts was tried first. Before noon on Friday, after testimony from Chileans and others, including some perjured testimony on Roberts's behalf in which it was claimed that he was in bed sleeping the night of the attack, the "Lieutenant" and ringleader was convicted on all four counts. The rest of the gang was tried during the next few days on the same charges as Roberts. Some were acquitted entirely, but eight others were convicted on one or more counts. Most of the eight were found guilty only of the first charge, conspiracy.

After the verdicts were in, the sentences were announced. Roberts and one other Hound were sentenced to ten years each at hard labor. The rest mostly received fines ranging from $250 to $1,000. What happened to the prisoners after that is not entirely clear, but it seems that none ever served his sentence or paid a fine. Roberts's conviction specified that as soon as circumstances allowed he be returned to some port in the United States, "never to return under pain of death." So his real sentence, and that of the others, appears to have been banishment, all in all rather light treatment considering the brutality they had inflicted and the havoc they had caused. The question is why were the Hounds in essence let go. True, the local jail was inadequate for confining a prisoner for ten years. But an unstated answer, at least in part, might be racism. Many Americans, although they wouldn't have resorted to violence to carry out their beliefs, viewed the Latinos in town as the Hounds did: as interlopers who were taking American gold. Although they were disgusted by what had happened they had little sympathy for Latinos overall. One wonders if, had the Hounds attacked American citizens, the punishment would have been as light. Two subsequent vigilante groups, the Vigilance Committees of 1851 and 1856, meted out more lethal punishment, hanging wrongdoers for lesser crimes. The victims of the wrongdoers in those instances were Americans.

Although documentation is scant, the rest of the answer as to why the penalties were lenient might lie in what could be called "friends in high places." Some historians have accused alcalde Thaddeus Leavenworth of being in league with the Hounds. Although he had used them on occasion to carry out his orders, such as once employing Roberts and his men to publicly flog a sailor who had pulled a knife on his captain, Leavenworth had no real reason to spare the Hounds punishment in view of their earlier threat against him. But others may have. *The Annals of San Francisco*, which appeared in print only six years after the Hounds affair, contained a cryptic reference that partially explains why not only no real punishment was meted out but also why no steps were taken to quell the band before things got out of hand: ". . . influential parties in San Francisco . . . to further their own personal interests . . . were known to have secret intimacies and mysterious dealings with certain leaders of the 'hounds. . . .'" *The Annals* didn't identify these men because they all were still around. But the "influential parties" seemingly refers to members of the "Legislative Assembly," a group of prominent citizens and businessmen that had formed earlier in the year. They largely were opposed to Alcalde Leavenworth and his policies, so their alleged backing of the Hounds contains elements of a political struggle. And it should be noted that not all of the Hounds, or "The San Francisco Society of Regulators," were thugs. Indeed, J. C. Pulis, the town's sheriff at the time, was a member of the Hounds (but appears to have taken no part in the rampage). So there certainly were ties between the Hounds and leading citizens.

The Hounds affair, along with the fact that San Francisco's population was rapidly increasing on a daily basis, threw into sharp relief the fact that the town badly needed a paid, full-time police force. In August, a new city council that had replaced the Legislative Assembly recommended that Malachi Fallon, a recent arrival from New York, be appointed chief. Fallon, an Irish former tavern owner was hired apparently based on his experience as a former keeper of New York's Tombs prison. An assistant chief, three sergeants, and 30 patrolmen were also hired. The latter were to receive wages of only six dollars a day. Carpenters and other skilled laborers were making as much $15 to $20 a day at this time, which shows that the city authorities, in not paying competitive wages, were still reluctant to spend public funds for needed services.

In the months immediately following the Hounds episode the city was especially peaceful and crime free. Many new arrivals in the summer and fall marveled at how safe the place was. Goods of all kinds could be found stacked in the open, left lying about for days unguarded and unmolested. The new police force may have had something to do with that, but most forty-niners, with a kind of blind faith in frontier democracy, seemed to attribute the serenity to the citizens' own roundup of the Hounds which had placed "a wholesome check on roguery." And they fully expected to continue relying on their own resources, even with a police force. One young man, tempting fate, was caught stealing a trifle, and had his ears cut off. "A second offense would string him up," noted this observer. Another commented: "Taken as a whole life and property were fairly safe but crimes against property were more severely dealt with than those against life." Those who had made it to California had taken big risks and had worked hard to accumulate what possessions they had. They weren't going to tolerate anyone trying to take them away.

The crime statistics for the last half of 1849 generally bear out the peaceful nature of the town as presented in anecdotal accounts. Between August 12, when Malachi Fallon was appointed the police chief, and September 25, ninety-seven arrests were made, or an average of about two a day. A few were for petty theft, but the vast majority was for drunk and disorderly conduct. (Some drunks were held overnight, but most were fined $25—a substantial sum—and released.) One irate reveler, who was thrown into the schoolhouse on the Plaza, which late in the year served as a jail, was indignant to think "that a citizen of the United States, seventeen thousand miles from home, could not get as drunk as he damned pleased, and make a little noise, without being put in a bloody country school house with a parcel of negroes."

A few crimes of a serious nature made the news. In August, a Frenchman was arrested for murdering his partner to steal his gold. In October, a Chilean stabbed a black man to death in a tent saloon. The following month, in a rare instance of what appears to be premeditated murder, a trussed up John Doe murder victim with bullets in his head and chest was found on the beach. And on the last day of the year, a body of a man who had been stabbed 24 times was found in bushes near Mission Dolores. Some deaths that were assumed to have been the result of natural causes could of course have been the result of foul play, but on the whole, a handful of homicides in the crowded and rough and tumble town that San

Francisco was in the second half of 1849 is a remarkably low number.

Things would get worse in 1850, and perhaps anticipating that, in October 1849 the town council, or ayuntamiento, in a less than arms-length transaction, approved the purchase of a deserted brig in the harbor, the *Euphemia*, from one of its own members, William Heath Davis, for $3,500. By early December the vessel had been refitted as a prison; 50 sets of balls and chains for prisoners would arrive in late January. The *Euphemia* started receiving prisoners on February 1, 1850. Besides convicts, the ship held any "suspicious, insane, or forlorn persons found strolling about the city at night."

8

Scoundrel Time:
Civic Chicanery

If it hadn't been for the Hounds' rampage and growing pressures on the military governors of California, it is difficult to say how long it would have taken for San Franciscans to get serious about organizing an effective city government. There had been a local American-run government in place since the U. S. takeover on July 9, 1846, but well into 1849 San Francisco had little to show in the way of public improvements or functioning civic infrastructure. A police department had only been formed in the wake of the Hounds incident.

There were several reasons why civic affairs had been neglected. One of them was that this was the era of Jacksonian democracy, whose mantra was "The government is best, which governs least." Americans had an abiding faith in democracy, but that did not include a love of regulation and bureaucracy. Another reason was obvious: everyone in this superheated business climate was busy with his own affairs. As long as they weren't interfered with, people paid little heed to government. But the main reason why locals took little interest in civic affairs and paying for improvements such as planked sidewalks and streets was the common mindset. Most were not planning to stay: they wanted to make their "pile" and go back home where they came from. The thinking was, why spend money fixing up a place where you were not going to hang your hat? San Francisco residents did not yet think of themselves as "San Franciscans"; they were still New Yorkers or Bostonians temporarily away from home.

Compounding the inattention of the locals was the fact that the military governor, the city officials' nominal superior, was located in Monterey, a three-day horseback ride from San Francisco. So city politicians, largely unencumbered by "state" government oversight or public scrutiny, were left to pursue things as they saw fit. Given the "get all you can get" climate it's not surprising that they succumbed to "gold fever." They didn't need to mine gold, however. They held the keys to a treasure right under their feet and surrounding them on all sides—the city's real estate. San Francisco's alcaldes, in charge of granting city lots, were sometimes tempted to take advantage of their privileged position to pursue their own self-interest at the expense of the public interest.

San Francisco's public officials had different titles and different duties than those of other American towns and cities of the time. That stemmed from the area's Spanish/Mexican heritage. Although California had been part of Spain's colonial empire in the western hemisphere since the 1500s, a semblance of government in San Francisco only got started in the 1830s, after Mexico had declared its independence from Spain. The senior official for California was the governor, whose title and function resembled that of American governmental systems, but below that things diverged. Carrying out the governor's orders and reporting directly to him was a prefect. The prefect's broad charge was to "take care of public order and tranquility." More specifically, he appointed justices of the peace and acted as the governor's watchdog in a supervisory role over local officials, particularly as to the administration and expenditure of town funds.

Reporting to the prefect was the top city official, the alcalde. This strange (to American eyes and ears) title had its roots in Moorish Spain, where the Al-Cadi served as a kind of village judge. An alcalde in Mexican California incorporated executive, judicial, and sometimes legislative functions into his office. The alcalde served as a combination judge, prosecutor, police magistrate, recorder, notary public, and coroner. As a judge he presided over both civil and criminal cases. Other duties included witnessing signatures, probating wills, and appointing executors of estates. The alcalde's most important function, however, especially after the American takeover, was his power to make grants of land.

The alcalde also served as presiding officer of the ayuntamiento, or town council. Ayuntamientos, according to Mexican law, were only to be constituted when a town's population reached 4,000, a level that San Francisco didn't reach until about mid-1849, but the town went ahead with one before that anyway for a variety of reasons. The ayuntamiento was responsible for keeping the streets clean, for providing burial grounds, prisons, hospitals, and schools, and for maintaining records of vital statistics such as births and deaths. Its most important function was managing the municipal treasury. It was charged with providing an annual financial report to the prefect that he would then send on to the governor.

While Americans could identify with a prefect, or a kind of lieutenant governor, and with an ayuntamiento, or town council, the office of alcalde, with its multiple roles, was different. Alcalde justice during the Mexican era was well suited to that time because it was rooted in community harmony, which was an important objective in Mexican California's village-like patriarchal society. Compromise, conciliation, and consensus were considered desirable and necessary parts of the governing process. Maintaining social harmony took precedence over protecting individual rights, a sequence Americans would have put in reverse order.

After the American takeover, in 1846, U. S. military authorities, in a measure designed to ensure continuity and stability in the wake of the war, which was still ongoing, decreed that all civil officers were to administer the laws "according to the former usages of the country." This was designed as a temporary expedient until the government of the territory could be more definitely arranged. That would take longer than anyone at the time anticipated.

In the meantime, the major problem was that no one knew what the laws of Mexican California were. The only copy was in the governor's office in Monterey—and it was in Spanish. Without a code of laws to guide them, alcaldes in San Francisco and other towns ended up pretty much doing what they individually thought was right. Many had no legal training. This type of seat-of-the-pants jurisprudence did not sit well with some San Franciscans, Sam Brannan most notable among them. In the inaugural issue of his *California Star* newspaper in January 1847 he thundered: "WHAT LAWS ARE WE TO BE GOVERNED BY . . . all suits are now decided according to the Alcalde's NOTIONS of justice. . . ." He had a point. It would take until San Francisco was officially chartered and incorporated in 1850 before the Mexican legal system—and nomenclature such as alcalde and ayuntamiento—would finally be junked, but in the interval, modifications to it would be made. The alcalde retained his multiple duties, but court proceedings, in contrast to the Mexican preference for mediation and conciliation, took on an adversarial cast: Americans preferred clear cut winners and losers. Lawyers were brought into the courtroom to represent both sides in disputes, and in 1847, juries were employed as well. Still, the alcalde retained quite a bit of clout and power, especially in his role as judge—and with his authority to grant lots.

With the American takeover in July 1846, and in keeping with the desire to effect a smooth transition, Commodore John D. Sloat, the senior U. S. military officer in California at the time, invited Mexican alcaldes to continue in office if they so chose. Most did not. In San Francisco, alcalde José de Jesus Noe left rather than submit to American authority, so Captain John B. Montgomery of the *Portsmouth*, anchored in Yerba Buena Cove, appointed one of his officers, Lieutenant Washington A. Bartlett, to Noe's vacant post, making Bartlett the first American alcalde for San Francisco. In September an election was held for the job and Bartlett won, mainly due to the votes he received from his shipmates. The position paid no salary, but in lieu of that the Americans decided to continue the Mexican practice of allowing an alcalde to retain the fees he charged for the petty duties of his office, such as witnessing signatures.

In November 1846 Bartlett, after receiving confirmation from his superiors that he had the power to make grants of land (his Mexican predecessors had done so), started granting lots to those who petitioned him to do so. The requirements for a grant were that the petitioner had to agree to fence in the lot and build a house on it within one year. Only one grant per purchaser was allowed. These terms were a reflection of the agrarian nature of land grants made in Spanish and Mexican California. They were designed to encourage settlement in what was a sparsely occupied country. Grants in pueblos (towns) were typically made in blocks of either 50 varas or 100 varas. One vara equaled 33.3 inches, so a 50-vara square block, or lot, measured 137.5 feet by 137.5 feet. A 100-vara lot measured

275 feet square. After the American takeover a fixed price of $12.50 was set for the 50-vara lots and $25.00 for the 100-vara lots, or only twice as much, even though the latter were four times the size of the former. Fees and recording costs of $3.62½ were added to each transaction.

Prior to Bartlett's alcaldeship, only 64 lots had been granted between 1836 and 1846 in the pueblo of Yerba Buena. And during that time only 12 lots had transferred ownership. But things quickly heated up after the Americans took over. By the time he left office in February 1847 Bartlett had granted nearly 60 lots, or almost the same number that had been granted in the previous ten years. Some of Bartlett's successors would grant at least that many in their first month in office.

At about the same time that he started to grant lots, Bartlett asked Jasper O'Farrell, an Irish civil engineer and surveyor and town resident, to do a proper survey and expand the scope beyond the current downtown area clustered in the few blocks surrounding Portsmouth Square. Nearly all the one hundred-plus lots between California Street on the south, Powell Street on the west, Broadway on the north, and Montgomery Street on the east, at the water's edge, would be granted by the time Bartlett left office in February. Clearly, with the demand for lots growing, the area surrounding the current town limits was ripe for expansion.

There had been a previous survey, which was why there were lots laid out already. In 1839, a few years after William Richardson and Jacob Leese had built their homes overlooking Yerba Buena Cove, Mexican Governor Juan Alvarado instructed Alcalde Francisco De Haro to survey and lay out a plan for the new pueblo of Yerba Buena. De Haro hired Jean Jacques Vioget, a Swiss émigré, who was the only one in town with the necessary surveying tools to do the job. Since central plazas were a feature of all Spanish/ Mexican towns of the New World, Vioget chose a former potato patch one block from the beach for his plaza, which, as previously noted, after the American takeover was named Portsmouth Square. Vioget laid out several streets surrounding the plaza, but he gave none of them names on the map he drew. Although Vioget had laid out a traditional grid pattern of blocks and streets, oddly they were set at a pitch two and a half degrees from a right angle. O'Farrell, in his survey, corrected Vioget's two and a half degree pivot—known as "O'Farrell's swing"—and made all the blocks conform to right angles. (This made it necessary for some homeowners to move portions of their buildings out of the newly aligned streets.)

O'Farrell was barely a month into his survey when Lt. Bartlett was recalled to his ship. Allegations of malfeasance in office were to plague virtually every American alcalde, and Bartlett became the first. A columnist in Brannan's *California Star* accused him of misappropriating funds belonging to the town. The drumbeat of allegations continued until a formal inquiry was held under the direction of the senior naval officer in the harbor, Captain J. B. Hull. No incriminating evidence was produced in support of the allegations, and Bartlett was cleared. Perhaps because of this military entanglement with civil matters Bartlett was replaced by a civilian, Edwin Bryant. Before leaving office, Bartlett did do the town one lasting service: he issued a proclamation changing its name from Yerba Buena to San Francisco.

Edwin Bryant, who was born in Massachusetts in 1805, spent his early adulthood in Kentucky working as a journalist and newspaper editor. Seeking a change, he headed west in 1846, joining other emigrants on the California–Oregon Trail. He made it to California that fall and spent a couple of months in San Francisco before heading south to help American forces battle Mexican troops in Los Angeles. He returned to San Francisco early the following year, at which time General Stephen Watts Kearny, the new military governor of California, appointed Bryant to succeed Bartlett as alcalde. Both Kearny and Bryant had served in southern California during the recent fighting, but the two men had only come to know each other in San Francisco before Bryant's appointment.

On the day Bryant was sworn in, February 22, 1847, his predecessor, Bartlett, granted (meaning sold, in this case for $12.50) him a 50-vara lot, on the southeast corner of Montgomery and Pine streets, and in return, Bryant four days later granted the outgoing alcalde a 50-vara lot, this one on the northwest corner of Broadway and Stockton. As an indicator of how fast real estate prices would start to escalate, less than a year later, one-half of Bartlett's lot sold for $100, a gain of 1,500 percent in only nine months.

One lot was not enough for Edwin Bryant, but with the restriction still in force of only one lot per grantee, he employed a stratagem that would soon be copied by all but one of his successor alcaldes as well as by other speculators—he used "straw men,"—friends and cronies—to take title for him. On at least four occasions (and probably more during his tenure) during the months of March and April, Bryant granted lots to various individuals only to turn around that day or the next and buy those same lots from them. On March 19, 1847, for example, Bryant granted a 100-vara lot to John C. Buchanan, who happened to be his clerk, for the set rate of $25, and the next day Buchanan sold the lot to his boss for "28 dollars plus one *real*," meaning that Buchanan sold it back for the purchase price, since the extra three dollars plus one *real* equaled the recording fees. On April 14 Bryant granted a 50-vara lot to a John M. Stanley for $12.50, and that same day Stanley re-conveyed it to Bryant for a payment of $20, netting Stanley an easy profit for his efforts. Lusting after San Francisco real estate was under way—a good year before the gold discovery.

Bryant and fellow speculators so eagerly took to snapping up city lots at relatively low fixed prices that the alcalde was to grant 96 lots in March, his first full month on the job. While buyers were looking at property in the sand hills ever farther away from the center of town at Portsmouth Square, as Jasper O'Farrell proceeded with his survey, town residents looked at the shallow cove with an eye toward filling it in and creating more lots. It was obvious to many that, with little flat land for warehouses and other commercial structures, filling in Yerba Buena Cove and expanding to the east would fill that need. In mid-February 1847 a public meeting was held in Portsmouth Square to address the issue. Sam Brannan (who was to be an aggressive buyer of lots over the next few years) and others put forth a resolution proposing that the cove be divided into business lots and sold for the benefit of the town.

The only problem with creating lots in the cove was that under Mexican law, which continued under American rule, a strip of the beach and the harbor beyond were reserved for the exclusive use of the government. But under pressure from Brannan and like-minded individuals, Bryant made the case with his patron Kearny. The governor, citing the authority invested in him by the president of the United States, on March 10 released the area of the cove between Fort Montgomery at Green and Battery streets on the north, to Rincon Point on the south, to be divided into lots and sold at auction. Kearny had no such authority from the president or Congress, but as the supreme military commander in California, and three thousand miles from Washington, no one was in a position to challenge his decree. Jasper O'Farrell surveyed the cove, divided 50-vara lots into thirds (50 by 16 2/3 varas each) and created 444 new lots, which encompassed the area between the high and low watermarks. Four fifths of these lots, which became known as the "Beach and Water Lots," or more commonly just "water lots," were fully underwater at high tide.

A proper interval being allowed to post notice of the sale, the auction was held from July 20 to 23, 1847. About 200 of the lots sold. Terms of the sale were one quarter of the amount to be paid in cash on the date of purchase, with the balance to be paid in equal amounts three, six, and nine months hence. The highest price paid was $610, which is what William Leidesdorff, soon to become San Francisco's first treasurer, bid for each of three lots on the north side of California Street between Montgomery and Sansome, which at that time was a prime location right at the water's edge. He seems to have overpaid compared to what other lots sold for, but he had to have these properties because previously, apparently as a squatter, he had built a warehouse on them for his trade in cattle hides. Lots sold for much less away from the immediate shoreline area of Yerba Buena Cove near Portsmouth Square. A couple of submerged lots on the west side of Beale Street between Market and Mission, for example, which were far from downtown, sold for a "high bid" of five dollars each. No records seem to exist as to how much this auction raised in total, but it was enough for the town to be able to start paying for some modest civic improvements, including financing a jail and a schoolhouse, and opening up a few streets through the sand hills.

The release of the water lots for public sale without official sanction from higher authority than Governor Kearny highlighted the issue of whether valid titles could be given to purchasers of these lots. Indeed there was a question as to whether the purchasers of any of the lots that had been granted, including the 50-vara and

100-vara land-based ones, could claim that they held legal title. Since California was still a war zone at the time, under the rule of the U. S. military, many wondered if, after the Mexican War was over, their grants would be confirmed. No doubt in the back of the buyers' minds was the old adage: "Possession is nine-tenths of the law." Because of the lack of certainty, all sales after the initial grants were made were done only with quit claim deeds, not warranted deeds, meaning that the property was sold "as is," with no recourse if the title proved faulty.

Beyond the matter of California's status as a conquered province in wartime was an unresolved real-estate question specific to San Francisco. That was the arcane but germane question as to whether San Francisco had been properly constituted as a pueblo under Spanish/Mexican law and thus whether city officials had the legal authority to make grants of land. This question took years to finally resolve, and proved a field day for lawyers. A great deal of research was needed, much of it in the Mexican archives, which were in disarray, leaving city residents with a cloud of uncertainty hanging over them as to the validity of their titles. A U. S. Land Commission was established in 1851 to deal with the problem and with the whole question of Mexican grants and tangled land claims in general. After at least one adverse ruling by the courts, in 1854 the commission ruled that San Francisco had been properly constituted a pueblo and that all the grants of land made by the alcaldes were legal. Appeals by the U. S. Government ground on for additional years, but were finally resolved in San Francisco's favor.

This knowledge, years down the road, was of course of little help to real property owners in San Francisco in the late 1840s. Even after the war with Mexico was concluded in 1848 California's legal status was undefined: it was part of the United States but was not yet a state or even a territory. Despite the lack of clarity, buyers of real estate were not deterred. Speculation in San Francisco lots increased rapidly, especially in 1848 and 1849 after news of the gold discovery spread. And speculation is what it was, to a large degree, especially in lots farther away from Portsmouth Square, which were left largely unimproved. The thinking for most buyers was to hold the lots a short time for appreciation in the frenzied market and then sell them for a quick profit. William Tecumseh Sherman asked Governor Mason why he didn't put a stop to what Sherman viewed as reckless speculation. Mason told Sherman that he "did not believe the titles given by the alcaldes were worth a cent . . ." but his rationale for letting them proceed was that they served to help settle the towns and public lands and that that on the whole was a benefit to the government. This was the same reasoning that Mason had used in his argument that miners should be allowed to hunt for gold unmolested on government land.

Edwin Bryant had left San Francisco by the time the auction of the water lots took place. Anxious to return to his home in Louisville, Kentucky, he resigned as alcalde in late May. He stopped near Sutter's Fort on his overland journey, where he joined General Kearny who was also on his way back east, to a new military posting at St. Louis. With Kearny was John C. Frémont, who was under a kind of house arrest for insubordination during the Mexican War. (On the way, the three men and their party stopped at Donner Summit, north of Lake Tahoe, where they buried the remains of the Donner party victims, who had perished in the snows of the previous winter.) Bryant wrote a book about his experiences, including briefly about his alcaldeship in San Francisco, called *What I Saw in California*. With the start of the gold rush and the existence of a great hunger for news about the fabled land, Bryant's book became a bestseller and went through multiple printings, earning him a nice income.

Bryant was replaced as alcalde by George Hyde, whom Kearny had appointed in Bryant's place just before he left town. Hyde had served as alcalde before, for one month early in 1847, when Washington Bartlett had briefly been taken prisoner by the Mexicans. Hyde, born in Philadelphia in 1819, trained as a lawyer as a young man. After practicing law in his hometown for a few years, in late 1845 he signed on as a clerk to Commodore Robert F. Stockton, who was preparing to depart on the frigate *Congress* for California. They arrived in Monterey in July 1846, and the following month Hyde made his way to Yerba Buena (as San Francisco was still then known). Hyde arrived in town just days after Sam Brannan. The two crossed swords almost immediately. Brannan and his Mormons on the *Brooklyn* had arrived a few weeks after the

U. S. had raised the American flag at Yerba Buena. Being a large group from a sect viewed warily by some, and having close to 200 muskets with them, their loyalty to the United States came into question, as did their motives for coming to California. Hyde, described as being arrogant and having an officious manner, served as prosecutor when the military government filed charges against the Mormons for "high treason." A trial was held, and Brannan and his flock were cleared. Hyde further earned Brannan's ire a couple of months later when the former represented one of Brannan's shipmate Mormons as a plaintiff who was unhappy with the tight control the Mormon elder held over his followers via a contract they all had agreed to before coming to California. Hyde lost that case too, but Brannan held a grudge ever after. He would attack Hyde in print in his newspaper whenever he found an excuse to do so.

Shortly after taking office in late May 1847, Hyde appointed six men as a kind of town council to help him manage civic affairs. Colonel Mason, who had replaced the departed General Kearny as military governor of California, told Hyde that his appointees could stand if he so chose, but Mason also suggested that an election be held for an ayuntamiento, which would serve until the end of 1848. Hyde deferred to Governor Mason; an election was held in mid-September. Among the six elected were such leading citizens as William D. M. Howard, the town's best-known merchant, Robert A. Parker, proprietor of the Parker House, and William Leidesdorff, owner of the City Hotel. Leidesdorff was selected to be town treasurer. The councilmen drafted San Francisco's first official laws, and they also appointed two constables (later reduced to one) as a police force.

One of the new ayuntamiento's first acts was to remove the restriction on having to fence in and build on lots within a one-year period after their being granted by the alcalde. More important, the council repealed the law limiting any purchaser to one lot only. Sam Brannan's *California Star* applauded this move in an editorial and justified it partly on the excuse that owners would be wasting valuable lumber putting up shanties just to qualify their lots so as not to risk forfeiture. The *Star* disingenuously conceded that this repeal would aid speculators. Sam Brannan would be one of those speculators, as would most of the newly elected ayuntamiento. Jasper

O'Farrell having completed his survey in August 1847, which greatly expanded the town's available real estate (to a total of more than 800 acres), a land grab was quick to get underway.

In late October the ayuntamiento passed a resolution ordering that all lots, whether on land or water, be sold at auction. This edict marked the beginning of a power struggle between various town councils and alcaldes over the next two years for control of city government, or more to the point, control of the city's real estate. Except for a small auction of 52 lots in early March 1848, which netted less than $1,200, this resolution was to be virtually ignored by both Hyde and his successor, Thaddeus Leavenworth. They naturally were reluctant to give up one of their key powers, which was the ability to grant lots at a fixed price to whomever they chose. The town of San Francisco would have been better served, of course, if all lots had been auctioned at market prices, but those wielding the reins of power had their own self-interest foremost in mind. The members of the ayuntamiento also don't seem to have pushed too hard at this point to enforce their auction decree; they all potentially stood to benefit from receiving grants of land at fixed prices.

With money coming in from lot sales, in late 1847 Alcalde Hyde was voted a salary of $50 a month. (This was probably in addition to, and not in replacement of, fees paid him for various services.) While he no doubt appreciated the stipend it was peanuts compared to what he would make from real-estate deals over the next few years. During his tenure as alcalde in 1847 and 1848, Hyde not only granted lots to others in his official capacity but he also actively bought and sold lots for his own account. In one especially profitable deal, a choice 50-vara lot near Portsmouth Square that Hyde had granted to Nathan Spear in December 1846, probably for the going fee of $12.50, he purchased from Spear in June 1847 for $90. Two months later he sold just one-third of that lot to a Rowland Gilston of New York City for $500. Other deals didn't produce nearly that rate of return, but Hyde appears to have made profits to some degree on all of his lot sales in the late 1840s as prices continued to escalate.

George Hyde also continued the practice started by his predecessor Edwin Bryant of granting lots to cronies and then quickly purchasing them back for a small consideration. As an example, on

January 14, 1847 Alcalde Hyde granted a 150-vara lot at First and Mission streets to Henry Harris. Five days later Harris "granted and conveyed" that lot to Hyde. Whether "granted and conveyed" means that money changed hands is not known. In any event, Hyde held the lot until March the following year when he sold it to his friend Robert A. Parker for $150. In another instance, six months later Hyde granted a 50-vara lot on the corner of Broadway and Sansome streets to J. Howard Ackerman, likely for $12.50 (plus fees of $3.12½). The next day Ackerman sold it back to Hyde for $20. Two years later Ackerman and Hyde would be part of a group that would attempt to depose Thaddeus Leavenworth, Hyde's successor as alcalde.

Thaddeus Leavenworth not only would eventually succeed Hyde, but while Hyde was First Alcalde, Leavenworth served under him as Second Alcalde. Hyde, hungry for more real estate, concocted a scheme to have his second-in-command, who surely had no such authority, to grant *him* lots. It would have looked unseemly, even in that greedy time, for the alcalde to be seen granting lots to himself. But in a transparent attempt to do just that, Hyde had Leavenworth deed over to him no fewer that 27 lots, most of them during a one-week period in early October 1847. Fifteen of the lots were in the 50-vara survey, the rest, save one in the 100-vara survey south of Market Street, were water lots. (The latter were lots that had gone unsold during the July auction.) One has to wonder: in these strictly inner-office transactions between Hyde and Leavenworth did any money actually change hands, or was it done with just a wink and a nod?

By the time Hyde left office at the end of March 1848 he had granted over 500 lots, including the 200 or so water lots that had been auctioned, more than doubling the amount granted in total by all of his predecessors combined. At least 29 of those lots he essentially granted to himself.

Even before Hyde went on his "shopping spree" for lots in October of 1847 he had come under attack on various charges. During the water lots auction in July several purchasers complained of the excessive fees he charged. One sea captain who purchased some water lots thought the $6.12 recording fee per lot excessive. And army quartermaster Captain Joseph L. Folsom, who was one of the most aggressive buyers of lots, both before and after the repeal of the one lot per purchaser rule, accused Hyde of "official extortion," for charging a separate fee for each one-third of a 50-vara lot when Folsom considered a lot to be a whole 50-vara block. Rumors also started circulating that alleged that Hyde was not selling lots to the first applicants to apply for them, suggesting that he was either selling to preferred buyers or was holding out for the best offers (and perhaps pocketing the difference between the selling price and the official grant price.)

Sam Brannan, eager to do whatever he could to undermine Hyde, made a number of accusations against his foe. Back in February 1847, months before the auction of the water lots, Brannan had accused the alcalde in print of conspiring to appropriate them for his own. There may have been some truth to that, since Hyde had opposed auctioning the lots. (Two years later Brannan would stand accused of much the same thing that he was pointing the finger at Hyde for in 1847.) Brannan further attacked Hyde in the *California Star*, accusing him of being soft on crime for letting drunken Indians roam the streets and accost women, a charge not supported by any evidence.

Other episodes that raised a flap were Brannan's allegations that Hyde had altered the numbers on certain lots on the official map and that the alcalde had granted a lot to another applicant after it had been promised to Brannan's mother-in-law by Edwin Bryant. Hyde, in a memoir, defended himself on those two charges by saying as to the first one that his clerk had merely restored numbers that had been obliterated by his predecessor, Bryant, and as to the second allegation, he said that his clerk had made an innocent mistake. He claimed that Brannan was satisfied with that explanation. Nevertheless, after the town council voted in late September to investigate the rumors of malfeasance on Hyde's part, Brannan, on October 1, 1847, petitioned Governor Mason, along with more than fifty others, to have Hyde removed from office. Mason, after an investigation, took no action and Hyde remained alcalde.

In early March 1848 William Leidesdorff, who was known for having a temper, got into an altercation with another man over a bet on a horse race. Hyde had both men bound over for trial, which earned him the enmity of Leidesdorff, who prior to this had been one of Hyde's allies. Shortly after this, Brannan, in his newspaper, made the serious charge that Hyde had not given an accounting of the funds received from the sale of the water lots. Town Treasurer William Leidesdorff's official journal shows only that when he became treasurer on October 7, 1847 he had had turned over to him a gross amount of $2,912 from Alcalde Hyde as revenues received from the water lots auction. (The alcaldes received the monies from lot sales and *then* turned them over to the treasurer, a situation ripe for abuse.) Hyde appears to have kept no individual records as to what monies were received from which purchaser for which lot, and since it is unknown exactly how much money was raised in total it is impossible to know if there is any truth to the charge that the alcalde had not turned over all of the money. Brannan was certainly skeptical that he had. The *California Star* claimed flat out: "A large amount of funds . . . deposited in the hands of the Alcalde . . . have not been turned over to the Treasurer of the Town. . . ." The net result of all these controversies is that having made enemies of Brannan, Leidesdorff, and other leading citizens of the town, Hyde threw in the towel and resigned.

George Hyde was replaced as First Alcalde not by Second Alcalde Leavenworth but by Dr. John Townsend, who was appointed by Governor Mason. Leavenworth remained as Second Alcalde. John Townsend, a Mormon and a friend of Sam Brannan, was a doctor who had come overland with his wife to California in 1844 and had settled in San Francisco two years later. Townsend was granted a 50-vara lot late in 1846 on California Street between Montgomery and Sansome—for which he paid the requisite $12.50 plus fees—across the street from Leidesdorff's warehouse and a stone's throw from the bay. (The site is now the heart of San Francisco's financial district.) Townsend built a house on his lot and opened a little medical practice in it. The stocky doctor with his Lincolnesque beard would be a familiar sight over the next couple of years as he made his rounds on horseback, treating both American and Mexican patients.

Townsend became alcalde on March 31, 1848 just as the gold discovery excitement was starting to sweep San Francisco. Unlike his predecessors he granted no lots, the main reason likely being that there were no buyers, with virtually everyone leaving town to go to the mines. Townsend's main failing as alcalde was that after only two months on the job he couldn't resist the gold fever either, and he decamped for the Mother Lode as well. (The town's residents apparently did not hold this against him, since he was elected to the ayuntamiento in 1849, having returned unrewarded by his gold-digging efforts.) About the only significant thing that happened during his administration was that a few days after taking office, William Leidesdorff, in his capacity as a member of the ayuntamiento, introduced a resolution calling for a committee to organize and index the books and papers of the alcalde's office, which gives some indication as to the sloppiness of the record keeping. Nothing apparently was done in this regard. Leidesdorff died the following month, and gold fever quickly put everything else in the shade.

After John Townsend's departure for the gold mines, Thaddeus Leavenworth, who had been Second Alcalde under both Hyde and Townsend, finally got his chance as First Alcalde. Dr. Leavenworth, a native of Connecticut, was both a physician and an Episcopal minister. He was just shy of his 44th birthday when he arrived in San Francisco in March 1847 as chaplain for Colonel Stevenson's regiment, which made him older than most of those in his new milieu. He doesn't seem to have actively practiced medicine, but in line with his medical skills he opened San Francisco's first pharmacy.

Like most of his fellow alcaldes Leavenworth took a liking to real estate. He had a long life, and upon his death in 1893, at age 89, his obituary in the *San Francisco Chronicle* said in part: "At one time he owned a large portion of what is now San Francisco and gave away property there now worth more than $1,000,000," which gives an indication of just how much he accumulated. Ironically, he took office in the summer of 1848 just as real estate values were starting to dip. Buyers had largely departed town, and the feeling of those remaining was that maybe San Francisco would decline in importance as the action moved to the Mother Lode. That didn't happen, and Leavenworth and others who bought lots in 1848 made out very well. By November of that year, when miners returned to town to wait out the winter rains, real-estate prices had increased as much as ten-fold in less than a year. Lots that had sold in the spring of 1848 for $100 to $2,000 now went for $1,000 to $10,000. Structures that rented from $10 to $20 a month now commanded $100 a month, or more.

Leavenworth, as Hyde had done before him, totally ignored the ayuntamiento's order of the year before that city lots should only be sold at auction. During his alcaldeship from mid-1848 to mid-1849, at a time when real estate was skyrocketing in value and the city would have greatly benefited from the auctioning of lots at market prices, Leavenworth continued granting them at the old fixed prices of $12.50 for 50-vara parcels and $25.00 for 100-vara ones. Many of these were granted to friends and cronies, with Leavenworth, in some instances, then taking back title in his own name.

Not long after assuming office, for example, on July 25, 1848 he granted four 50-vara lots at Jones and Chestnut streets, which was then right at the water's edge in North Beach, to a Charles Cobb for $25. The next day he bought them from Cobb for $30. It's true that these particular lots were a long way from the downtown area of Portsmouth Square—ten blocks as the crow flies—and thus not then very valuable, but even so, the initial sales price amounted to a half-off sale, since four 50-vara lots would normally have sold for $50, not $25.

About a month later Leavenworth granted a 50-vara lot on the northwest corner of California and Stockton streets to Mills Callender, his clerk, for $12.50. At some point Callender "transferred" the lot back to the alcalde. Leavenworth reaped a huge gain when he sold this parcel less than a year later to a John Allig on May 30, 1849 for $3,800. (This last price could well indicate that a house or some other structure had been built on it, thus hiking its value.)

In a final example of sharp trading, in late September 1848 Leavenworth granted a 50-vara lot on the corner of California and Powell streets to William S. Clark, one of the town's prominent citizens and a member of its first elected ayuntamiento, for $12.50. Within a day or two Clark sold it back to Leavenworth for the same $12.50. Only five months later Leavenworth sold the lot to an Andrew Hoeppner for $1,000. The lot wasn't worth that much—

Hoeppner sold it six weeks later to a different party for only $500. Why would Hoeppner buy a property that even in that inflated market was overpriced? The answer seems to be that it was part of a "I'll scratch your back if you scratch mine" deal, because in early March 1849, just days after Hoeppner had paid Leavenworth the $1,000, Leavenworth paid Hoeppner $9,000 for 800 acres that Hoeppner owned in Sonoma County.

These three examples are probably just the tip of the iceberg of Leavenworth's real-estate dealings. During his tenure as alcalde he granted nearly 550 lots. How many of these he was able to convert to his own use is impossible to say. He may also have used other stratagems to enrich himself. George Hyde, in a memoir he wrote some thirty years after the incidents in question, claimed that if Leavenworth had already granted a lot at a fixed price and a buyer came along with a better offer, Leavenworth would destroy the first deed and pocket the additional money. What other moneymaking schemes did he engage in? Alfred Green, a veteran of Stevenson's regiment, visited Leavenworth in his office one day to complain about dealings he had had with a local merchant, and was startled when the alcalde asked him how much money he had. Thinking that Leavenworth was soliciting a bribe he stormed out in disgust. A few months earlier a British sea captain, Anthony Easterby, who befriended Leavenworth during a brief visit to San Francisco in early 1849, wrote of the alcalde: "He made me several interesting business propositions . . ." The deliberate three-dot ellipsis Easterby placed at the end of this sentence suggests that these propositions were not entirely above board. Easterby never elaborated, so those conversations are lost to history.

Leavenworth's self-enriching deals seem to have been common knowledge even if the details were lacking. Town resident Dr. Victor Fourgeaud referred in a letter to Leavenworth when he wrote: "The office of Alcalde in San Francisco is unfortunately held at present by a man utterly unworthy of it—accused by all of base and unprincipled conduct." The *Alta California* (a newspaper formed at the beginning of 1849 by the merger of the *California Star* and the other paper in town, the *Californian*) didn't mince any words: "It was well known that the Alcalde in defiance of law and justice had been in the habit of selling town lots, and other property of the town, and that the proceeds of such sales had been for a long time unaccounted for." Not surprisingly, although he had a few supporters, Leavenworth was widely disliked and distrusted.

At the end of 1848, the term of the ayuntamiento of six members that had been elected in 1847 when George Hyde was alcalde was set to expire. Accordingly, an election was held on December 27 to choose a new ayuntamiento for the year 1849. Seven new members were elected, but the old council, citing fraud at the polls, refused to recognize the new council. The first council refused to yield office and called for a new election. Thus a third ayuntamiento was voted into office on January 15, so for that one day, San Francisco had three different town councils, each vying for legitimacy. At the end of that day the first council of 1848 resigned, leaving just two. Alcalde Leavenworth, watching these proceedings with a wary eye, started sleeping with a loaded gun by his bed at night.

Not long after this, Leavenworth was approached by a committee from the newest council and was asked to give an accounting of the revenues he had collected on the sale of town lots. He had no records of how much the sales had brought in, and further he had used some of the money to pay his salary and his clerk's salary, as well as office expenses. None of the expenses was documented. Based on these findings the town council passed a resolution in early February and published it in the *Alta*, stating that for anyone indebted to the town of San Francisco, it was "strictly forbidden to pay any money to said Leavenworth, his order, or request."

With the gauntlet now thrown down between the two branches of city government, something had to give. A public meeting was held in Portsmouth Square in mid-February to resolve the issue of the two competing councils. As a result of that meeting, on February 21, both councils resigned. In their place, three justices of the peace and a new council of fifteen members were elected; one of the new councilmen was former alcalde George Hyde. They called themselves the Legislative Assembly (of the District of San Francisco). They swore themselves into office on March 5 and wasted little time getting down to business. The new council called for an audit of Leavenworth's accounts, and on March 22 they passed a bill abolishing the office of alcalde entirely. They delivered a copy of this act to Leavenworth and demanded that he deliver to the Legislative Assembly all of his books, records, and official papers. The alcalde refused to do so, and instead approached General Persifor Smith, the senior military official in town, to seek his advice. Smith instructed Leavenworth to not cede his office and to hold onto his books and documents. Smith said Governor Mason, who was in Monterey, would rule on the matter. Mason, however, who had applied late in 1848 to be relieved of his duties in California and to be ordered back East, finally got his wish, and so on April 13 he was replaced as governor by General Bennet Riley. Riley visited San Francisco, and after meeting with the Legislative Assembly and hearing their arguments, suspended Leavenworth from office on May 6.

With Leavenworth still refusing to turn over the town's records—he had more than a passing interest in keeping secret what they would reveal—the Legislative Assembly sent a group of men led by their sheriff, John Pulis, (who was also a member of the Hounds) over to the alcalde's office. In a scene worthy of a "B" movie, when Leavenworth spurned their request to turn the records over, he and Pulis drew revolvers on each other. Outnumbered, Leavenworth surrendered the records. After the ledgers had been loaded into a waiting dray, the driver they had hired, in keeping with the greedy nature of the times, demanded two ounces of gold for his services. When Pulis and his party complained that that was exorbitant, the drayman held the most valuable record book hostage until his demand was met.

When Governor Riley got word of the seizure of the records, fearing that things were getting out of hand, he reversed course and reinstated Leavenworth. A few days later, on June 4, Riley issued a proclamation that labeled the Legislative Assembly an illegal body that had "usurped powers which are vested only in the Congress of the United States." He continued by stating that no matter what one thought of the present alcalde, the office was legally constituted and had to be respected. He called on the Legislative Assembly to return the city's records to the alcalde. Faced with defeat, the Assembly disbanded, having been in existence for just three months. The next day this whole "opera bouffe" came to an end when Leavenworth, under strain and fed up with all the turmoil, submitted his resignation to Riley. It was contingent upon a replacement taking over. That wouldn't happen until August 1, so in the interim Leavenworth stayed in office—and continued to grant more lots.

Meanwhile, California governance, which had a direct influence on San Francisco, was experiencing its own rockiness. While the war with Mexico was still on, Colonel Mason had ruled as governor with a firm hand and unquestioned authority. When the news of the treaty ending the war reached Mason on August 6, 1848, the situation changed. Mason's authority as a military leader no longer held sway, but a real civil government couldn't yet exist since California was neither a territory nor a state, so he couldn't legally rule in a civil capacity either. So he, and then his successor, General Riley, carried on as de facto governors of a conquered province that was now part of the United States, but with undefined legal status.

Mason had hoped that, with the end of the Mexican War, Congress would act swiftly to bring California into the Union. President Polk had, in fact, asked Congress in the summer of 1848 to provide for a territorial government for California. But the possible expansion of slavery into new territories was a hot button issue. There were thirty states—half of them slave, half free. A new territory, leading to statehood, would tip the balance one way or the other. Southerners opposed California's joining the Union, because a provision of the 1846 Wilmot Proviso prohibited slavery in territory gained in the Mexican War. There the matter would stand until a Congressional compromise was reached in 1850 and California would be admitted directly as the thirty-first state—and one free of slavery.

Californians in late 1848 and into 1849 were left hoping that the situation would be resolved much sooner. They were longing for self-government and were growing restive. They disliked being ruled by the military and having to abide by the old Mexican system of laws and offices, including sometimes corrupt and arbitrary alcalde rule and justice. By mid-1849 pressure was growing on Governor Riley to do something. Matters came to a head on May 28 when the *Edith* steamed into San Francisco Bay with the word that Congress had adjourned without establishing territorial status for California. Even worse was the news that Congress had passed a bill making California subject to U. S. revenue laws and thus taxation. The reaction in San Francisco was one of fury: "No taxation without representation" came the cry. Faced with a seething population and lack of leadership from Washington, on June 3 Riley issued a proclamation calling for a convention to choose delegates for a provisional state government and to draft a constitution. He set August 1 as the date for elections not only for representatives to the convention but also to elect new local officials where there were vacancies, which in San Francisco included a replacement for the outgoing alcalde, Thaddeus Leavenworth.

Prior to Riley's proclamation, Californians had wanted territorial government. After it they clamored for statehood. Delegates were duly elected from various districts around California. They assembled in Monterey in early September. After five weeks of discussion and negotiation they hammered out California's first constitution. At a grand ball the concluding evening the delegates heartily thanked General Riley, who had attended the convention in full uniform complete with a yellow sash he had earned for battle heroics during the Mexican War. With the ratified constitution in hand, Riley informed his superiors in Washington that he intended to turn California over to civilian control. When there was no objection he called for an election for November 13 to ratify the constitution and elect a governor and members of a bicameral legislature. The duly elected representatives met on December 17 in San Jose, which had been designated as the state capitol. Three days later Peter H. Burnett was sworn in as California's first governor, and military control of governmental affairs in the region came to an end. Official statehood, however, would have to wait until September 1850.

Even with all the political turmoil, there was one place in San Francisco throughout the late 1840s where the governors' minions ruled unchallenged—the Custom House on Portsmouth Square. Tariffs applied to foreign goods imported into the United States were strictly a federal matter, so when the U. S. military established its authority in California during the Mexican War, junior officers were appointed as collectors at the Custom House. Navy Lieutenant Washington A. Bartlett served first in that role, after which he was succeeded by Army Captain Joseph L. Folsom. All customs revenues were placed in a "Civil Fund" to help finance the military government in California. The Civil Fund grew rapidly after the word of the gold discovery brought ships to San Francisco from all parts of the globe. By the end of 1849 revenues were averaging $100,000 a month.

With the end of the Mexican War the office of Collector of the Port was turned over to civilian control, although it was still under the supervision of the military. Edward H. Harrison, a mustered-out veteran of Colonel Stevenson's regiment, replaced Folsom in September 1848. When Vicente Pérez Rosales arrived a few months later on a ship from Valparaiso he described how the "port captain," a corpulent man with a black eye and reeking of whiskey, came aboard with his assistants to inspect their cargo. After sending a spray of chewing tobacco juice overboard he announced in a loud voice: "Welcome to the land of gold." When the ship's captain handed the passengers' passports to him the customs official glinted at him with his good eye and snarled that he didn't need to see them. The skipper then offered the inspector wine. The official replied that he only drank champagne. After downing a bottle of bubbly he departed, leaving his assistants to follow up. Rosales didn't name the "port captain," but this unflattering characterization appears to refer to Edward Harrison.

Harrison was so informal and so indifferent about security that the gold and silver coins he collected as tariff duties were kept in canvas and buckskin bags and were left casually lying about the Custom House. One observer remembers seeing Harrison's employees sitting around the office on sacks of Mexican dollars three feet high. Because space was tight, other bags of coins were stored under a shed on California Street, according to that same witness.

When James Collier arrived in November 1849, having been appointed the new collector of the port by President Zachary Taylor as Harrison's replacement, he was appalled by the lax security and the lack of bookkeeping. The old Mexican adobe Custom House had doors that were nearly off their hinges and a roof that leaked when it rained. Collier felt that anyone with theft in mind could have carved through the adobe walls with a knife in twenty minutes. Collier also found that Harrison had little interest in keeping records and did not even know how much money he had on the premises. Harrison paid government expenses, his salary, and those of his clerks and inspectors out of the coin bags as the need arose. Collier, a much more officious sort, made a point of counting all the money in the 24 sacks of coins he found there. An audit later determined that customs receipts between August 6, 1848 when San Francisco learned of the Mexican War's end, and November 12, 1849, the day after Collier's arrival, came to $1,365,000. Whether Harrison (for whom Harrison Street is named) dipped into the money sacks surrounding him to supplement his annual salary of $2,000 is not known, but *The Annals of San Francisco* claimed that Harrison became wealthy as a result of his Custom House employment.

San Francisco city officials, with their under-funded treasury, could only look longingly at the bulging coin bags in the Custom House right across the street from them. Thaddeus Leavenworth, while he was alcalde, approached Governor Mason to see if some of the money could be used to aid the sick and needy in town, but Mason had denied his request. Mason regarded the Civil Fund as federal government money and thus not for the use of civilians in California. When city officials tried again in the summer of 1849 they found Governor Riley more receptive. He authorized a payment of $10,000 on the condition that San Francisco raise an equal sum and that the money be used only for constructing a jail and courthouse.

With Governor Riley's call for a new election on August 1 and with Thaddeus Leavenworth having submitted his resignation, the office of alcalde was vacant and up for grabs. Instead of there being competition for the job, however, San Francisco's citizens quickly rallied around one man to be their new leader: John W. Geary. Geary is depicted in most histories of San Francisco as being initially uninterested in political office. His Caesar-like seeming lack of interest was probably a pose, because the ambitious Geary was a politician to his core. In this case he didn't need to express his desire to be alcalde because he was indeed popular for a variety of reasons. The two most obvious were that he was a war hero and that he had been the bearer of good tidings when he had brought to San Francisco something everyone wanted: mail from home. Beyond that, although a Geary scholar says that among his negative attributes were "an unforgiving personality, quick anger, and an obsession with discipline" (probably qualities that only came fully to the fore during the Civil War), Geary was seen by locals as a man of fairness and integrity. He also was described as soft spoken, even dispassionate—just the opposite of another leading figure in town, Sam Brannan, with all of his theatrics and bombast. But Geary didn't need to raise his voice; he commanded attention merely because of his size. He weighed 260 pounds and stood 6 feet 5 inches. Other men literally looked up to him. Another reason Geary was admired was that, unlike most men, he had brought his wife and family to California. With females and children scarce, deference was paid to those with families. And finally, in perhaps a perverse way, Geary was esteemed because he was a teetotaler. In hard-drinking San Francisco anyone who had the discipline to avoid imbibing was seen as worthy of one's respect.

For all these reasons Geary was elected alcalde virtually by acclamation. His election came at a good time for him because his stint as postmaster had just ended. He had supplemented the salary from that with profits from his commission merchant partnership with O. P. Sutton and William Van Voorhies, but with his election he left them to devote his time to his new duties. Geary noted in a letter to his wife, who had returned to Pennsylvania with their two young sons by this time, that the office of alcalde paid much better than the post office. Not enough to satisfy Geary's wants certainly, but he would soon remedy that.

When Geary was sworn in on August 6 by Governor Riley so were twelve new members of an ayuntamiento. Among them were Sam Brannan and former alcalde John Townsend. Within the next two weeks other leading townspeople were appointed to fill newly created city offices, among which were city treasurer, city attorney, city physician, captain (chief) of police, city surveyor, and collector of taxes. San Francisco was finally putting in place the makings of a real government.

Geary lost no time getting down to business. He called for all relevant documents, including real-estate deeds in private hands, to be turned in to city officials to be kept as public records. In his inaugural speech he painted a bleak picture of the town's standing and finances:

> At this time we are without a dollar in the public treasury, and it is to be feared the city is considerably in debt. You have neither an office for your magistrate, or any other public edifice. You are without a single police officer or watchman, and have not the means of confining a prisoner for an hour; neither have you a place to shelter while living, sick and unfortunate strangers who may be cast upon our shores, or to bury them when dead. Public improvements are unknown in San Francisco.

Geary was exaggerating for effect, but not by much. His speech was meant to justify his call for taxes on numerous goods and services to finance much-needed improvements. By mid-September the ayuntamiento had passed sweeping legislation that provided for licensing and fees for many occupations, including auctioneers, merchants, peddlers, and draymen. Small businesses such as taverns were assessed monthly fees of fifty dollars. Owners of billiard tables and ten-pin alleys had to be licensed and pay $20 a month. Gambling was especially targeted: operators of monte, faro, roulette, and other games were required to pay $50 monthly for *each table* they owned. Even owners of boats and launches on the waterfront had to pay; they were assessed forty cents per ton for each vessel. All these fees were payable in advance.

It was the selling of city real estate, however, that served as the main attraction for San Francisco officials and that would bring in the majority of the revenue for the next year or so. Jasper O'Farrell in his 1847 survey had plotted 773 50-vara lots, 136 100-vara lots, and 444 beach- and water-lots. But with virtually all of those granted by mid-summer of 1849 and with real-estate speculation still in full flower, the ayuntamiento instructed City Surveyor William M. Eddy to survey additional lots beyond the boundaries of the O'Farrell plan. Eddy, a native of New York, had only arrived in town in June. Little is known of his background, but he must have had the credentials for the job (he used the initials C.E.—for civil engineer—after his name), since only two months later he was appointed to the surveyor's post. How much of the actual survey-ing he did is debatable. One of the surveyors working for him kept a diary, and in a March 1850 entry wrote: "Went to office 2nd time p.m. and found him (Eddy) drunker than usual." Eddy likely stayed in the office while his subordinates did the actual fieldwork. Whatever the case, the Eddy survey about doubled the number of lots sur-veyed by O'Farrell. North of Market Street the 50-vara survey was extended west to Larkin Street. South of Market the 100-vara plan reached to about Seventh Street on the west and to between Harrison and Townsend streets on the south depending on the loca-tion of the shoreline. The water lots north of Market were expanded to the east past Front Street, and south of Market to the east of Beale Street to a depth of 12 feet at low water.

Eddy's survey paved the way for the sale of this additional real estate. But there was to be a major change: these lots would be sold by auction. Governor Riley, in an earlier proclamation, had offi-cially restored San Francisco's ayuntamiento, and that body, after its investiture in August, quickly asserted its authority by prohibit-ing the alcalde from selling or disposing of any town or public lands without its consent. The alcalde would still be the official grantor of lots, but he could only do so now with the sanction of the ayuntamiento. The days of the alcalde selling lots for fixed prices on his own initiative were over.

The ayuntamiento lost no time in introducing resolutions call-ing for the sale of Eddy's additional lots. Auctions were held in late 1849 on November 19, November 28, and December 10 for the land-based lots. Nearly 200 lots were sold each time. A few appear to have been re-sales of property by the original grantees, but the vast majority was newly offered unimproved lots. Most were 50-vara lots west of downtown between Taylor and Larkin streets, stretching from Nob and Russian hills in the north to Market Street on the southern border, encompassing much of today's Tenderloin district. As many as 79 of the lots in the December 10 auction were 100-vara lots, south of Market Street. Virtually all of these were west of Fifth Street, an area far removed from the center of town. The three auctions brought in a total of $183,065, an average of about $332 per lot overall with the 100-vara lots averaging north of $400 each.

One observer, William F. White (alias William Grey), who maintained that he was shut out of the process in trying to bid on lots at these sales, charged that surveyor Eddy favored a "ring" of individuals including Sam Brannan and John Geary by tipping them in advance as to which lots were more desirable. He claimed that Eddy did two maps, one for the ring, each of whom paid Eddy $50 to look at the map marked with such comments as "A nice building lot," or "On a high sandhill, covered with oak timber." White further alleged that the process was rigged because Sam Brannan had gotten his brother-in-law's partner, George Tyler, appointed as auctioneer. The insiders got their hands on the choicest lots because under auctioneer Tyler "no outsiders bid *was heard*, except the lot was not wanted by any member of the ring," according to White.

Ayuntamiento member Sam Brannan also introduced a resolution calling for an auction of the additional water lots, all of these being farther out in the cove beyond the boundary of the original water lots of the 1847 auction. That sale took place on January 3, 1850. Three hundred and forty-four lots, each amounting to one-third of a 50-vara lot in size, were sold, with about 50 of them appearing to be re-sales of earlier grants from the O'Farrell survey. Prices overall here were higher than for the land-based lots inasmuch as everyone agreed that the potential appreciation for these would eventually be much greater once they were filled in. Prices ranged from a low of $250 to a few in the $4,000 range. One lot, at a choice location on the beach at First and Mission streets, and an apparent resale, sold for $7,200 (the high price indicates that there likely was a structure such as a warehouse on it).

The total revenue raised from the January 3 auction came to $468,780, making for an average sale price per lot of $1,363. Although George Tyler had wielded the gavel and acted as auctioneer, John W. Geary, as alcalde, was the official grantor. He signed the deeds and collected the money. The three auctions of late 1849 were cash-only transactions payable in full at the time of purchase, but the subsequent water-lots auction of January 3 offered terms of one-fourth in cash at time of purchase with the balance due in three installments, three, six, and nine months thence, with a mortgage on the property until the final payment was made.

A little more than half a year after the four auctions, specifically on August 12, 1850, a large block advertisement appeared in the *Alta California*. Being offered for sale the next day, by a local auction company, was a mixture of at least 20 properties, most of which were 50-vara and 100-vara lots. There were also a few water lots that measured $16\frac{2}{3}$-varas by 50-varas. To accommodate the still strong demand for real estate, the land-based lots had now been subdivided, with the 50-vara lots being partitioned into 12 tracts and the 100-vara ones being sectioned into 36 parcels. The total came to 406 lots being offered for sale. At the bottom of the ad under the terms requiring one fourth cash down and the rest in three installments was this sentence: "TITLES GUARANTEED, being the property of JOHN W. GEARY." The day of the sale, prospective buyers and members of the press gathered in the auction company's showroom on Montgomery Street and dined on a lavish spread of food along with plenty of liquor to get bidders in the mood. A newspaper reporter in attendance wrote of Geary:

> . . . the gentleman has made good use of his time and opportunities as Alcalde . . . for as Mayor of the city he has as yet received no salary. The industry of Mr. Geary is worthy of all praise, for he has amassed in a very short space of time, an amount of property that it takes other men less energetic and less fortunate, years of labor to acquire; and that, too, while burdened with the cares and duties of a very onerous office.

This probably sarcastic description highlights Geary's sudden wealth but doesn't answer the question as to just how he managed, with no salary, to acquire all that valuable real estate. So how did Geary get his hands on all those lots, especially in light of the fact that Wheeler's *Land Titles*, the semi-official record of who was originally granted what lots shows Geary as being the purchaser of only one 50-vara lot? The answer lies in to whom the lots were originally granted. Over three-quarters of the lots in the advertisement had been granted by Geary himself as part of the auctions of November and December 1849 and early January 1850. Of those advertised lots for sale granted by Geary, more than ninety percent were granted to one man, a David Logan. David Logan was Geary's brother-in-law.

Logan had accompanied Geary and his wife (née Margaret Ann Logan) and family to California. He had taken a brief stab at gold mining, but after not too long Logan returned to San Francisco and ended up working in the city surveyor's office under William Eddy. Obviously, at some point between late 1849 and August 1850, David Logan simply deeded back to Geary the lots granted to him. That question answered, another arises: did David Logan really pay for the lots to begin with? If so, one wonders how a salaried employee in the city surveyor's office came up with the more than $20,000 that Logan bid in total for these lots. One also suspects that Logan himself didn't actually pay for the lots, since the records show him as being virtually the only bidder to pay all four installments of the water lots sale in one lump sum.

Purchase money for all of these sales was handed directly to the alcalde, Geary, who would later turn it over to the treasurer. Were the Logan purchases "nod and a wink" transactions between two city officials who also happened to have family ties? We can't know for sure, because although Geary periodically turned over aggregate amounts of money to the city treasurer, there is no record of his documenting which cash was being turned over to pay for which specific lots. If the Geary grants to his brother-in-law were "phantom" transactions, with no money changing hands, then Geary and his brother-in-law, who kept a few lots, apparently as his reward, made out well indeed.

And what about the other lots Geary advertised for sale that he had not deeded to his brother-in-law? Some of them had been granted by his predecessor, Thaddeus Leavenworth, to various other individuals, including two grants of 50-vara lots that, interestingly, were made to David Logan. Some of the remainder of the lots that Geary himself had granted—in the water-lots auction of January 3—were made to Charles L. Ross. Ross and Geary were presumably friends, Geary having used a portion of Ross's store as his first post office when he arrived with his sacks of mail in April 1849. As to the other grantees, those with no known ties to Geary but whose lots ended up in Geary's hands, perhaps the only inference that can be made is that anyone with important business with the city had to deal with Alcalde Geary. With his senior position and multiple responsibilities, he was the most powerful man in San

Francisco. Payments and gifts to politicians from those wishing to curry favor is a practice hardly unknown today, let alone in the more freewheeling 19th century.

There is no doubt Geary wanted to become wealthy. When gold fever raged on the East Coast, starting in late 1848, he became "infected" like virtually everyone else. He hustled down to Washington, D.C., presented himself at the White House, and as a war hero received a commission from President Polk to become postmaster in San Francisco, ground zero of the new golden land. Upon arrival, dazzled by the speculation and fortunes being made, he wrote to his parents, starting one sentence with: "When I get rich . . ." Instead of heading for the Mother Lode after his postal job ended he went into politics, for which he had a natural affinity. And that, in turn, opened the door to real estate, a field in which he already had some experience, having successfully engaged in land speculation in Kentucky while working as a surveyor there as a young man. So the plum job of alcalde got him the wealth he had sought.

Secondary sources, most notably Hubert Howe Bancroft, claim that Geary amassed at least $200,000 in the less than three years he was in San Francisco. That doesn't sound unrealistic. The August 1850 auction of Geary's properties lasted two days. The first day's sales fetched $105,000 and included the more valuable water lots, the highest priced of which went for $4,400. The lots sold the second day were comprised mainly of sandy wastes at the far western edge of town or in the swampy regions south of Market Street. A complete tally doesn't exist, but most of those sold for only from $20 to $30 apiece (this was for one twelfth of a 50-vara lot and unknown amounts for one-thirty sixth of a 100-vara lot). An educated guess would place the second day's take at maybe only $15,000, giving a grand total of about $120,000. Not a bad two-day haul considering that Geary likely paid little or nothing for the lots.

In fairness to Geary and his predecessor alcaldes, not to excuse their ethical lapses and illegal behavior, they had demanding, stressful jobs under trying, even chaotic, circumstances. In addition to his judicial duties for both criminal and civil cases, which, by one estimate, totaled more than 2,000 during his tenure as alcalde and mayor, Geary performed many routine services for his constituents, including such things as witnessing declarations of intent to become U. S. citizens, notarizing powers of attorney, and signing off on lease agreements, as well as on satisfactions of mortgages. In one instance he was even called upon to witness the manumission of a slave named George, whose owner, a Texan, appeared before Geary to testify that he was freeing him in return for payment of $1,000.

To help lighten Geary's load, another judge was appointed in mid-December, with the governor's approval, to handle only civil cases for sums in dispute in excess of $100. The man selected was William B. Almond, who quickly gained a reputation as one of the more colorful characters in town. Almond, a former peanut vendor from Missouri, appears to have had no legal training. He eschewed traditional courtroom demeanor, puffing on a cigar while court was in session and offering it to anyone needing a light. He paid little attention to courtroom testimony, since he was frequently busy signing papers, writs, and executions. He once adjourned court for ten minutes to drink whiskey with a juror. Whatever else may be said of Almond's administration of justice, litigants could not complain about "the law's delay." He rarely gave attorneys more than half an hour to make their cases, and sometimes not even that; he would cut them off in mid-argument if he had heard enough to make up his mind. As the *Annals* noted, Almond had "a sovereign contempt for Buncombe speeches, legal technicalities, learned opinions, and triumphantly cited precedents."

Many of the cases Almond heard involved claims against owners and masters of ships. There were numerous suits by arriving passengers involving breach of contract over bad food and mistreatment during long, grueling sea voyages. Judgments in these cases usually went against the defendants because, as some observers cynically noted, they were best able to pay not just the judgments themselves but the court costs too, a matter naturally of concern to Almond. Ships' captains who couldn't pay judgments would end up having their ships seized and sold by the sheriff.

Disputes over cargo also sometimes ended up in court. Captain George Coffin told how he had trouble clearing his cargo because the consignees couldn't be found. The freight bills had been paid in advance in New Orleans, so once the goods were put on lighters in Yerba Buena Cove he had no further control over or responsibility for them. But when the lightermen landed the goods on shore and found no one to receive them—a not infrequent occurrence in the hustle and bustle of the waterfront—the merchandise was left in the mud. The owners sued Coffin for their lost or ruined property, and he had to "employ a lawyer, and dance attendance at court myself to save the ship from loss."

Gardner Quincy Colton, another new judge, took office not long before William Almond was appointed. Colton was appointed a justice of the peace by Prefect Horace Hawes, with authority to handle civil cases involving amounts of less than $100. G. Q., as he was more commonly known, was the younger brother of Walter Colton, the alcalde of Monterey. A native of Vermont, G. Q. Colton had come to California by sea in February 1849, and after an unsuccessful stint in the gold mines had returned to San Francisco. After his appointment to the bench, Colton lost no time in using what he assumed was his power to grant lots. He surely must have known that nearly all the city's real estate had been sold, but without a grantees list in front of him he went on a spree over the next few weeks, granting several hundred lots, most of which had already been deeded to others by John W. Geary and previous alcaldes. Colton grantees were typically those who had been latecomers to San Francisco and had missed out on the earlier granting of lots. They were only too happy to get in on the action, issues of prior ownership be damned.

Once word got out about Colton's grants the ayuntamiento, on December 21, instructed City Attorney Archibald Peachy to file suit against him to cease and desist. Three days later the ayuntamiento declared Colton's grants null and void, but Colton, undissuaded, continued on, even keeping his office open on Christmas Day to accommodate purchasers. The jig was soon up. After an arrest warrant was issued, Colton fled San Francisco and returned to the East Coast, apparently taking with him the purchase money he had received from buyers, since none seems to have made it to the city treasury. Reestablishing himself in New York, Colton, who had had some medical training, gained notoriety as a pioneer in the use of nitrous oxide, or "laughing gas," as an anesthetic for painless tooth extraction. San Franciscans were not left laughing in the wake of his departure, since the "Colton grants" led to a tangle of competing claims of ownership and a lot of finger pointing among city officials.

Prefect Horace Hawes, who had appointed Colton, found himself on the hot seat over Colton's transgressions, and as a result he quickly became embroiled in a power struggle with the ayuntamiento. Hawes, a native of New York state, had come to San Francisco in early 1849 from Honolulu after serving as consul to various South Sea islands for two years. An able lawyer, he had served as one of the two prosecutors in the trial of the Hounds. As prefect, he served as the governor's right hand man, charged with overseeing the doings of local officials.

By early 1850 Hawes had become concerned about the state of San Francisco's finances. Rumors were circulating about how leading officials were enriching themselves at the city's expense. In mid-February, Hawes convinced Governor Peter Burnett to issue a proclamation suspending sales of city lots until a proper accounting could be made. Hawes complained to the ayuntamiento that he had not received an accounting of the water-lots auction of January 3, and furthermore he wanted a tally as to how many of those lots had been purchased by the town council's members. The defiant ayuntamiento ignored his demands and indicated that it planned to proceed with further lot sales regardless. As a deadline approached on March 1 for the ayuntamiento to provide a report on the town's fiscal condition for the previous year, as required by law, and with no report forthcoming, Hawes notified the governor. Governor Burnett had his attorney general put pressure on the ayuntamiento, which, soon after, came up with an accounting of revenues and expenditures for the period from December 6, 1849 to March 4, 1850.

Hawes meanwhile had completed an investigation into the water-lot sales of January 3, 1850, and had discovered that members of the ayuntamiento had purchased 120 of the lots. Sam Brannan and his partner J. W. Osborn had bought 57 of those. On March 15 Hawes sent a scathing letter to the ayuntamiento detailing what he had discovered, and that he had further found that the council's secretary, the auctioneer, business partners of the members, and "one of the Alcaldes" (he surely was referring to Geary) had also purchased lots. This was a clear violation of their fiduciary duty and of the law, and as such Hawes declared those purchases to be null and void. The ayuntamiento members could not deny the truth of the findings, so they proceeded to blacken Hawes's reputation. They accused him of collusion with G. Q. Colton, and alleged that Hawes himself had illegally accepted grants of land from his protégé. There was no evidence to support that allegation, and Hawes publicly refuted the charges. He might have prevailed in this tit-for-tat with his rivals, but he was a quarrelsome sort who had prickly relations with almost everyone, apparently including even the governor. With all of the town's leading citizens aligned against him and with no friends at court, so to speak, when the ayuntamiento petitioned Governor Burnett to remove Hawes from office, Burnett did so at the end of March, writing an end to that bitter contest.

After the sale of the water lots in early January, with the thought of several hundred thousand dollars soon to be coming in to supplement what had already been raised in the November and December lot sales, the ayuntamiento went on a spending spree. There was a crying need for wharves. Although the privately owned—and highly profitable—Commercial Street Wharf (or Long Wharf as it was commonly called) was now extending some 800 feet out into Yerba Buena Cove, more wharves were urgently needed. Most goods were still being brought ashore via lighters. This was a time consuming and expensive process; it could take weeks or months to fully unload a ship. And by the time that occurred the cost of doing so sometimes equaled the cost of freight from Atlantic ports. A ship tying up at a wharf could unload in only a few days at much less expense. With that in mind, Sam Brannan and other council members pushed through resolutions appropriating $200,000 for a California Street wharf, $100,000 for a wharf that would extend from Pacific Street, and a like amount for a Market Street wharf. Brannan had more than just his civic duties in mind. Some of the water lots he purchased that January just happened to lie along the line of the proposed California Street Wharf. The ayuntamiento did not stop there. It voted another $100,000 for street improvements. Brannan would profit from this too because all city residents would be assessed to pay for grading and eventual planking that would improve the value of the real estate adjoining those streets—and Brannan owned a lot of real estate.

Sales of town lots from the three auctions late in 1849 had delivered almost $111,000 to the town's treasury in December, while revenues from license fees and taxes had added more than $24,000 that same month. But the city's cash balance on December 31 stood at just under $41,000. Cash was going out the door at a rapid clip, and that was the last month for years that there would be a surplus. The major expenditures were for street improvements, police force expenses including maintenance of the prison brig *Euphemia*, city hospital and city physician charges, and surveying fees from William Eddy and his crew. Soon to be added to those were the enormous outlays for wharves, not to mention $200,000 budgeted for a new city hall.

Even if the revenue from lot sales had materialized in total it still wouldn't have been enough to fund all of the city's upcoming expenses. But that money came in in amounts much less than expected. After the auction of water lots on January 3, 1850 an article in the *Alta* reported that sales from it had totaled $635,130. The real amount was only $468,780, not an insignificant sum but more than $160,000 short of the stated figure. A second and even greater shortcoming was that the actual amounts collected from the auctions of late 1849 and early 1850 fell far short of what was gaveled down and stated on the deeds issued. As noted, sales from the three auctions of late 1849 were recorded as having totaled $183,065, while the water-lots sale of January 3, 1850 added $468,780, for a grand total of $651,845.

The city treasurer's cashbook, which recorded actual money taken in, tells a different story. From late November 1849, when money from the first auction started to come in, to November 30, 1850, when the monies from all four auctions should have long since been deposited, the treasurer's ledger book recorded only $438,975 in lot sales receipts, a shortfall of over $200,000. Not only that, almost half of what was taken in was not even in cash but was in the form of notes, due bills, and vouchers—in other words, IOUs.

Payments from lot sales diminished steadily as the year 1850 progressed. From September through November, a period when the fourth and final installment of the January water lots sale should have, by John Geary's own estimate, brought in $107,602, only a pitiful $972.80 was recorded for "Water lots 4th installment," as having been received from "J. W. Geary."

Those bleak numbers raise questions that remain unanswered. Did Geary simply pocket the money and not report it, or did the buyers of water lots already have their deeds in hand (which would have been a violation of the terms of sale) and they simply didn't bother to make further payments? It remains an unsolved mystery. The net result of prodigious spending with slack revenues was predictable: the city quickly became bankrupt. By August 31, 1850 the deficit was nearly $200,000, and the city was issuing scrip to pay its bills. Even at three percent interest per month the scrip rapidly depreciated to about half its stated value, so bleak were San Francisco's prospects. Things got worse in 1851. By March 1 the debt had climbed to $1.1 million. Just about this same time, to add insult to injury, Dr. Peter Smith, the city physician, who had been paid, like every other creditor, in scrip, sued to have his redeemed at full value. The court sided with Smith. Forced to produce the cash, city authorities had to sell off real estate and other property it owned to pay the judgment against it. It would take most of the 1850s before San Francisco was able to return to financial health.

And what happened to John W. Geary? As mayor, he became chairman, in 1850, of the appropriately named "Sinking Fund of the City of San Francisco," a body established to consolidate the city's debt, issue bonds, and hold in trust its remaining lands and property until it could right its financial ship, one that John Geary, to a certain degree, helped nearly sink.

9

Glimmers of Civilization

With the every-man-for-himself mentality infecting everyone from city officials on down, and with few San Francisco residents planning to stay, social and community organizations were slow to develop. Religious and educational institutions were among those.

Sunday, the traditional day of worship, was the only day treated as a day off. Even then, for some, it was work as usual because the pressure to make money was relentless. For those who did take the day off, most used it to catch up on sleep, write letters home, or do domestic chores such as darning socks or washing shirts. Others, removed from the influences of family and church and thus feeling less pressure to conform to traditional norms and values, socialized with friends, drank, gambled, visited prostitutes, or took in popular amusements. So church attendance took a back seat to other leisure-time activities. One resident captured the feeling of many in justifying his decision to go to a bullfight rather than to church on Sunday when he wrote: "We are not burdened by religion here in California."

A number of preachers and ministers came to San Francisco along with the hordes of gold seekers. The previously mentioned William Taylor was one of those. Taylor drew notice for his open-air street preaching in Portsmouth Square. With his booming voice he attracted attention and crowds but with mixed results. One day when men lined up to get mail at the post office, one of them asked Taylor: "Is this the line to the A and D window?" Taylor replied: "I don't know, sir. I am forming a line, sir, to travel to the Kingdom of Heaven. I shall be very glad to have you fall in our line, sir, and go with us." "I don't want to go there yet," the man replied. "I want my letters from home."

Still, an unknown but apparently small number of San Franciscans did attend church services, especially as formal congregations became established. Religious faith and spiritual practice for them served as a much-needed counterbalance to the hurly-burly of their milieu of stress, competition, and temptation. A Sunday morning seated in a church pew could provide such a release that Presbyterian minister Albert Williams watched some parishioners weep through the entire service. Attendance at church also offered another advantage in that it provided a place to socialize with others apart from the gambling halls or saloons. It was also a locale where men were more likely to see the women in town who were not prostitutes.

The first clergyman to arrive in the wake of the gold discovery was Timothy Dwight Hunt, who had come to San Francisco from Honolulu in October 1848 after he heard the news. The following month he was chosen to serve on a non-denominational basis as "Protestant chaplain to the citizens." His salary was to be $2,500 a year, which would be paid by subscription. The schoolhouse on the Plaza was used as a place of worship.

Hunt only served as the "city chaplain" for a few months. Other clergymen soon arrived, and when they did, Hunt's Protestant interfaith services split into separate congregations—Methodist, Presbyterian, Baptist, and Episcopalian. Hunt, whom forty-niner Daniel Coit described as "an unbearable windbag," started his own First Congregational Church in mid-1849.

Catholics had been without a place to worship since Mission Dolores had shut down when the missions were secularized in the 1830s, but in June 1849 two Jesuit priests arrived from Oregon and established St. Francis Church on Vallejo Street in North Beach. (A sole Indian priest seems to have carried on out at the Mission, but apparently had few, if any, parishioners.)

Jews also migrated to California to hunt for gold. In September about thirty Jews, collectively from the United States, Europe, and Australia, gathered in a tent-store on Jackson Street to celebrate the Jewish New Year, Rosh Hashanah. Ten days later an even larger group gathered in the same location to observe Yom Kippur, the Day of Atonement. These initial services would lead to the formation of Temple Sherith Israel and Temple Emanu-El, both of which

are still active today in San Francisco. One of the Protestant churches, Grace Episcopal, founded in late December 1849, is going strong
today as well. It had its first service in a shack on Powell Street.
Today its landmark cathedral sits on the crest of Nob Hill.

With lumber in short supply, and expensive, early church services were held in existing structures, such as the schoolhouse, or in
tents. Some of the tents were quite large and could hold as many as
500 people. The interiors were spartan. Seating consisted of benches
of unplaned boards extending the width of the space, with walks at
either side. The minister would officiate at a small desk behind a
plain wooden railing. As more goods arrived by sea from around
the Horn, some congregations were able to bring in small organs or
pianos for their services. And for those who remained confined to
vessels in the harbor, clergy of all denominations took turns conducting shipboard services for seamen.

Clergymen also found that there were other demands on their
time besides just conducting Sunday services. Pastor Albert
Williams dealt with requests for assistance with finding employment or other relief, and responded to inquiries from abroad on various issues. He also visited the sick and performed the last offices
for the dead, many of whom, in contrast to life back in the States
where a minister knew all the members of his congregation, were
strangers. All of the above left Williams with little time for "undisturbed leisure."

Another civilizing institution, formal education, also started to
take root in San Francisco in the late 1840s, albeit fitfully. Despite
the heavy preponderance of male adults, San Francisco did have
some children. In January 1847 the *California Star* observed that
there were about 40 of them, ages 5 to 13, playing in the streets, and
editorialized that a school should be built. The writer of the editorial
pledged $50 and one half of a 50-vara lot as part of a private sub-
scription to get a school started. A private school did open a few
months later under the tutelage of William Marston, a Mormon. It
wasn't until September, however, that a committee of three leading
citizens was formed to take action to construct a schoolhouse. In
early December 1847 San Francisco's first schoolhouse, made of
redwood, was erected on the southwest corner of the Plaza, across

from the Custom House. It took a few months for a teacher to be hired and books to be procured. Thomas Douglas, a graduate of Yale who had recently arrived from Hawaii, was employed as a teacher at a salary of $1,000 a year. Tuition was charged to those able to pay, with any shortfall apparently made up by public-spirited townspeople.

The school opened on April 3, 1848. Six pupils attended the first day, but that number quickly grew to 37 within a few days. Classes didn't continue for long. By the end of May, with gold fever in full bloom in San Francisco, enrollment had dwindled to eight students. Four of five of the school trustees and their families had left for the mines. The remaining trustee advised schoolmaster Douglas to go there as well. He took that advice and didn't return to town until early in 1849. That left San Francisco without a school until late April, when the Reverend Albert Williams reestablished classes in the Plaza schoolhouse. It was a private school supported by tuition paid to Williams, but it closed in September because it was taking too much of the minister's time and because the town wouldn't supply any aid.

John W. Geary, in his inaugural address in August 1849, championed the cause of public education. With the city short of funds, it was left to the Reverend O. C. Wheeler of the Baptist Church and a teacher recently arrived from Andover, Massachusetts, John C. Pelton, to restart a school in San Francisco, which they did in late December. Wheeler provided the use of the church's chapel without charge, and Pelton kicked in savings of his own along with donations from supporters to make the school free to local children. California's 1849 constitution provided for a state superintendent of public instruction, an enlightened position considering that only four states at that time had a similar official. San Francisco led the way for the state; by 1851 a school board had been established and four schoolhouses had been constructed, one in each of four districts of the city. Even more remarkable is that despite the city's precarious finances, starting in the 1850s it maintained its schools at public expense. Up until the 1850s, when the idea of tax-supported public instruction finally took root, education of children was considered to be the responsibility of parents and the churches.

10

Ethnic Stew

What we know of gold-rush San Francisco comes mainly from the accounts of white Americans. This is due to the fact that they came in overwhelming numbers compared to all others; they spoke and wrote in English, the dominant language, and a great many were literate. Stories told from the viewpoint of the minorities of the time—Indians, Latinos, Asians, and blacks—are few, primarily because individuals among these groups lacked the high degree of literacy of their white counterparts. Some of their stories may lie undiscovered in foreign archives or among family papers. Lacking those, we have to rely mainly on what we know about these groups from the accounts of white English-speakers and take into consideration their prejudices in their observations.

White Americans in California ranked foreigners in a hierarchy of likeability. Europeans were foremost, with the English, Scots, and Germans at the top, followed by the French. The Irish were suspect, partly because many had come from Australia and were therefore assumed to be ex-convicts. At the bottom of the scale were Latin Americans, Chinese, and Negroes (as they were called then, or worse). Latinos and the Chinese were disliked because they were clannish groups who dressed differently and spoke a foreign language. Blacks were reviled because of inherited deep-seated racism associated with their heritage of slavery.

Lowest on the pecking order were those immigrants who had preceded everyone, the Native Americans. Likely descendants of Asiatic people who had crossed a land bridge that had once existed between Russia and Alaska, they had lived in California for thousands of years prior to the Gold Rush. The Indians were aware of the gold. They were in fact its true discoverers, since they had brought shiny pieces of it, plucked from mountain streams, to the missions years before Marshall's discovery. But the mission priests, to whom they gave the nuggets, did little with them, other than bury them under the floorboards of their churches, because in those remote, self-contained outposts there were few people, little to buy, and virtually no commerce.

When news of the January 1848 discovery started to spread, Indians were affected just as much as whites, perhaps even more so since a number of tribes occupied land in the Sierra foothills, site of the main gold discoveries. When Governor Mason visited the gold country in the summer of 1848 he estimated that at least half of those engaged in mining were Indians. The ratio of Indians to whites may have in fact been as much as two to one. Some worked for their own account but most labored for whites, either selling their services for as little as fifty cents an ounce or at a fixed rate of a dollar a day. With such cheap labor available, some unscrupulous whites corralled Indians into large groups. Seven whites from Monterey, upon hearing the news, arrived at the gold fields and put 50 Indians to work for them. After seven weeks the group had mined 273 pounds of gold, which at $16 an ounce gave a value of nearly $70,000—equivalent to over $2,000,000 today. The miners, after expenses, netted about $1,350 a week each, while the Indians earned the equivalent of about $10 a week. Some Indians fared even worse. Local ranchers who employed Indians as servants and vaqueros, and consequently looked at them as part of a rancho's stock, just like cattle, took them to the gold fields and treated them like peons, forcing them to work and paying them only in food, clothing, and whiskey.

The Treaty of Guadalupe Hidalgo was signed in 1848, ending the Mexican War. Under its terms, Indians were grouped with the Californios, and thus theoretically became U. S. citizens. Not only were they never treated as such but rather were seen by many whites as less than human—little more than wild animals. Forty-niner Samuel Upham, en route to Stockton on his way to the gold fields, encountered some "Digger Indians" (so called because they used their fingers and sticks to forage for food). His ignorance and prejudice starkly revealed itself in the following description: "The Digger eats very little animal food. Like his brother, the gorilla, he is a vegetarian and subsists on wild berries and acorns, occasionally luxuriating on snails and grasshoppers."

Relations between whites and Indians in 1848 had generally been harmonious. Despite taking advantage of their cheap labor and sometimes charging them "Indian prices" (meaning that they paid more for their food and supplies), whites already established in California were used to living in close proximity to Indians. While the whites may have viewed Indians as strange and inferior, they engaged in no gratuitous violence toward them. But in recognition of the aphorism "We fear things in proportion to our ignorance of them," the advent of forty-niners like Samuel Upham, who had little knowledge of California Indians, caused matters to take a turn for the worse.

In the spring of 1849 a band of white gold-seekers from Oregon arrived at the Mother Lode. Accounts differ as to exactly what happened, but they had engaged in clashes with Native Americans on the way. Some Indian women were likely raped, which may have played a role in the attacks on the whites. In any event, when the Oregonians reached Coloma they shot and killed a number of Indians who were working for James Marshall. Part of the reason for the slaughter, other than prejudice and fear, may have been that while Marshall and others who employed Indians viewed them as an economic asset, new arrivals saw these low-wage laborers as a threat, since it gave their masters a distinct advantage. If that was the motivation it worked, because use of Indian gang-labor soon came to an end. Some Indians began working for their own account, and having become wiser as to how much gold meant to whites, started getting better value for their efforts. But as more and more whites arrived in the diggings—and as violence between the two groups increased—Indians became scarcer as they fled to higher elevations or to lowland areas not yet frequented by whites.

In the Bay Area there were few clashes that led to violence, but Native Americans were viewed with suspicion and mistrust and were kept under close watch. In the fall of 1847 Henry Halleck, Governor Mason's Secretary of State, issued an edict stating that in order to distinguish between "friendly" Indians and marauders and horse thieves, all employers of Indians were required to give them certificates verifying their status. Any Indian found outside the town or rancho of his employment without such a certificate would be liable to arrest as a horse thief. And the theft of horses was a problem. The Indians used them for hunting game and also as food. Edwin Bryant, when he was alcalde, wrote that the Indians had developed quite a taste for horseflesh.

Native Americans had lived in scattered villages, mainly near the shore around San Francisco Bay, for centuries prior to the coming of the Spanish. William Richardson, when he first settled at Yerba Buena in the mid-1830s, employed some of the natives to pilot launches around the bay in the trade that was just starting to develop between the ranchos and arriving ships. A decade later the Mexican authorities used Native Americans to make the adobe bricks used in constructing the Custom House on the Plaza. In June 1847 journalist Edward Kemble conducted a census of the town and found that 34 individuals, or 7 percent of San Francisco's 459 residents, were Indians. Some were still employed making bricks for the adobe structures going up in the vicinity of Portsmouth Square, while others worked as servants and porters. Some of them may not have been working of their own free will. There were reports of Indians being treated as virtual slaves by their "owners"; some were even rumored to have been sold as property transfers. Captain John B. Montgomery was concerned enough that he issued a proclamation condemning "forced Indian labor in the District of San Francisco." Sam Brannan, in his *California Star*, showed a total lack of sympathy. He viewed Indians through his own prejudiced lens, and wrote that they were "an idle, intemperate race, laboring only to procure the means for gratifying their passion for rum and monte."

By 1849, with the gold-rush hordes arriving, Indians were largely absent from San Francisco. There were a few, however. When the Reverend Albert Williams opened a Sunday school in June, one of the attendees was "'Sammy,' a Digger Indian boy, 8 or 9 years old." He was a friend, or perhaps a ward, of one of the local families. Out at Mission Dolores, by 1849 a dilapidated ruin, a solitary Indian priest, Francisco Santillan, held sway. He lived in a structure adjoining the church, which is where the Reverend Williams found him lying ill in his bed. The minister deemed the native priest to be simple and sincere. He spoke English and a little Latin.

Across the street from the church was the bullring. Perhaps the most celebrated bullfighter of 1849 San Francisco was an Indian named Valentin, who was famed for his skill in dispatching bulls. Fluent in Spanish, Valentin might have been a vaquero on a nearby rancho when, with the gold-rush throngs to cheer him on, he found his true calling as an entertainer in the bullring. He drew standing ovations and thunderous applause for his fearlessness, waiting until the last second before dodging a charging bull and plunging his sword into the beast. Spectators showed their appreciation by showering the ring with gold and silver coins, which Valentin scooped from the sand.

The first foreigners to arrive in San Francisco in the wake of the gold discovery were Mexicans from neighboring Sonora and nationals from Chile and Peru, countries on the west coast of South America that had received word of the new El Dorado from ships calling at their ports in the summer of 1848. Many of those immigrants, from Sonora and Chile especially, were experienced placer miners. The more well-to-do brought peons with them, which enabled them to work large stretches of riverbed in the Mother Lode. This did not sit well with American miners, who felt that these semi-slaves gave the foreigners an undue advantage similar to that of Indian gang-labor.

Resentful Americans, who viewed Spanish speakers of whatever nationality as "descendants of Africans" (after the Moors in Spain), looked down on them as being lazy and degraded and referred to them as "greasers." When the Americans became numerically superior in the gold fields in 1849 and 1850 they lost no time in driving most Hispanic miners out of the Sierra foothills. Few, if any, Anglo miners saw the irony in that just a few years previously Americans had been the foreigners in Mexican California.

Both before and after being driven from the mines, Latin immigrants congregated in San Francisco in "Chiletown," where they became victims of the brutal attack of the Hounds. Chilean Vicente Pérez Rosales established a business in San Francisco, and thus had first-hand dealings with Americans. The experience left him with a jaundiced view of them, especially when it came to their ways of settling disputes. Pérez Rosales described the alcalde in February 1849 (it must have been Thaddeus Leavenworth) as a drunken Yankee, who, if two Yankees were quarrelling, tried to smooth things over. If the quarrel was between an Anglo and a Spanish speaker he would rule in favor of the former. If the dispute was between two Hispanics he would rule against the one with money, so that he would be able to pay the court costs—including the fee for the interpreter.

African Americans followed the siren song of gold just as so many others did. The first blacks in California were four men who had been with English buccaneer Francis Drake during his stay on the Marin coast in 1579 while circumnavigating the globe. They were probably slaves who had been captured from the Portuguese or Spanish. Two centuries later, the de Anza expedition that brought Spanish settlers to San Francisco had people of mixed ancestry. Some of the leading Californios, including the last governor of Mexican California, Pio Pico, could count Africans among their ancestors. Mexico had preceded the U. S. by abolishing slavery in the early 1820s. As a result, some free blacks arrived in California aboard sailing ships before the discovery of gold. Those in port in Yerba Buena Cove when the news came out were some of the first to go to the mines.

In San Francisco, the census taken in 1847 found nine black men and one black woman in town, which amounted to only two percent of the population. William Leidesdorff may not have been one of those nine. Leidesdorff, who seems to have been able to pass for white because of his mixed heritage—he was the offspring of a Danish sailor father and a mulatto mother from the West Indies—was one of the prominent men of early San Francisco. He had come to the village of Yerba Buena in 1841 by sea from New Orleans, where legend has it he had become engaged to the daughter of a wealthy white merchant. But when he revealed his African ancestry to her, she returned his engagement ring. Broken hearted, and wanting to get as far from the scene of his humiliation as possible, he piloted a vessel he owned around the Horn and up the west coast of the Americas, and decided to settle in the obscure Mexican

pueblo on the shore of San Francisco Bay. Leidesdorff established himself as a waterfront trader and real-estate speculator. He
received a 35,000-acre land grant on the American River near Sacramento, and purchased a number of lots in San Francisco as well. He
built the City Hotel, the town's premier pre-gold-rush hostelry. A
member of the first ayuntamiento, he was serving as San Francisco's treasurer when he took ill and died suddenly in May 1848 at
the age of 38. Had he lived, his real estate holdings no doubt would
have made him the wealthiest man in the land. He died without
leaving a will, which left his estate entangled in conflicting claims
and litigation. Joseph L. Folsom, as rapacious as anyone when it
came to acquiring real estate, ended up with most of Leidesdorff's
land holdings. (According to forty-niner William F. White, no fan of
John W. Geary, Folsom only managed to take title to Leidesdorff's
property after paying Alcalde Geary a "commission" of $10,000.)

William Leidesdorff doesn't appear to have faced anything in
the way of racial discrimination in San Francisco, but in antebellum
America hostility towards blacks was well entrenched. Many
Americans, not just Southerners, accepted the inferiority of the
Negro as a fact. Typical of the kind of expressions used in those
days was the remark of a white miner, who after a stint of
back-breaking labor in the gold fields gave up, declaring that it was
"only fit for niggers to do."

In San Francisco, blacks likely faced less overt discrimination
than elsewhere in the U. S. for the simple reason that most people
were too busy with their own affairs to spend much time and
energy enforcing racial barriers. Another reason perhaps is that
since blacks were few in number in the early days (even by 1852
there were only about 2,000 blacks in the whole state of California,
or about one percent of the population) they were not seen as a
threat, as the Latinos were initially, or the Chinese were later. At the
Constitutional Convention of 1849 the issue of slavery had naturally arisen. The convention delegates, surprisingly even the southern sympathizers, voted overwhelmingly to prohibit slavery in
California. They did it not so much for humanitarian reasons, however. Some felt that if slavery were allowed, gangs of slaves would
be brought in and used to unfairly compete with individual white
miners. Monterey alcalde Walter Colton had another theory. He felt

that the real reason the anti-slavery clause was enacted was that white miners would resent it if they had to dig gold beside slaves.

The prohibition of slavery in the 1849 constitution did not mean that African Americans would enjoy the same civic privileges as whites. It specified that only white males could vote. Restrictions increased further in April 1850 when the California legislature passed a law prohibiting blacks, mulattos, and Indians from testifying in court against a white person. That this law was enforced is shown in a news item that appeared in the *Alta California* a few months later. A white man was brought up on charges of larceny, "but the proof resting on the testimony of a colored witness, he was discharged."

Despite the prevailing attitudes, some white San Franciscans viewed African Americans in a positive light. Lieutenant William Tecumseh Sherman thought highly of the blacks he knew because they were loyal and they kept their promises. Sherman described how on a number of occasions he would see General Persifor Smith walking down Montgomery Street, where he would "take off his hat on meeting a Negro, and, on being asked the reason of his politeness, he would answer that they were the only real gentlemen in California." Smith's attitude may have been influenced by the fact that his black cook and servant "Isaac" was the only member of his household staff who didn't desert him to go off gold hunting.

Artist William Redmond Ryan also viewed African Americans without prejudice. In Monterey he had met a black man, Antoine, with whom he had become friends. In the spring of 1849 when he ran into Antoine in San Francisco he gave him a friendly handshake—to the disapproving looks of passersby. Antoine, to make his living, procured a horse and cart and soon was making twenty to forty dollars a day doing light hauling. When he was faced with increasing competition he sold his rig and returned to Monterey, having saved up close to $6,000.

Discrimination or no, the Gold Rush, with its promise of the opportunity for anyone to better himself, had a salutary leveling effect when it came to perceived race and class distinctions. One day in September 1848 a newly arrived Yankee hailed a passing black man and asked him to carry his luggage ashore. The black pulled a bag of gold dust worth close to $100 from his shirt and said: "Do you think I'll lug trunks when I can get that much in one day?"

African Americans engaged in all sorts of employment. A common occupation for free blacks in antebellum America was that of cook. Since good cooks were always in demand on sailing vessels it was also a good way for blacks to move freely from place to place and take advantage of opportunities as they arose. Alexander Forbes, a white man who joined the steamship *California* as purser on its journey from Panama to San Francisco in October 1849, was astonished to learn that the cook, "a negro named George Washington, was receiving the princely salary of $500 per month." This was the same wage as that of the chief engineer and more than that of the captain of the vessel who was only being paid $250 a month on a contract basis. The cook's pay was that high to discourage him from deserting to the mines.

Captain George Coffin, when he anchored his ship *Alhambra* in Yerba Buena Cove in October, found himself fielding offers from hotel keepers and restaurateurs who bid as much as $300 a month for the services of his black cook. The Reverend Albert Williams in his memoirs recalled a "colored professional cook" known as "Uncle Peter" who opened an eating house in a tent on Pacific Street. His good cooking drew favorable notices. The menu lacked variety but the dishes were well prepared, according to Williams. Potatoes were scarce, but when they were available "Uncle Peter" would pass around the table with a dish of them and, using a fork, would place one on each guest's plate. They were barely bigger than walnuts.

Of all the arrivals the Chinese stood out the most. Sometimes referred to as "Celestials," because China was known as the "Celestial Kingdom," these exotic newcomers from the Orient with their buttoned up blue jackets and long, slender pigtails trailing down their backs naturally attracted attention. Many forty-niners mentioned them in their diaries and letters.

The first Chinese to land in San Francisco arrived in early 1848, shortly after the gold discovery. The party of three—two men and a woman—came from Canton as servants with Charles Gillespie, who was supercargo aboard the brig *Eagle*. Gillespie and his wife moved into a house on Washington Street adjacent to Portsmouth Square, where their Chinese woman servant, named Marie, could be seen in the yard tending the family cow. Shortly after he arrived, Gillespie wrote to his friend Thomas Larkin praising the Chinese as "a sober and industrious people . . . ." He felt that they would be a great asset to California, and that if enough of them could be induced to immigrate, property values would increase as a result.

Although the Chinese were to play a large role in San Francisco's history, they did not arrive in large numbers until after 1849. By the end of that year there were fewer than 800 in San Francisco. They were almost exclusively men. (One of the handful of women, besides Marie, was the prostitute Ah Toy.) Although news of the gold rush had reached China in 1848 it didn't seem to have the same galvanizing effect as it had elsewhere. It was only starting in the early 1850s, when crop failures and the Taiping Rebellion led to upheavals in their native country, that Chinese started to come in appreciable numbers. Once they did start coming it became almost a flood; within a decade Chinese would make up about one-third of all the miners in the Mother Lode.

Most of the Chinese who came to California appear to have come on their own account but, unlike other immigrants, a number of them came as indentured servants, that is as individuals who agreed to work for a certain period of time in return for payment of their passage. About a dozen Chinese who worked at the City Hotel for John Henry Brown in early 1849 seem to fall into this category, since they had an English "owner" who received $1,200 a month from Brown for their services. Early resident Jacob P. Leese is recorded as having brought a Chinese man named Ansung to San Francisco in 1849 "to work as a coolee" for him under contract for three years. In return, Leese paid Ansung's passage and agreed to provide him with room and board in addition to paying him the small salary of $12 a month.

Those Chinese not working as indentured servants or under contract labored at various occupations, just as other nationalities did. Many worked in construction, where demand for workers was great. San Francisco was growing rapidly, especially in the summer and fall of 1849. James Tyson, a physician who arrived in September, wrote: "The saw and the hatchet were constantly heard,

the work being in many instances solely performed by Chinese. . . ."
The *Pacific News* was impressed by the industriousness and personal habits of the Chinese, whom they also found to be a quiet and
orderly people: "Search the city through and you will not find an
idle Chinaman, and their cleanliness exceeds any other people we
ever saw." A few Chinese opened restaurants and served their
native cuisine to all comers. Their food and tea won acclaim.
William Redmond Ryan visited one Chinese restaurant and was
surprised to find how clean and neatly arranged it was—he had
been led to believe that the Chinese were dirty and unclean. The
prices were moderate and the food was good. With his artist's eye,
he noted how every dish consumed was written down in Chinese
characters by a waiter using a long brush dipped in India ink.

By early December the Chinese had formed enough of a community that three hundred of them gathered at a restaurant on
Jackson Street. There they appointed a committee of four to ask
Selim Woodworth, a leading businessman with an interest in
Chinese affairs, if he would act as their advisor and mediator with
the white community. Woodworth agreed and a few days later he
and local officials, including Alcalde John Geary, were guests of
honor at a party hosted by the Chinese. This reaching out to the
white power brokers may have been in response to an incident that
had occurred the week before, when a fight had broken out at
Clark's Point between groups of Americans and Chinese. The
Pacific News wrote of the melee: "The Chinese got a pretty good
'hammering,' and entered a complaint with the Alcalde. The case
was however, dismissed for want of testimony." It seems that no
white man was going to testify in favor of a Chinese against another
white. This clash presaged hostility on the part of a vocal and
aggressive white minority against the Chinese that would only
grow in the coming decades.

11

Quagmire

By the second half of 1849 news of the gold discovery had been conveyed around the globe. Ships filled with newcomers from all over the world arrived daily in San Francisco, disgorging a ceaseless human stream from the vessels in the harbor to the shore. With each passing month Yerba Buena Cove became increasingly clogged with vessels: several hundred of them, abandoned, riding at anchor, their masts shorn of sails. Trader and merchant William Heath Davis, who had been in town since the 1830s, and for whom Davis Street is named, thought that the harbor resembled "an immense forest stripped of its foliage." Davis lived uphill at Stockton and Jackson streets. When he looked down on the panorama below in the cove he saw "a living mass of human beings moving to and fro, seeming in the distance not unlike an army in battle on the fringe of a forest. . . ."

By September, some 200 new people on average were arriving every day, and they all needed accommodations. Many of the newcomers headed for Happy Valley, which extended from the water's edge at First and Mission streets, south of Market, and comprised an area about two blocks or so to the south and west. New arrivals, saddled with excess baggage, discarded their unwanted stuff on the nearby beach, which quickly became strewn with cast-off goods of all kinds, including worthless gold-washing machines, casks and tins of ships bread, and other merchandise not worth the storage charges.

Happy Valley seems to have gotten its name from the fact that it was located in a sheltered valley between the sand dunes, and it had, at least initially, a few springs of good clean water. As more and more people put up shacks and pitched their tents there, the lack of sanitation led to the springs becoming polluted and, as a result, many residents suffered from diarrhea and other intestinal complaints. "Two swallows of the water in the valley gave me the dysentery," wrote one. Numerous rats, fleas, and flies added to the misery. The name "Happy Valley" changed from one with good connotations to one of derision.

Those who camped there didn't have better alternatives. The area around Portsmouth Square had gotten increasingly crowded and expensive. One forty-niner noted that it could cost ten dollars a day to live in the city (meaning the area around the Plaza), but he found that he could get along on only one dollar a day in Happy Valley by living in his tent and cooking his own meals. Conditions were Spartan. A. W. Geming, who along with three companions arrived in late September, put up a tent that measured ten by twelve feet. The trunks they put on each side "served for tables at meals, seats during the day, & bedsteads at night. . . ." In the tradition of doing what they could to make money, tent dwellers in Happy Valley established businesses of all kinds, using their dwellings during the day as restaurants or saloons, or as lodging houses at night. Others dealt cards, bought and sold gold, or even ran small slaughterhouses.

Part of the reason that Happy Valley residents were able to live economically is that most were squatters living there rent-free. Virtually all the lots in the vicinity had been granted in early 1847, but with a steady stream of new arrivals and constant comings and goings it was difficult for landlords to keep track of whom their tenants were. Many also had trouble identifying exactly where their property was, because wind-blown shifting sands obscured the surveyor's stakes denoting lot lines. Thus most property owners appear not to have bothered trying to collect rent.

Those who had arrived as paying passengers on ships were at liberty to land and pursue their fortunes of their own free will. Those arriving as crew were no less infected with gold fever, but they had a harder time realizing their dreams. Confined to their ships, they remained virtual prisoners, a tantalizing short jump to land. The lure of gold proved so overpowering for some that they risked their lives to get away. After a ship from Adelaide, Australia arrived in September, four Malay crewmen attempted to get ashore in a whaleboat. They were stopped, and the ship's officers pulled in all the landing boats to prevent future attempts. But the men were not to be deterred. They made their escape by floating away on stray planks they had lashed together. Their golden quest came to an end shortly after, when a strong wave swept them off their precarious craft and they drowned.

Another tragic example occurred about the same time. Desertion by sailors for the mines was a constant worry for the U. S. Navy, which had a number of vessels in port. One day in late September five sailors on the Cutter *Ewing*, after having landed a party in town in a launch, threw their officer, a midshipman, overboard on the way back. When he attempted to climb back in they struck him on the head with an oar and rowed off, making their escape. The five were captured several days later near Pittsburg, at the mouth of the San Joaquin River, heading for the gold region. Returned to the *Ewing* they were placed in irons and, after a trial, were convicted of desertion, mutiny, and attempted murder (the midshipman survived). All five were sentenced to death by hanging.

Two days after the sentence was handed down, two of the five, Peter Black and John Black (not related), confessed that they were the guilty ones, so Commodore Thomas ap Catesby Jones commuted the death sentences of the other three. The three men fell to their knees and thanked Jones for his clemency. They may have wished that they hadn't been spared, since they received one hundred lashes each and were sentenced to hard labor in irons without pay for three years.

On October 22, the day before the executions, local clergy, including Albert Williams and J. L. Ver Mehr, came aboard to hear the condemned men's confessions. Commodore Jones took communion with the prisoners. Peter and John Black, their chains rattling, knelt down to receive the bread of life. The next morning, each man having been placed on a separate ship, they were brought up on deck from their prison holds to find all of their shipmates standing at attention—their comrades had been ordered to witness the spectacle as an object lesson. City residents had been alerted to the executions. As hundreds of spectators watched from Telegraph Hill and other vantage points on shore, nooses were placed around the doomed men's necks. Reverend Williams tried to comfort John Black, telling the 19-year old, whose eyes were welling with tears:

"Don't cry, don't cry." "I did not want to murder him, indeed, sir, I only wanted to go the mines," said Black. He further worried about what his parents would think if they ever found out what end he had come to. Hoods were then placed over both men's heads as heavy weights were attached to the other ends of the ropes. Over on the *Savannah*, where Peter Black was held, as the cannon boomed signaling the first execution, the weight dropped, and he was "twittered up like a fish," spiraling rapidly up to the yardarm. Seconds later on the *Ewing*, as Reverend Ver Mehr related: "Boom! Sounded just under me, and John Black went up with lightning speed to the end of the yardarm, swung up and fell."

Aside from spectacles such as the shipboard hangings, what many observers remarked about San Francisco in late 1849 was the rapid change, the way the town was transforming itself before people's eyes. When Bayard Taylor arrived in August he estimated that there were probably 500 structures, including not only houses but sheds and tents as well. He was gone for three weeks, and when he returned in September it seemed to him that the town seemed to have doubled in size. Up on the hills where before there had been only sand and chaparral, there now stood clusters of houses. New warehouses had sprung up near the water, and streets outside the downtown area, which formerly had been so indistinct that residents had pitched their tents in them, were now well-defined, and buildings had been erected along lot lines. Taylor estimated that from 20 to 30 new houses a day were going up. He was astonished by how fast a ready-made house could be erected. He wrote about himself in the third person: "He walks over an open lot in his before-breakfast stroll—the next morning, a house complete, blocks up his way."

The incessant hammering and sawing may have ceased at dusk, but other activity and noise carried on after dark. Boardinghouse keeper Mary Jane Megquier captured San Francisco at night in a letter she wrote home in late November: ". . . it is a mighty busy place, it is now past midnight, I can hear guns firing, music, some calling for help. I think by the sound they are having a drunken row, but it is so common it is of no account. . . ." Aside from the threat of crime, it could be risky to be out after nightfall, because once outside the immediate area of the Plaza, where lights from the many gambling saloons provided illumination, it was very dark indeed. One man, stumbling about one night, fell into a mortar bed: "I wish San Francisco were finished," he wailed, expressing a common desire for relief from the constant change and turmoil.

San Francisco's rainy season usually starts in November. But in 1849 the first winter storm struck without warning on October 9, and lasted for two days. Tent dwellers were especially affected: canvas became soggy and water collected in pools inside and out, forcing some to evacuate. Shopkeepers suffered when their stores were flooded. Those with goods stacked in the open had to write them off as a total loss. Although there was a hiatus of several weeks before the next storm, the rains then started in earnest. The winter of 1849–50 would go down as one of the rainiest on record. It didn't rain every day. It only seemed like it did. By mid-November Edward Kemble, editor of the *Alta California,* was already editorializing about the "miserable, suicidal, despicable weather!" Making things even more uncomfortable was that it was also cold. Rain sometimes turned to hail, and snow could, on occasion, be seen on the hillsides around San Francisco. The cascading storms also wreaked havoc with the ships in the harbor. Unmanned, and packed close together as they were, high seas and winds would cause some ships to drag their anchors, leading to collisions. Ernest de Massey saw one ship struck so violently by three other vessels that it caved in a section of her stern.

All the rain turned San Francisco's unplanked dirt streets into muddy sloughs. O. P. Sutton, John W. Geary's former partner, recalled seeing two men that winter walking toward each other in front of his store on Montgomery Street during a storm. Because their slouch hats had been pulled down over their eyes they couldn't see each other coming. The two men collided, caught at each other, and went overboard into the street into two feet of soft mud, locked in each other's arms. "They went out of sight in fact, and when they struggled out, they were entirely covered with mud, and had to rub the mud out of their eyes," Sutton wrote in a memoir. The larger of the two was very angry, but the smaller one smiled and joked about it, Sutton noted.

The constant churning of the thoroughfares by drays loaded with cargo and men on foot tramping back and forth, along with the continuing rain, only served to deepen the mud, which was made even more intolerable because it was composed not just of dirt and water but garbage and human waste as well. By some estimates the muck was as much as five feet deep in places. The heart of the commercial district, stretching from Montgomery Street at the water's edge up to Portsmouth Square, became a virtual quagmire. Someone posted a sign at the corner of Kearny and Clay streets that read: "This street is impassable, not even jackassable!" Anyone venturing in was in danger of getting stuck. Some literally lost their boots when the glue-like mud sucked them right off. Margaret De Witt's husband came home from his store one evening "with mud above the knees" and declared, "he had been where there was no bottom."

The appalling conditions did provide some moments of mirth. Spectators laughed as a slurry of mud carried a small boat down the street toward the bay. Humorous stories started making the rounds, most on the order of "the mud was so deep that . . ." Perhaps the best was this droll tale by William Shaw:

> It is reported that a man's hat having been seen floating above a notorious quagmire in Pacific Street, on raising it, the head of the wearer was seen underneath; when extricated from this 'Serbonian bog,' he begged that the horse which was beneath him, might likewise be rescued, but his steed was too deep down to be got at. I cannot vouch for the veracity of this story. . . .

In an attempt to try to ameliorate the situation and provide some stability and traction, all sorts of goods for which there was little current demand and were not worth storing were thrown into the mire: kegs of nails; wire sieves; cement; barrels of beef. Boxes of Virginia tobacco, much of it ruined by the rains, were tossed in as "stepping stones" to aid pedestrians, who would jump from one to the other. Those that missed a box would end up being fished out by their companions. While such measures aided men on foot, other materials, especially smaller debris such as twigs and chaparral, only served to entangle the feet of horses and mules as they attempted to drive on through. One observer wrote that such matter "often proves a dangerous snare to the incautious teamster, who driving on with undiminished force soon finds the mud rise to the belly of his horse." Lieutenant Sherman, who was living on Montgomery Street that winter, actually saw several mules stumble and drown in the liquid mud before they could be rescued. In early 1850 the bodies of three men were pulled from the mud on Montgomery Street. They had been out at night, were likely intoxicated, and had fallen in and smothered.

Most forty-niners who made it to San Francisco were no strangers to death: many had seen it first hand on their journey to California. Whether they had come around the Horn, overland, or via the Isthmus, they had buried acquaintances or even loved ones along the way, whether at sea, along the trail, or in the jungles of Panama. A substantial number of those who did make it to San Francisco alive arrived in ill health. Charles Howe, an American who arrived in October after a trek through Panama, provides one such example. Weak from a fever he had picked up in the tropics, he pitched his tent on a damp hillside near Stockton Street. Tempted by the gambling emporiums, but down to his last ten dollars, he decided to risk it all in an attempt to boost his fortunes. He lost the whole amount playing monte (he was perhaps the only diarist to actually admit losing money gambling) and retreated to his tent. Two days later, wet through with perspiration, he crawled out and slid down the muddy ravine that was Sacramento Street toward town. The rain was falling in torrents, his spirits "darker than the mud hole before me." Exhausted, broke, and ravenously hungry, he entered a tent restaurant and begged the proprietor for a fifty-cent meal of pork and beans on credit, but was refused. Fortunately for Howe, as he stumbled along the beach, he found a discarded box of baloney sausages, which he devoured. That led to a turn in his prospects; he recovered his health and found employment. Others would not be so lucky.

Many new arrivals quickly went to the mines to try their luck. Most got more than they bargained for. Few realized just how hard gold digging was until they set to it. It was especially challenging for those who had led sedentary lives. They found themselves swinging pickaxes and shoveling hundreds of buckets of dirt a day while laboring under a hot summer sun. Back strain, blistered hands, sore muscles, sprained ankles and fingers, and sunburned skin were all part of it. The miners endured all kinds of weather while living in tents or rough cabins for months at a time. This harsh regimen, combined with a poor and limited diet, left many of them ill and old before their time. Those with mirrors might not have recognized the images staring back at them—men with deeply lined faces, rotting teeth, and hair turning prematurely gray.

Compounding their troubles was that the gold-mining season of 1849 was a much more crowded affair than the previous year. In 1848 there were some 6,000 miners in the diggings. By the end of 1849 some 40,000 plus were covering the same ground. The overcrowding led to increased competition and declining takings per man. With the majority of miners now making only enough to cover expenses or less, many returned to San Francisco, where some joined the new arrivals in Happy Valley. Many of the returnees were in poor health. Bayard Taylor described one such emaciated miner he saw who had just been set ashore from a launch:

> He was sitting alone on a stone beside the water, with his bare feet purple with cold, on the cold, wet sand. He was wrapped from head to foot in a coarse blanket, which shook with the violence of his chill, as if his limbs were about to drop in pieces. He seemed unconscious of all that was passing; his long, matted hair hung over his wasted face; his eyes glared steadily forward, with an expression of suffering so utterly hopeless and wild that I shuddered at seeing it.

A contributing factor to poor health was the prevalence of liquor and the frequency with which many indulged. One forty-niner felt that ". . . men, who in the States never drank, are here irreclaimable *drunkards*." That heritage started in San Francisco even before the Gold Rush. In 1847 the Reverend Chester Lyman arrived from Hawaii just in time for the Fourth of July. The locals were celebrating in boisterous fashion. Lyman thought that about every third person was drunk. As a minister he may have been more easily offended by such behavior, but he clearly was indignant at what he saw. He passed a grog shop "from which the sounds of drunken revelry & awful profanity were issuing most hideously." Four days later the carousing was still in full swing, as sailors on shore leave were making merry in the City Hotel. Proprietor John Henry Brown got thrown out a window of his own establishment when he tried to restore order. The city fathers, in reaction to all this riotous behavior, shortly afterward passed several resolutions calling for penalties against public houses for allowing such conduct, but with virtually no enforcement authority the ordinances had little effect. It was only in August 1849, after the formation of a city police force, that some attempt was made to rein in drunken behavior.

Many San Franciscans needed little excuse to imbibe. Drinking provided a release from stress and a chance to socialize with friends. Some drank for other reasons. With food and restaurant meals expensive and with liquor fairly cheap by comparison, some drank to allay their hunger. Others drank liquor to avoid the local drinking water, which was always at risk of being contaminated. Whatever the reason, drinking in early San Francisco, as in many a frontier town, was commonplace and was frequently done to excess.

Heavy drinking sometimes had tragic consequences. Ernest de Massey told the story of one of his shipmates, a fellow Frenchman, who, while working as a waiter in a café, fell down some stairs while intoxicated and broke his neck. The man died after fifteen days of agony in a vermin-infested attic. Resident Robert Smith Lammot, in a letter to his father, wrote of a friend named Frank who had promised to stop his "bad habits," but after helping put out a fire took a drink, and then another and another. That evening Frank called at a friend's house nearly naked, and very drunk. The friend took him in, re-clothed him, and started him off toward home. But on the way Frank "sold all his clothes for liquor, staggered into a tent . . . and died during the night of delirium tremens." In a similar incident, another young man, who had gambled his money away, got very drunk and was found lying on the ground in a stupor. Passersby tried to revive him but were too late. In going through the dead man's few belongings they found an ounce of gold, a notebook, and a Bible. In the Bible was a card with gilt edges that had been used as a bookmark. On it, in a woman's handwriting, was the poignant inscription: "A sister's prayers go with you."

Alcohol abuse led to some deaths, but illness and disease claimed many more lives. Diarrhea caused by dysentery was by far the most common complaint, and not infrequently led to death. One victim who survived wrote graphically of the "blodey disentary" that left him wasted and "discharging nothing but blood and slime." Rheumatic diseases, and fevers of various kinds such as typhoid, were other sources of illness. "Brain fever," or meningitis, was another one. That was what killed William Leidesdorff. Cholera had stalked the Argonauts who made the trek overland to California in 1849 and killed some of them, but the disease did not arrive in San Francisco until October 1850, and then was brought by ship. All of those diseases could have been prevented by proper sanitation, but sanitation was in short supply in gold-rush San Francisco.

Also in short supply or even totally lacking in many cases was insight into what caused these diseases and other ailments. Medical knowledge would increase enormously over the next hundred years, but in the mid-19th century it was still in a fairly rudimentary state. Doctors of the time knew nothing of bacteria, viruses, or of sterilization. Since they didn't know what caused various diseases they also couldn't really know how to cure them. Some tried the ancient method of "bleeding," thinking that draining the body of "bad blood" would effect a cure. Others favored purging in an attempt to drive toxins out of the body. Harsh laxatives such as calomel, which contained mercury, were prescribed. But calomel, if given in too large a dose, could cause a patient's teeth to fall out or cause other damage. In short, the cures were sometimes worse than the diseases, since many of the treatments only served to weaken already enfeebled patients. One drug that did have some salutary effects was quinine, which was useful in reducing fever caused by malaria. As the "miracle drug" of the day it was much in demand, hard to obtain, and thus expensive. One batch sold at auction for four times its weight in gold.

Sick individuals also had no way of knowing whether the doctor treating them was qualified as an M.D. By one estimate, at least half of the gold-rush "physicians" had never even attended medical school. There were no professional standards, and it would be years before physicians would be licensed in California. Any man could hang out a shingle and call himself a doctor. Vicente Pérez Rosales saw a tent occupied by a fellow Chilean that had "So and so, Physician and Surgeon" painted on its flap. The man had never been more than a gravedigger in his native Chile. The lack of credentials didn't prevent that former gravedigger, or others, from setting up a practice. With perhaps up to half the population suffering from one ailment or another, doctors were in great demand and they profited accordingly. Most charged an ounce or more for a simple house call. One doctor, who arrived in March 1849, set up an office in the Parker House where, according to one observer, he was making from $150 to as much as $500 a day. With income like that it's no wonder so many unqualified men hung out a shingle. On the other end of the scale, it didn't pay to be a patient. As one recovering individual wrote: "A man cannot afford to be sick here long, at sixteen to twenty-four dollars a day."

Those who became so ill that they could no longer walk the streets or care for themselves would be brought to the city hospital, which consisted of a couple of ramshackle buildings on Stockton Street. City officials contracted with a series of local doctors to run the facility and care for the indigent sick. Preacher William Taylor visited the hospital one fall day in 1849 and was appalled by what he found. The upper floor housing the "choice" rooms, that is for those who could afford to pay, were filthy enough, but when he descended to the indigent ward the stench was so bad it was all he could do to force himself to go in. It was an airless building in which men lay on cots with just enough space between them for a person to pass. The male nurses were a vile lot who were poorly paid and who supplemented their income by stealing from their defenseless patients. Taylor tried to provide comfort to the sick—men of all nationalities—by singing hymns, talking, and praying with them. When he passed out religious tracts free of charge some expressed surprise: they thought that nobody in California ever did anything but for money. Given the poor health most of the men suffered from when they entered the hospital, and the squalid conditions, many died. If they expired late in the evening or if the weather was bad, the corpse was simply left on its cot until it could be removed. It would then be placed on a dead cart, usually in the company of several others, and hauled to the cemetery in North Beach. That cemetery, which had been established in 1847, rapidly filled up. It closed in early 1850 when the burials reached close to one thousand.

Deceased forty-niners of means found that death was as expensive as life in San Francisco. Dr. John W. Palmer wrote that a coffin of rough boards cost not less than $30, the grave itself, not including the gravedigger's charge, cost $60, "and one got but a clumsy hole at that price." A lopsided cross of knotty pine painted white with black letters cost an ounce, and a priest, if desired, another ounce. Even with such a payout the dead were not guaranteed eternal rest. Coffins were placed in graves so shallow that winter rains washed the soil away and left the caskets exposed.

By late in the year stark differences were discernible among San Francisco's citizens. A few individuals had made fortunes beyond imagining and lived extravagantly, while many more ended up destitute. Some of those differences were due to skill, hard work, or good luck, and some of them to poor planning, misfortune, or bad luck. Mary Jane Megquier put that contrast and the results in perspective when she wrote:

> . . . some will get into business the moment they put foot on land, in three months will find themselves worth fifty thousand, while others whose prospects are much brighter, will in the same short space of time be breathing their last in some miserable tent without a friend or a single dime to pay their funeral charges. . . .

Men who were connected in some way to others, whether through family, friendships, or through membership in some social or fraternal organization, generally fared better than those completely on their own. The Masons, for example, established a lodge in San Francisco in October 1849. They provided for their members who were sick or destitute and arranged for decent burials for those who died. Religious groups also provided support for members of their congregations. Jewish pioneers benefited when the First Hebrew Benevolent Society was founded in December "to assist

poor and needy Hebrews in sickness and want." Those without
such ties, and who had not succeeded, faced the full brunt of the
Darwinian struggle for survival that characterized San Francisco in
1849 and into 1850. That struggle hardened into a callous indifference on the part of some. With everyone busy with his own business
affairs and with illness widespread and common, people became
inured to the sufferings of others. One unnamed San Franciscan
expressed that in stark fashion when he wrote to a newspaper in
Massachusetts:

> A man's life here is worth about fifty cents on the dollar.
> While I am now writing, a poor fellow lies tied hand and
> foot, raving mad, with the brain fever, and very little
> attention is paid to him. He is a stranger to all in this house
> . . . twenty-four hours or so will close his troubles.

Similarly, Captain George Coffin captured not only the effect on
a victim but on his loved ones back home:

> Nobody feels any interest in the affairs of the other. Many
> a poor mortal breathes his last alone, without a friend to
> smooth his pillow or convey his last message to his
> friends, who will never know when, how, or in what place
> he ceased to struggle with his fate. All they will ever know
> will be that at such a time his correspondence ceased.

Some attempts were made to alleviate the suffering. Former
Alcalde Edwin Bryant, who had returned to San Francisco from
Kentucky in 1849, no doubt to monitor his real estate, headed a
relief committee that raised some money for the down and out. The
group also arranged for some pro bono medical care on the part of
local doctors. And some individuals were known for spontaneous
generosity when approached for handouts. Sam Brannan was one
of those known as a "soft touch." But all such efforts were way short
of the overall need.

Given the extent of suffering and the abysmal conditions San
Francisco experienced during the winter of 1849–50, it's also not
surprising that some individuals became depressed. ("Deranged"
was the term used then.) George Dornin, appalled by the selfish-

ness and indifference to the suffering and death he had witnessed, tried to put some distance between himself and what was happening all around him. One winter day, thinking to escape the mud hole of downtown San Francisco, he hiked to the top of Russian Hill. After a hard slog he arrived at the summit only to find the graves of the Russian sailors buried there. Surveying the plain wooden crosses with their Cyrillic lettering, feeling like a stranger in a strange land, homesick and in low spirits, the 18-year-old sank to the ground and started to cry.

The psychological toll for others proved fatal. While it's certain that the broad category of illness and disease was the leading cause of death in San Francisco in 1849, it seems clear from frequent mentions in diaries and letters, and in newspaper reports, that suicide was the second leading cause of death. (Accident and homicide, likely in that order, were distant runners-up.) Besides the prevalent illness and the squalid conditions there were other reasons for despair. By the end of 1849—a year that had started with such promise and high hopes—the golden dreams of many had turned to ashes. Forty-niners who had promised family and friends that they would return home rich, and had not made their "pile," now had to face the bitter reality of failure. In San Francisco they found themselves in an alien, artificial world, one largely devoid of women, one of extreme competition and great stress, and one lacking well-developed governmental and social institutions. They were far from home, cut off from the nurturing bonds of family, and surrounded by strangers. Faced with all of these strains an unknown but not insignificant number of men took their own lives. "There were no less than four suicides this last week," wrote one resident in mid-November.

The easy availability of deadly weapons facilitated self-destruction. Many used their own pistols or sharp instruments readily at hand. Captain George Coffin told the story of a man named Ward who had borrowed a large amount of money and had become overextended. In a final attempt to recoup his fortunes he agreed to a loan at one percent interest per day for thirty days. On the day the note became due he was unable to pay. A shot was heard in his room. Men hearing it rushed in to find him with a discharged pistol lying by his ear, his left eye and forehead blown out. Similarly, Dr.

John Palmer was summoned to the adobe house of a friend of his, Karl Joseph Krafft, a native of Germany, who was cashier at the Custom House. Palmer had seen his friend's behavior change recently, cause unknown, to one of anger, suspicion, and devil-may-care spending that had led to wild speculation at the gaming tables, followed by creditors banging on his door. Visitors staying in Krafft's guestroom heard a shot one morning. Called to the scene, Palmer found that his friend had taken his favorite pistol, and while sitting up in bed, had shot himself. The resulting explosion had taken off the top of Krafft's head. Palmer described the aftermath in grisly detail: "The wall behind the head was blackened, and bespotted with brains and blood. Fragments of the skull, with hair still attached, were hanging from the walls on every side, and from the ceiling in the farthest corner." In another example, a young New Englander in Happy Valley, distraught by financial losses, left his tent, went to a secluded spot, undid his cravat, took a razor from his case, placed the case on his cravat, and then slit his throat.

Whether death was due to illness, suicide, or other causes, the best estimates are that from five to ten men died every day during the winter of 1849–50. Some individuals, out of money, literally died of starvation. Men would be found stiff and lifeless in their tents, having expired during the night. At sunrise, others would be found lying in the streets or on vacant ground. Those who were destitute would be tumbled into the dead cart in the clothes they died in and hauled off at city expense to the cemetery in North Beach.

Despite the tribulations of some, life went on for the rest of the city's residents, even with the continuing miserable weather. Charles Howe recalled how he was tapped on the shoulder one day and asked to come to the alcalde's office. Thinking that he was going to be arrested he was relieved to find instead that he had been selected to serve on a jury. Because of lack of space in the courtroom, Howe and his fellow jurors had to conduct their deliberations out back in a fenced-in enclosure, this despite the fact that it was pouring rain and hail. After reaching a verdict, Howe, who had been made foreman, divided payment of 12 ounces of gold among the six jurors. Howe used his share to buy a pair of boots to get him through the winter. Local merchants kept on going too. To get passersby into their shacks or tents from the muddy streets they set wooden planks or barrel staves across the mud so that customers could get to their doors. Entrepreneurs with no fixed locations persevered as well. German immigrant Johann Knoche, along with a partner, operated an outdoor coffee stand. They cut firewood at a little copse on Bush Street, which they used to boil the coffee. When the rains came they brought out their umbrella to cover the kettle to keep the fire from going out, but the umbrella wasn't big enough to cover them too, so they squatted in the dirt while the rain soaked their shoulders and ran down their backs.

As San Francisco's population and business activity increased late in the year, so did its construction boom. Tents were still prevalent, but were giving way to more substantial wood-frame structures. Bricks, despite their high cost, were imported and used to build several two- and three-story commercial buildings near the waterfront. Those who had seen San Francisco earlier in the year and returned later were astounded by the changes. Henry Hiram Ellis, in a letter to his mother in late November, wrote: "The canvas town of last spring has disappeared and in its place have sprung up as if by magic a wooden city. . . ." Wandering reporter Bayard Taylor, who had been amazed by the changes just from August to September, was even more impressed when he returned to town in December. The city had expanded far beyond the immediate cove area up to the peaks of the surrounding hills. Tents and shacks had given way to finely furnished homes. Three new hotels had opened—the Ward House, the St. Francis, and the Graham House—each of which in Taylor's opinion far surpassed in comfort the earlier leading establishments, the Parker House and the City Hotel. Restaurants now offered a broad array of fine cuisine. Men who could afford it had improved their dress. Slouch felt hats gave way to black beaver top hats, flannel shirts to white linen, and frock coats came out of sea chests. High boots, however, were still de rigueur. The town's populace had changed and grown too. At the start of 1849, San Francisco had numbered perhaps 2,000 souls. By the end of the year the count had increased more than tenfold to 20,000 to 25,000. A subtle but important change also occurred late in the year. San Francisco's civic leaders, who had heretofore always referred to the municipality in official proceedings as the "Town of San Francisco," started calling it "The *City* of San Francisco."

12

Fire!

As the end of the year approached, newcomers continued to arrive steadily by sea in San Francisco. Like their predecessors, they had stars in their eyes upon arriving in the famed El Dorado. After a long journey from France, Ernest de Massey, whose ship dropped anchor in Yerba Buena Cove in mid-December, described his first impressions with something approaching rapture: ". . . all these lights in the city, as well as those from the ships in the harbor, reflected in the waters of the bay, seem to have a supernatural and magical air about them . . ."

Two weeks later a young lawyer from New York, Stephen J. Field, arrived via steamer from Panama. Field had only ten dollars left to his name, and he used seven dollars of that to have his trunks hauled to a room on the west side of the Plaza. The next morning he purchased the cheapest breakfast he could find—for two dollars, leaving him with just one dollar. Despite his straitened circumstances, and the fact he had no idea how he was going to make a living, he felt a sense of exhilaration. He was convinced that he was going to make a fortune, and so did all the other newcomers he encountered. The word "glorious" was heard in conversations everywhere, with people he encountered exclaiming "Isn't it a glorious country?" or "Did you ever see a more glorious country?" (Field's ebullience may have been enhanced by the fact that he arrived during a brief interval of beautiful weather.)

Fortunately for Field, while he was strolling around Portsmouth Square the next day, he saw a sign that read: "Jonathan D. Stevenson, Gold Dust Bought and Sold Here." Field had known Stevenson in New York, and in fact carried a note in his pocket from his brother Dudley against Stevenson for close to $400. He entered Stevenson's office, and the two men heartily shook hands. After

Stevenson made the obligatory reference to it being "a glorious country," he boasted: "I have made two hundred thousand dollars." Field told Stevenson that he was delighted to hear of his good fortune, and then pulled out his brother's note and presented it to him. Field, in his memoirs, wrote—with delight—that Stevenson's facial expression suddenly changed from "wreaths of smiles" to one of dismay. Stevenson carefully examined the note, concluded that it was his signature, calculated the interest on the sum, and then paid Field $440 in Spanish doubloons and gold dust. That was the start of Field's good fortune, because, as he noted: "If it had not been for this lucky incident, I should have been penniless before night." Field went on to a meteoric legal career. He was elected to the California Supreme Court in 1857, and became chief justice two years later when David S. Terry resigned to engage in his famous duel with David C. Broderick. In 1863 President Abraham Lincoln appointed Field to the U. S. Supreme Court, where he went on to become one of its longest serving justices.

Just a few days before Field arrived, San Francisco had suffered its first major catastrophe. The town had been threatened by any number of hazards in 1849. Probably the one most remarked upon by many residents in letters home throughout the year was the ever-present risk of fire. The city was a virtual tinderbox, composed as it was of highly combustible tents and flimsy wooden structures, all in close proximity to one another. Compounding the danger was the lack of easily obtainable water and the fact that there was no fire department. It all added up to a recipe for disaster. In the early morning of December 24, just before dawn, the inevitable happened. A small fire broke out on the second floor of Dennison's Exchange, a saloon on the Kearny Street side of Portsmouth Square, and ignited the painted cotton ceiling. It quickly spread to the Parker House next door. Dense clouds of smoke rolled out of the hotel's windows and doors and shouts of Fire! Fire! arose as city residents tumbled out of bed. Spectators quickly gathered to watch as flames rose through the roofs of the two buildings. Amid the sound of "gongs, bells, and trumpets," men sprang into action. Businessmen in the immediate vicinity commandeered drays to help remove merchandise from their threatened buildings. A bucket

George Hyde.

Lt. Washington A. Bartlett.

General Stephen Watts Kearny.

Colonel Jonathan D. Stevenson.

General Bennet Riley.

General Persifor Smith.

Dr. John Townsend.

Thaddeus M. Leavenworth in later years.

The leading businessmen of gold–rush San Francisco.

Front row, left to right are Jacob Primer Leese, Thomas O. Larkin,
and William D. M. Howard.
Upper right is a relaxed and confident–looking Sam Brannan.
From a daguerreotype taken about 1850, probably in San Francisco.

John W. Geary.

The last alcalde and first mayor of San Francisco.

William A. Leidesdorff.

Jasper O'Farrell.

John C. Frémont.

Jessie B. Frémont.

Thomas L. and Mary Jane Megquier.

Thomas opened a medical practice while his wife, Mary Jane,
ran a boarding house. From a daguerreotype
taken in the early 1850s, probably in San Francisco.

David C. Broderick.

Reporter Bayard Taylor.

The Rev. William Taylor.

Malachi Fallon.

San Francisco's first police chief.

Chilean forty–niner Vicente Pérez
Rosales.

George Dornin, age 18.
Dornin tried many different occupations
to try and stay afloat in gold–rush San Francisco.
From a daguerreotype taken in January 1849 in New York
before Dornin left for California.

Dr. John W. Palmer stitches up the wound of
a prostitute stabbed by another prostitute.

Horace Hawes.

Justice Stephen J. Field in later years.

brigade formed to pass water from hand to hand from a nearby well. But fire fighting came to an abrupt halt when a rumor circulated—false as it turned out—of "stored powder" at the Parker House. (It was not uncommon for businesses to keep kegs of gunpowder on their premises.) That led to a general stampede away from the fire; several thousand men gathered in quickly overheating Portsmouth Square. There they stood idly by and watched the city burn. Only when someone offered the rich sum of three dollars an hour could some be persuaded to enter threatened buildings and save goods from the advancing flames.

The fire leapt from the Parker House to the El Dorado, the four-story gambling emporium next door at the corner of Kearny and Washington. "Canvas partitions of rooms shriveled away like paper in the breath of the flames," wrote one. As the walls of the El Dorado collapsed, the fire marched down the south side of Washington toward Montgomery Street and the waterfront, consuming one building after another. One witness described how at this point former New York fireman David C. Broderick came to the fore. His "stentorian voice, shrill as a trumpet, could be heard above the crashing of the falling buildings and the din of the excited crowd," providing direction to those fighting the blaze. Partially due to his efforts the buildings on the north side of Washington Street were saved when proprietors draped wet blankets on their roofs and facades. This action prevented those buildings from being consumed but still left their fronts blackened and charred due to the immense heat and smoke generated.

Alcalde John W. Geary also swung into action. In an attempt to stop the fire he ordered that a number of buildings, not immediately threatened should be removed to create a firebreak. Some structures were blown up; others were literally pulled down using ropes and pulleys or were reduced to splinters with axes. There were also at least two small fire engines in town at the time. They had been sitting on the waterfront waiting to be shipped to the gold fields to pump out flooded mines, but when the fire broke out they were quickly put to use. They seem to have done good service, and helped to stop the fire's progress.

Despite the lack of participation of many residents, the heroic efforts of those who did contribute managed to confine the fire zone to Kearny Street between Clay and Washington and Washington between Kearny and Montgomery. This was the core of downtown, however, and gone with the flames were the city's leading hotel and rendezvous point, the Parker House, and the largest gambling saloon, the El Dorado. One of the town's newspapers noted that tenants of these structures "paid as high rent probably, as any buildings in the world." Some two dozen buildings burned to the ground. Damage was estimated at $1,000,000. The human toll was slight; only a few men were killed or injured. The destruction could have been a lot worse. San Franciscans were fortunate that the fire started in the morning before the usual afternoon winds kicked in and that it was the rainy season. The buildings were not tinder dry and the ubiquitous mud was used in some cases as a fire retardant.

Most individuals acted with honor and good intentions during the crisis but a few took advantage of the situation to engage in petty theft, resulting in a few arrests. Merchants hauled their safes and large sacks of gold to the Custom House on the Plaza for safe-keeping, and a few miscreants were caught there with their fingers in the cookie jar, so to speak. Englishman William Shaw, making the somewhat dubious claim that he was helping rescue goods from destroyed buildings, told how he discovered in the ashes "a heap of potatoes roasted to a nicety. . . ." He considered this a find better than gold or silver since he had not tasted baked potatoes in ages. He gorged on them until advancing flames forced him to flee.

A fortunate few spectators found themselves favored by serendipity. Two wine merchants, their buildings threatened by approaching flames and about to be blown up as a firebreak, invited bystanders to come in and help themselves, which of course required no second invitation. Some men emerged with boxes of claret, others with baskets of Champagne. All took pride in their taste and selection. They rapidly carried off what they could until the authorities gave the signal to clear out. Then the buildings were blasted to pieces, while the treasure hunters carried off their booty and at the same time tried to dodge the falling debris.

The cause of the fire was never determined with certainty, but John Henry Brown wrote in his memoirs that the cause of the blaze was arson, started by a black man who was beaten with a club by the racist lessee at Dennison's Exchange. The lessee, Tom Bartell, apparently didn't want blacks in his establishment, and he made that forcefully known. The victim apparently ran afoul of this, which led to his beating. During the weeks he took to recuperate he allegedly was heard to say that he would get revenge.

On Christmas Eve, with the flames barely extinguished, the ayuntamiento met in special session to decide how best to protect property and aid the victims of the fire. Just as the formation of a city police department didn't occur until after the crime spree of the Hounds, it took a major fire before action was taken in forming a fire department. The town council called for organizing a fire protection brigade, and voted to spend $800 for the purchase of axes, ropes, hooks, ladders, and a wagon. The new volunteer-manned company was given the quaint name of "The Independent Unpaid Axe Company." Thus the San Francisco Fire Department was born.

If the fire was a disaster for some—there was no such thing as fire insurance in San Francisco, for the risks were simply too great—a few clergymen looked at the event as an opportunity to preach. They saw the fire as a sign from God that the populace should mend its sinful ways. Hadn't the fire's destruction been largely confined to the gambling hells and brothels? Several of them mounted tubs at the scene, cried "Woe unto Sodom and Gomorrah," and exhorted the people to turn from the errors of their ways and to erect houses of worship. Their plea fell on deaf ears. The fire had barely subsided when burned-out gamblers offered $6,000 a month for use of a nearby undamaged hotel. They had saved their gambling paraphernalia from the flames, and before the day was out they were doing business as usual.

Others couldn't wait to rebuild and resume operations. The ashes had hardly cooled before deals with contractors were struck. One owner even signed an agreement for his building's reconstruction while it was still on fire. He promised the builder a bonus if he finished it within fifteen days. That was the carrot. Then he used the stick: the contract called for the builder to pay a penalty of $500 for every day beyond day fifteen until the work was completed. Time was money. Ernest de Massey made note of the determination of those who had lost their businesses:

> One calamity more or less seems to make no difference to
> these Californians. Far from being discouraged, their
> faces do not even show the slightest emotion when they
> see their houses and wares reduced to ashes.

Within three days all the debris had been cleared away and new
structures were already under construction. Two hundred carpenters were at work, earning premium wages of $15 to $20 a day. The
sound of hammers, axes, and saws was incessant. Only one week
after the fire the El Dorado and Dennison's Exchange were completely roofed, weatherboarded, and almost ready for occupancy.
The Parker House would take longer, since it would be rebuilt with
brick. The reconstruction of the burned area took place so quickly
that Ernest de Massey wrote: "Within 10 days no one would have
ever known a fire had been there."

For those businesses not affected by the conflagration, business
went on as usual. Even Christmas was treated like any other day, as
lawyer R. P. Effinger noted in a letter home to Ohio:

> December 25th: No Christmas here, just as I expected. Men
> can't afford to shut up their business houses and enjoy
> holy days here; it costs too much money. Plenty of persons
> got gloriously drunk and ate big dinners, but these are
> everyday occurrences.

On the last day of 1849 a Sam Adams wrote in his journal:
"What an eventful year it has been to me as well as thousands of
others! It seems like a dream." For some it had been a dream; for
others, a nightmare. For Bayard Taylor it was a reporter's dream:
adventure and colorful stories almost without end. Taylor would be
returning home to New York the following day. He had in fact tried
to leave two weeks earlier but his ship, a patchwork Peruvian brig-
antine, delayed a full week by bad weather and unfavorable winds
and tides, sprang a leak as it was heading out through the Golden
Gate on Christmas Eve and had to return. Taylor had witnessed the
fire from the bay where, after climbing into the rigging, he saw the
flames shooting up through the fog enveloping the city. But what
most struck him was the noise: people shouting, the crackling

sound of blazing timbers, the smothered sound of collapsing roofs, and finally, the explosions.

On January 1, Taylor, through the kindness of a ticket agent, managed to secure a spot on an overbooked steamer, the *Oregon*, which was leaving San Francisco for Panama. On board was $2,000,000 in gold and a number of illustrious passengers, including California's newly elected first two senators, John C. Frémont and William Gwin, its first congressman, Edward C. Gilbert, several senior army and navy officers, and a score of leading San Francisco businessmen. The following day the *Oregon* stopped at Monterey, where William Tecumseh Sherman came aboard. He was on his way to New York with military dispatches. The ship sailed away, and with that a landmark year in American history—1849—in a dramatic place—San Francisco—was over.

"Of all the marvelous phases of history of the Present, the growth of San Francisco is the one which will most tax the belief of the Future. It's parallel was never known, and shall never be beheld again."

- *New York Tribune* reporter Bayard Taylor writing of San Francisco in 1849 in *Eldorado: Adventures in the Path of Empire.*

Epilogue

When forty-niner Hiram Pierce returned to San Francisco in October 1850, having been gone to the gold fields for over a year, he was astonished by the changes that had occurred. The city was barely recognizable to him. Where a few tents once stood were now substantial wood-frame and brick buildings. Streets and sidewalks in the area around Portsmouth Square had been graded and planked with redwood. Sand hills had been leveled and gullies filled. Wharves now extended into Yerba Buena Cove from virtually every street. The gambling houses were on a princely scale, complete with imported ornate back bars and chandeliers.

Pierce had missed the fire of December 24, 1849, as well as three subsequent conflagrations in May, June, and September of 1850, each of which had caused extensive damage and had led to new construction in its wake, further transforming the city. Two more major fires would follow in 1851, making for a total of six in the space of only a year and a half. The fires—and growth and change in general—so thoroughly remade San Francisco that by 1852 only one structure remained in the downtown area that dated from before the discovery of gold.

The relative calm that had prevailed in the second half of 1849 in the wake of the Hounds incident and the formation of the San Francisco Police Department also began to disappear as crime increased starting in 1850. Some of the disruption can be traced to an influx of "Sydney Ducks," ex-convicts from Australia. These and other hoodlums who came to San Francisco in the wake of the Gold Rush made their presence known with a rash of burglaries and robberies. Some may have also been involved in the major fires of the period, a few of which might have been the result of arson.

Partly in response to the perceived increase in crime and the losses suffered due to the fires, a number of leading citizens, mostly local merchants and businessmen, banded together in 1851 to form a vigilante group, which later became known as the First Committee of Vigilance. With a show of force that cowed local law enforcement they restored relative order by hanging four Sydney Towners (as the area where they congregated became known— soon to be called the Barbary Coast) for crimes ranging from burglary to murder. Five years later a Second Committee of Vigilance was formed, with some of the same members as the first one, in response to new threats to public order. Four alleged murderers were hanged and scores of other undesirables were deported or prevented from landing before this second group of vigilantes also disbanded after a few months in existence.

Despite the sporadic turbulence, by the mid-1850s San Francisco would take on a more settled aspect as a population of transient miners gave way to increased numbers of women and families with children. Laws were passed against prostitution and gambling, but they were rarely enforced. In keeping with a heightened sense of propriety and respectability however, establishments catering to such vices moved away from Portsmouth Square to more discreet locations. Theaters, circuses, and other legitimate entertainments grew in favor with those looking for leisure and amusement. Churches and social and fraternal organizations also increased in size and number and became a more prominent part of city life. The lone schoolhouse on the Plaza was gone but was supplanted by over a dozen schools scattered about town. By the end of the 1850s San Francisco's cosmopolitan population had increased to about 50,000, and supported thirteen newspapers in half a dozen languages.

The city's economy had by this time also become more broadly based. Oil, soap, and candle works opened, as did sawmills, factories of various kinds, meat and produce markets, and breweries and distilleries. Heavy industry also took root: at least half a dozen foundries blossomed south of Market, some in the former campground of Happy Valley. The employees of these businesses must have worked up a good thirst, because there was a great number of saloons—more per capita, according to historian Bancroft, than in any other U. S. city.

Gold mining remained an important part of California's—and San Francisco's—economy in the 1850s, although its nature changed. After only a few years the easy to find placer gold had largely disappeared. Plenty of gold still lay deeper down however, embedded in rock and quartz. New mining techniques that required deep tunneling and stamp mills to crush the gold-bearing rock came to the fore, and with it the need for capital investment, which was provided by banks and investors. Banks also proved valuable in providing financing for other enterprises, such as agriculture, ranching, and the larger industrial and manufacturing businesses. With the trend toward bigger, more capital-intensive mining however, the solo miner panning for gold in a mountain stream became an increasingly rare sight. Most of those who stayed with mining inevitably found themselves in the employ of larger concerns.

After the rapid growth of San Francisco in the decade following the gold discovery one might have thought that the city would settle comfortably into a role as a modest outpost on the western edge of the United States. But the 1860s proved almost as disruptive following the discovery of massive amounts of silver in western Nevada. Most of that wealth poured into San Francisco, triggering a building boom and more growth. By the time the silver rush was over, about 1880, the city's population had ballooned to 234,000 from only 57,000 two decades earlier. In 1906, by which time another 100,000 plus had been added to the roll of residents, San Francisco suffered the famous devastating earthquake and fire that destroyed most of the city. Also gone by 1906 were virtually all of the principal players in the drama that was San Francisco in 1849.

Here is what happened to them:

Washington A. Bartlett (1812–1871)

After being recalled to the *Portsmouth* in early 1847 in the wake of allegations of misappropriating town funds, Lt. Washington Allon Bartlett (not to be confused with Washington Bartlett, a later governor of California), the first American alcalde of San Francisco, resumed his military career. He seems to have been more interested in private entrepreneurial activities however, because his *Portsmouth* shipmates accused him of turning his stateroom into "a kind of hucksters shop" where he sold clothing and "segars."

Throughout the late 1840s and early 1850s Bartlett would be dogged by charges of financial mismanagement and self-dealing.

Among them were allegations that he sold an Indian shawl at an exorbitant price to an old woman in Monterey, that he smuggled goods into San Francisco without paying duty, and that he defrauded the U.S. Government by padding his expenses on a trip to France. True or not, it all got to be too much for the navy; he was drummed out of the service in 1855.

Pacific Street was originally named Bartlett Street, as shown on a map published during Bartlett's tenure as alcalde. When Jasper O'Farrell's survey and map were published in August 1847, after Bartlett had left office, Bartlett Street had been renamed Pacific. Bartlett's name today adorns a five-and-a-half-block-long street in the Mission District.

Samuel Brannan (1819–1889)

No one epitomized gold-rush San Francisco more than Sam Brannan. A man of gusto, boundless energy, and willpower, he was a risk-taker who achieved great wealth—only to lose it all in the end. Always highly visible, starting with his trumpeting the discovery of gold upon returning from Coloma and his rousing crowds to action during the Hounds affair, he served as president of the First Committee of Vigilance and was one of the leaders of the Second Committee of Vigilance. His mercantile operations in northern California, including the gold country, combined with his real-estate holdings in San Francisco and Sacramento, enabled him to accumulate a fortune. By 1857 he was likely the richest man in California, and he remained so until the mid-1860s. He developed sugar and fruit plantations in Hawaii, started a trading operation with China, and invested in mines in California, Nevada, and Utah.

But Brannan's magic touch and good fortune did not last. He started drinking heavily and made increasingly poor investments. In 1859 he purchased land in the Napa Valley. Developing it into a resort and spa he called Calistoga proved to be a financial drain that helped dissipate his fortune. His wife, fed up with his drinking and his extra-marital affairs, divorced him and moved to Europe with their children. In the ensuing settlement Brannan gave her his valuable San Francisco properties while hanging on to his money-losing resort. (One day Brannan surprised trespassers on his Calistoga estate; he was shot eight times, but recovered.)

By the 1880s Brannan had moved to southern California. He spent his final years promoting a land development scheme in the Mexican province of Sonora; at one point he was reduced to selling pencils door-to-door in Nogales to raise funds for the venture. Sam Brannan died a pauper near San Diego in 1889 at age 70 in the company only of his Mexican common-law wife. His tombstone reads: "California Pioneer of '46. Dreamer, Leader, and Empire Builder." He was all of those, and more.

Brannan Street, south of Market, is named for Sam Brannan.

David C. Broderick (1820–1859)

After cashing out his gold assaying and minting partnership with Frederick Kohler, and helping battle the fire of December 24, David Colbreth Broderick turned his attention to politics. His interest in that field had pre-dated his arrival in San Francisco; he had run unsuccessfully for Congress in New York in 1846. He had better success in California, getting elected to the state senate in 1850. In 1857 his colleagues in the legislature approved his bid to go to the U.S. Senate for a six-year term. (This was before senators were directly elected by the people.)

By the late 1850s, slavery was the most contentious national issue. In 1859 the anti-slavery Broderick was challenged to a duel by southern sympathizer and California Supreme Court Chief Justice David S. Terry. The two men met near Lake Merced, in the southwest corner of San Francisco, on the morning of September 13. When Broderick raised his Belgian dueling pistol he fired prematurely, sending the ball into the dirt in front of him. Terry took dead aim, and fired a bullet into Broderick's chest. Mortally wounded, he was taken by wagon across town to Fort Mason, where he died three days later. (The house on Franklin Street where he died still stands.) Broderick Street is named in his honor.

John Henry Brown (1810–1905)

In 1886 former innkeeper Brown published a book called *Reminiscences and Incidents of Early Days of San Francisco (1845–1850)*. He was a terrible speller, and after the passage of 40 years he got a few dates wrong, but he loved gossip and was a good storyteller. The book remains, with all of its vivid incidents, the best first-hand account extant of San Francisco on the eve of the Gold Rush.

Brown started as a humble bartender at San Francisco's first hostelry, the Portsmouth House, went on to run the City Hotel on two separate occasions, and in 1848–49 operated the Parker House. With lucky timing he sold his interest in the Parker House just four days before the December 24 fire burned it to the ground. Brown moved to Santa Cruz in 1850 and remained there for the next three decades. In the early 1880s he came back to San Francisco, where he ran a grocery store for a few years. He returned to Santa Cruz and died there in 1905 at the age of 94.

Edwin Bryant (1805–1869)

After resigning as alcalde at the end of May 1847, Edwin Bryant returned to his home in Kentucky. His book, *What I Saw in California*, which was published in 1848, and became a bestseller during the Gold Rush, produced a steady stream of royalties for him. Bryant traveled overland to San Francisco in August 1849, undoubtedly to check on the real estate he had accumulated while serving as alcalde. According to a secondary source, Bryant owned 14 city lots, which by then were worth $100,000. He didn't stay long, and went back to Kentucky after a visit to Oregon. Bryant returned to San Francisco one last time, in 1869, this time by train. His visit was a brief one. In ill health, he returned to Louisville, Kentucky where he committed suicide by jumping out of a third-story hotel window. Bryant Street, south of Market, is named for Edwin Bryant.

George Dornin (1830–1907)

Plucky George Dornin, who tried so many different occupations to stay afloat after his arrival, opened a grocery store in conjunction with a partner in the winter of 1850–51. Wiped out by the disastrous fire of May 4, 1851 Dornin opened a new store. It was only marginally successful, so the following year he moved to Nevada City, in the northern Mother Lode, where, ever adaptable, he tried his hand at a number of different jobs, working variously as a merchant, daguerreotype photographer, bookkeeper, and stagecoach line operator, before finally settling into a successful career as an insurance agent and adjuster. After such a life he truly could have claimed to "have seen the elephant." ("Seeing the elephant" meant you had made the journey, had experienced travails and hardships, and had survived.)

William M. Eddy (c.1818–1854)

William Matson Eddy (not be confused with William H. Eddy, a survivor of the Donner tragedy), was appointed city surveyor in 1849 and continued in that capacity for several more years, surveying lands ever farther away from the downtown, before being appointed surveyor general of California.

In San Francisco in 1852 he ran into attorney Hall McAllister one day around noon. That Eddy wasn't averse to naming streets after people in return for a favor is illustrated by the following exchange:

"Hello, Hall. Buy me a lunch and I'll do something for you."

"Yes?" replied the lawyer cautiously.

"I have a short street without a name. It runs from Market only as far as Larkin. Buy the lunch and your name goes on it."

As this little vignette seems to illustrate, Eddy could be bought and bought cheaply. It also points out that, contrary to today's convention wherein streets are usually named after people only after they die, back then, as the city was expanding out into the sand hills, new streets were named after living individuals, in this case, prominent men of the town. In 1849 Eddy named major new streets after such figures as George Hyde, Thaddeus Leavenworth, and

John W. Geary. Geary, in fact, granted lots in some cases adjoining the street already named for him. Eddy, of course, named a street after himself.

Eddy married in 1850, his fiancée having come via Panama from Ithaca, New York. Mayor Geary was one of the guests. The couple moved into a pre-fab house on Mission Street that Eddy had imported from New York. Harriet Eddy became a widow less than four years later when Eddy, an alcoholic, died in 1854 at age 35 of "mania [a] potu"(madness from drinking), or delirium tremens.

Malachi Fallon (1814–1899)

Fallon, who had been made captain, or chief of police, in the wake of the Hounds rampage, was elected city marshal in 1850 after San Francisco was officially chartered. In 1851 however, the political winds shifted and he was voted out of office. He left the field of law enforcement for good and instead became a waterfront saloonkeeper. In 1852 he bought a 17-acre parcel in the East Bay, where he built a home and enjoyed entertaining friends over the years with stories about the rowdy days of gold-rush San Francisco. Fallon Street, in downtown Oakland, on which his home was located, is named for him.

Stephen J. Field (1816–1899)

As noted in Chapter 12, Stephen Johnson Field's meteoric legal career led him to being appointed an associate justice of the U. S. Supreme Court only fourteen years after arriving virtually penniless in San Francisco in 1849. Field would go on to serve 34 years on the Supreme Court, finally retiring in 1897. During the latter part of his tenure Field served as the presiding judge of the California Circuit Court. In that capacity in 1888 he had participated in a ruling adverse to the interests of Sarah Althea Hill, a woman who claimed that Comstock millionaire William Sharon had secretly married her (and thus she was entitled to his estate when he died, in 1885). Hill's attorney—and husband—was David S. Terry, most notorious for the 1859 duel in which he killed Senator David C. Broderick. In a situation full of ironies, Field, who succeeded Terry as chief justice of the California Supreme Court when the latter resigned to fight the famous duel, had been a friend of Broderick's.

When the 1888 ruling against Sarah Althea Hill, confirming that she was not entitled to William Sharon's estate, was read in court in San Francisco, she and David Terry erupted in anger. Terry, a man with a long history of violence and assault, pulled a Bowie knife from his coat and attempted to slash a courtroom deputy who tried to restrain him. Terry and his wife were sentenced by Field for contempt of court. After serving their six-month sentences they both were heard making threats to kill Justice Field.

Matters came to a flash point the following year when Field returned to California from Washington, D. C. as part of his circuit court duties. While in transit by train from Los Angeles to San Francisco, Field and his bodyguard—a former marshal of Tombstone, Arizona—stopped at the town of Lathrop, in the Central Valley. While they were having breakfast at the station, Terry and his wife caught up with them. When Terry spied Field seated at a table he came up from behind and suddenly stuck the frail 72-year-old jurist in the face and on the back of the head. Before Terry could do further damage, Field's bodyguard pulled his revolver and shot him dead. Justice Field, senile near the end of his life, died peacefully of natural causes in Washington, D. C. in 1899 at age 82.

Joseph L. Folsom (1817–1855)

Army Captain Joseph Libbey Folsom, who arrived in San Francisco in March 1847 as quartermaster of Stevenson's Regiment, stayed in town as collector of the port until he was replaced by Edward Harrison in early September 1848. Folsom, who had taken as active an interest as anyone in acquiring real estate, left San Francisco in June 1849 for the West Indies on a quest to buy the estate of the late William Leidesdorff, the town's first treasurer, who had died the previous year. Leidesdorff had died $40,000 in debt just as the news of the gold discovery was gaining currency, but he owned the City Hotel and other choice lots in the Portsmouth Square area, as well as 35,000 acres on the American River in Sacramento. Leidesdorff, who had never married and had no children, left no will at the time of his death. Thus his heirs were his nearest relatives, his mother and siblings in the West Indies. Folsom returned to San Francisco after having purchased the estate for $75,000, far less than it was really worth, instantly making himself one of the richest men in California.

The uncertain state of land titles in California during the early 1850s left Folsom subject to lawsuits from others claiming the property. He also faced the problem of trying to evict squatters from his Sacramento-area holdings. Land rich but cash poor, Folsom was forced to borrow money to pay his legal bills in an attempt to fend off all the claimants. The apparent strain took its toll on his health. After complaining of chest pains for several weeks, Joseph Folsom died at a friend's house in San Jose at age 38. The unmarried Folsom left everything to his mother, sister, and a nephew. The sale of his estate, which started in early 1856, netted them over $1.4 million.

Both Folsom Street in San Francisco and the town of Folsom, once part of his Sacramento properties, are named for Joseph L. Folsom.

John C. Frémont (1813–1890) and Jessie Frémont (1824–1902)

After John Charles Frémont and his wife, Jessie, reunited in San Francisco in the summer of 1849, they set up house in Happy Valley. His star was on the rise, since some property he had purchased in the southern Mother Lode proved to contain a rich gold mine. The Frémonts stay in San Francisco was brief however, since John had political ambitions. They moved to Monterey so that John could attend the constitutional convention. There the new legislature elected him to be one of California's first two senators. He drew the short term that lasted until 1851, but was not re-elected. The couple and their children spent the rest of the 1850s dividing their time among stays in Europe, their gold-country ranch, called Mariposas, and New York and Washington.

In 1856 John C. Frémont received the newly organized Republican Party's nomination for president, but lost the election to James

Buchanan. The Frémonts and their children returned to San Francisco in 1860, where they lived in a small Victorian cottage at Black Point, Ft. Mason, on San Francisco's northern waterfront. Upon the outbreak of the Civil War Frémont returned to military service, but he resigned his commission after a controversial and undistinguished career. Meanwhile his Mariposas property had become entangled in legal and financial difficulties that forced him to sell it. Their wealth greatly reduced, the Frémonts largely supported themselves at the end of their lives through income received from books and articles that Jessie wrote documenting her husband's colorful exploits.

Fremont Street, located south of Market not far from the site of the small home the Frémonts occupied in the summer of 1849, is named for John C. Frémont.

John W. Geary (1819–1873)

After the establishment of San Francisco's first city charter, on May 1, 1850, John White Geary, who was the last alcalde under the old system, was elected its first mayor. He served a one-year term and, apparently tired of the stresses of office, declined to stand for re-election. Geary rejoined his family in Pennsylvania in early 1852. His wife, who was ill, died the following year. He never returned to San Francisco.

In 1856 Geary was appointed governor of Kansas Territory, which proved to be a trying experience because of all of the skirmishes over slavery plaguing the region. He resigned a year later. With the outbreak of the Civil War, Geary joined the Union Army, was promoted to brigadier general, saw action at Chancellorsville, Gettysburg, and other battles, and was wounded several times. He served under William Tecumseh Sherman (the one-time lieutenant was now Major General Sherman) on his march through Georgia.

After the war, Geary, always interested in politics and government, served two terms as governor of Pennsylvania, from 1867 to 1873. There was speculation that Geary might run for president, but just three weeks after retiring as governor he suddenly dropped dead of an apparent heart attack or stroke. He was 53.

Geary Street/Geary Boulevard is named for John W. Geary.

Horace Hawes (1813–1871)

When his tenure as prefect came to an end Horace Hawes embarked on a political career, serving several terms as a California assemblyman and then senator. Among his accomplishments was the bill he introduced in 1856 that split off the southern portion of San Francisco, creating San Mateo County and consolidating San Francisco into a combined city and county, one of the few in the nation. His alleged and somewhat cynical motivation for this law was that corruption could more easily be controlled in a smaller, defined area.

Upon his death, in 1871, the irascible Hawes, at odds with his wife and children as with so many others, bequeathed most of his estate, valued at $400,000, not to them but to a proposed college to be located in San Mateo and called Mont Eagle University. Hawes was quoted about not leaving money to heirs: "When the damned vampires gather around me after I'm gone they'll find nothing but dry bones." Hawes's widow sued to break the will, arguing that her husband was insane. There may have been some truth to that allegation: witnesses claimed that in the last few years of his life Hawes became increasingly suspicious, even paranoid; he accused his wife of trying to poison him. The jury had a lot of sympathy for her, and she prevailed in court. Hawes's university was not funded and never got off the ground.

William D. M. Howard (1819–1856)

Boston native William Davis Merry Howard arrived in California aboard a trading ship in 1839. By 1847 he had settled in San Francisco and partnered with Henry Mellus. The two of them purchased the old Hudson's Bay Company's two-story building on the waterfront at Montgomery Street, a structure that was the most notable landmark on that street when the gold-rush hordes arrived.

The building served as the headquarters of their very successful trading and mercantile business.

The Howard and Mellus partnership broke up in 1850, and Howard moved to a large estate he had purchased in the Burlingame, Hillsborough, and San Mateo area with the profits he had made in his business. During his time in San Francisco the public-spirited Howard served on the first ayuntamiento and was noted for his philanthropy, donating land and buildings for churches and schools.

Howard's health declined early; he died in 1856 at age 37. Howard Street, south of Market, is named in his honor.

George Hyde (1819–1890)

After resigning as alcalde in 1848, George Hyde returned to private law practice. He kept at it only until 1852, when he retired to devote himself to managing his real-estate holdings and several other business pursuits. He built a grand home surrounded by lawns and gardens on the triangular block bounded by Market, Kearny, and Post streets, lots of the 50-vara survey that he had had Second Alcalde Thaddeus Leavenworth grant him in October 1847. Hyde's retirement years seem to have been peaceful and unmarked by controversy. When he died in San Francisco, in August 1890, just a few days shy of his 71st birthday, he left a comfortable estate to his wife and six children. Hyde Street is named for him.

Stephen W. Kearny (1794–1848)

General Stephen Watts Kearny, after leaving San Francisco on May 31, 1847, stopped north of Lake Tahoe with John C. Frémont and Edwin Bryant and buried the remains of the Donner Party. They continued on to Ft. Leavenworth, Kansas, whence Lt. Col. Frémont was sent on to Washington D.C. to be court-martialed for insubordination during the Mexican War. The war was still on, and Kearny was soon sent south to become military governor of Vera Cruz and then Mexico City. He contracted yellow fever there, returned to the U. S., and died in St. Louis in October 1848. Kearny Street in downtown San Francisco is named for him, as is Ft. Kearny, Nebraska, where he had spent time early in his military career.

Thomas O. Larkin (1802–1858)

Thomas Oliver Larkin played little or no role in the political dramas that enveloped San Francisco in the late 1840s, but like many of the men who had city streets named for them in the downtown area, he owned a lot of real estate. Larkin had actually spent much of his time in Monterey (he had arrived there from Massachusetts in 1832) where he was a leading figure and successful businessman. He moved to San Francisco in 1848 just as the town was coming alive with gold fever. Larkin already owned a substantial portion of the north shore of San Francisco, having bought all of what is today's Cow Hollow and Marina District from the original Mexican grantee in 1846. (His title was subsequently declared void by the U.S. Supreme Court.)

The real-estate tycoon also owned a number of lots in downtown San Francisco, and he purchased large tracts along the American River in Sacramento. He additionally worked in concert with Robert Semple to develop the town of Benicia in the East Bay. At one point Larkin owned or controlled as many as 250,000 acres throughout northern California. Despite his wealth, near the end of his life he confided to a friend that he missed the old days prior to July 1846 (the start of the Mexican War and the American takeover) and all of its simple pleasures. Thomas Larkin died in San Francisco of typhoid fever in 1858, at age 56. Larkin Street is named for him.

Thaddeus Leavenworth (1803–1893)

After his turbulent reign as alcalde in 1848–49, Thaddeus M. Leavenworth largely dropped from public view. Not well liked in San Francisco because he had exploited his office to his personal advantage, Leavenworth retired with his wife to his 800-acre Sonoma estate shortly after purchasing it in 1849, although he continued to own numerous lots in the city. (His wife came to join him in California only after his term as alcalde ended.) He died at Santa Rosa, in Sonoma County, in 1893 at age 89.

Leavenworth Street in San Francisco bears his name.

Jacob Primer Leese (1809–1892)

Jacob Leese, the second resident of Yerba Buena in 1836, after William A. Richardson, only stayed in town until 1841 when he moved with his wife and family to Sonoma. Like so many other early arrivals he had an eye for real estate, and owned a number of choice lots in the Portsmouth Square area. In 1850 he traded a chunk of those to Thomas Larkin in exchange for Larkin's Monterey house and other properties. After a failed real-estate development scheme in Baja California in the 1860s Leese moved to New York, essentially abandoning his family. He did not return to California until after his wife, Rosalia (sister of Mariano Vallejo), died, in 1889.

Richard Barnes Mason (1797–1850)

Career military man Colonel Richard Barnes Mason left California in April 1849 after serving for almost two years as governor of California, first as a military commander and then, after the peace treaty with Mexico, as a quasi-civilian governor. He reported to his new posting at the Jefferson Barracks at St. Louis, Missouri. The following summer he contracted cholera and died only a few hours after coming down with symptoms. He was 53.

In San Francisco, both Mason Street and Fort Mason, the former army post now part of the Golden Gate National Recreation Area, are named in honor of Colonel Mason, and deservedly so since he served as governor of California in capable fashion during a critical time in the state's development.

James Marshall (1810–1885)

James W. Marshall, the discoverer of the first gold at Coloma, the man whose match lit the bonfire that became the great California Gold Rush, never profited from his discovery. Instead, it only brought him misery. Coloma quickly swarmed with gold hunters in the wake of the discovery, and would-be miners hounded him nearly to death, thinking that he knew where all the gold was. Marshall did a little prospecting of his own but with no success. He worked for a while as a blacksmith, and when that petered out he sold cards with his autograph to try to stay afloat. Along the way he started drinking heavily. He ended up alone and in dire poverty. After his death, in 1885, he was buried on a hill overlooking the site where he had made his momentous discovery. A stone monument with a 10-foot-high statue of Marshall pointing to the spot where gold was first discovered marks his grave.

Mary Jane Megquier (1813–1899)

Boarding house keeper Mary Jane Megquier, who arrived with her husband, Thomas, in 1849, didn't make a fortune, but the couple did do well enough to purchase 18 acres in their native state of Maine and build a large house on it with the money they made in San Francisco. Their marriage underwent a great deal of strain during their stay, and the two were essentially estranged by the time they left the city separately for good in the mid-1850s. Part of the reason seems to be that Mary Jane was changed by the open, tolerant, entrepreneurial society she found in gold-rush San Francisco. Although she worked hard, she liked being her own boss. She enjoyed an active social life and loved to dance. And she neither observed the Sabbath nor attended church.

In 1856, now a widow, she begged her children and grandchildren to come live with her in San Francisco. When they declined, although she was loath to return to small-town life in Maine, she reluctantly packed her things. "The very air I breathe seems to be so very free," she wrote of San Francisco as she bid goodbye.

Mary Jane Megquier died at her home in Winthrop, Maine in December 1899 just two days short of her 86th birthday and a half century after she first landed in gold-rush San Francisco.

Jasper O'Farrell (1817–1875)

Surveyor Jasper O'Farrell, who gave the town its first proper survey, in 1847, nearly got lynched for it because when his map was first published it showed a grand boulevard, Market Street, at 120 feet wide, bisecting downtown. This extravagant use of land—most other streets were only 60 feet wide—outraged the real-estate speculators who coveted the area. When a mob formed in protest and called for hanging O'Farrell, he took a boat for Sausalito and stayed away from San Francisco until the furor died down.

In 1848 O'Farrell tried his hand at gold mining; he had some success but soon returned to his surveying practice. His skills were in demand, and since he usually was paid in land rather than cash, he managed to acquire some large holdings, especially in the North Bay, where he retired with his wife and eight children to a 60,000-acre ranch near Sebastopol in Sonoma County. He visited San Francisco frequently, and on one such trip, in November 1875, he dropped dead of a sudden heart attack at age 58.

John W. Palmer (1825–1906)

Dr. John Williamson Palmer, appointed San Francisco's first city physician, in August 1849, resigned his post late that year. He wrote a cryptic resignation letter that made it hard to decipher the real reasons why, but given the thankless task that the job no doubt was, it's not hard to sympathize with him for resigning.

Palmer left San Francisco in the early 1850s and made his way to the Far East, where he became a surgeon with the East India Company. He returned to the U.S. a few years later, settled on the East Coast, and wrote a book about his experiences in both San Francisco and India. Palmer continued his literary efforts thereafter, writing stories and poetry that were published in various periodicals. He died in February 1906 at age 80 in Baltimore, Maryland, the city of his birth.

Robert A. Parker (1820–1865)

Bostonian Robert A. Parker came to California in 1847 as super-cargo on a trading ship. He settled in San Francisco, where in 1848 he opened a store in the Casa Grande, William Richardson's large adobe above the Plaza. The business was a success, and he used some of the profits to enter into a partnership with innkeeper John Henry Brown in the City Hotel. The two men soon embarked on building the Parker House, which in 1849 was the town's premier combined hotel and gambling emporium.

Parker, unfortunately, was generous to a fault when it came to helping less fortunate friends, and he also appears to have been a poor businessman, at least when it came to running his namesake hotel. By September 1849 he owed his partner Brown $80,000. He sold out to Brown to cover his debts, leaving Brown as sole owner. After running up still more debt, Parker left San Francisco in 1850 and moved to Humboldt County in the far northern part of the state. Subsequently he moved to Baja California. He died at San Diego in 1865 at age 45.

William A. Richardson (1795–1856)

William Antonio Richardson, the English sailor who in 1835 became the first resident of Yerba Buena, and who built the Casa Grande, a large adobe that was the fledgling town's most solid structure for almost a decade thereafter, didn't stay long. He sold Casa Grande in 1841 and moved to Sausalito, north of the Golden Gate, where he had been given a 20,000-acre land grant by the Mexican governor. He prospered for a while by acting as a customs inspector for the Mexicans and by selling supplies and water from his abundant springs to ships calling in port before and after the discovery of gold. When the gold-rush hordes arrived he had trouble keeping squatters off his land. After he experienced a series of bad business deals and fell victim to a land fraud scheme, he became essentially bankrupt. To add insult to injury, in 1855 all three of his trading vessels were lost to shipwrecks. Richardson died the following year from an overdose of mercury tablets that had been prescribed for his rheumatism.

Richardson Bay, north of Sausalito, is named for William A. Richardson.

Bennet Riley (1787–1853)

General Riley was the last military governor of California. After he turned over control to an elected civilian government in December 1849, he remained in California as head of the U. S. military there until the following year, when he was transferred to Texas. Shortly thereafter he retired to his home in Buffalo, New York, where he died of cancer in 1853. A street in San Francisco's Presidio, the former army post, is named for him, as is Fort Riley, Kansas.

Vicente Pérez Rosales (1807–1886)

Santiago-born Vicente Pérez Rosales was one of the few forty-niners from South America to record his experiences in San Francisco in 1849. He had a low opinion of Americans due to their prejudice against "greasers," but he kept his head down and concentrated on making a living. After an unsuccessful stab at gold mining he and several other Chileans opened a restaurant on Dupont Street. When the restaurant was destroyed by fire in the latter half of 1850 he returned to Chile. He traveled to Europe in 1858 where he was consul in Hamburg, Germany in charge of promoting immigration to his native country. Upon returning to Chile in 1876 he entered government and politics, and finished his career as a member of the Chilean Senate.

William Redmond Ryan (?–1852)

Artist William Redmond Ryan, who, like other prominent men in gold-rush San Francisco had arrived as a soldier in Stevenson's regiment in 1847, left the city for good at the beginning of September 1849. He was concerned for his health, and was tired of the increasing crowds, the squalor, and the high cost of living. The artist and ex-soldier intended to return to New York, and perhaps go on to his native England, but he stopped in New Orleans on the way. It's not clear if he continued his journey and came back to New Orleans or simply stayed, but he died there in 1852. Ryan wrote a book about his time in California, *Personal Adventures in Upper and Lower California*, which is notable for its perception, insight, and vivid details. The book was published in London in 1850 and became a bestseller, going through several printings.

William Tecumseh Sherman (1820–1891)

Three years after leaving California with military dispatches at the beginning of 1850, William Tecumseh Sherman resigned his army commission and returned to San Francisco with his wife and infant daughter to start a career as a banker by opening a branch of a St. Louis-based bank owned by his father-in-law's brother. Despite prudent management by Sherman, the venture lasted only four years. (The bank building itself still stands on the northeast corner of Jackson and Montgomery streets; a bronze plaque on its Jackson Street side identifies the historic structure as "Sherman's Bank.") He returned to the East, and when the Civil War broke out in 1861 he rejoined the U. S. Army as a colonel. Despite some setbacks early in the war he was promoted to general. In 1864 he led his famous march through Georgia, in which he physically laid waste all in his path. His Georgia campaign was considered important in shortening the war and in getting Abraham Lincoln re-elected.

After the war his colleague and mentor, President Ulysses S. Grant, promoted him to Commanding General of the Army. In 1876, while serving in that capacity, Sherman paid a return visit to San Francisco. The former junior military officer and relatively obscure banker was feted as a war hero and lionized as a native son.

Sherman retired from the army in 1884 and settled in New York City. He died there seven years later at age 71. A fine gilded bronze equestrian statue of him by the celebrated sculptor Augustus

Saint-Gaudens stands at the southeast corner of Central Park, just a stone's throw from the Plaza Hotel.

Persifor F. Smith (1798–1858)

General Persifor Frazer Smith was a native of Philadelphia. As a young man he studied law, then joined the local militia and saw action in the war against the Seminole Indians in Florida in the 1830s. When the Mexican War began he raised several regiments, which became part of the regular army. He fought in Texas with his friend Zachary Taylor (who later became president), was promoted to general, and served as military governor of Mexico City. Smith was appointed to head the army's western command in early 1849. At a stop in Panama on the way, he issued an edict prohibiting foreigners from harvesting California gold—a decree that served to fuel nativist sentiment.

After Smith arrived in San Francisco, Lieutenant Sherman became his adjutant. Smith set up at the Howard and Mellus warehouse on Montgomery Street, but he never cared for San Francisco, believing it to be a poor location for a military headquarters. In June 1849 he moved to Sonoma and established himself at the old Mexican barracks on the Plaza. Two years later he left California for a post in Texas; a few years after that to St. Louis; and finally to Ft. Leavenworth, Kansas, where the genial and well-liked Smith died at age 59, probably of dysentery caused by chronic diarrhea.

Jonathan D. Stevenson (1800–1894)

Colonel Jonathan Drake Stevenson arrived in San Francisco in March 1847 as head of a regiment of volunteers that he had recruited in New York to help in the war against Mexico. The fighting in California was largely over by the time he arrived, and thus his men mostly served garrison duty in key locations until the following year, when they were mustered out. Stevenson, along with some of the men from his regiment, joined the gold hunters in 1848 and did quite well in the Mother Lode.

After returning to San Francisco he engaged in real estate speculation, laying out towns and selling blocks of lots in locations as far
away as Santa Cruz and Suisun Bay, including a town at the latter
location he labeled "New York of the Pacific," which subsequently
was renamed Pittsburg. During the miserable winter of 1849–50
Stevenson rendered what assistance he could to the destitute in San
Francisco, which included reaching into his own pocket to try to
help. In 1851 he himself suffered financial reverses and went into
debt. He eventually rebounded and repaid his creditors. A wid-
ower, his first wife having died before he left for California, he also
remarried in 1851 and, by coincidence, had three daughters and a
son with her, just as he had with his first wife.

Stevenson lived to be 94, dying peacefully at his home at Van
Ness and Pacific avenues in 1894. One of his daughters died a few
years before he did. When asked by a friend what the cause of death
was, Stevenson replied: "Poor child! she died of old age."

John Sutter (1803–1880)

John Augustus Sutter, on whose land the first gold was discovered, suffered a fate similar to that of James Marshall, his partner in
the sawmill at Coloma. When the gold-rush hordes arrived, Sutter
lost his once extensive land holdings in the Sacramento Valley to
squatters and then speculators, who took advantage of his generosity and poor business sense to strip him of his property. He sued the
government to recover his land and establish title, but after the
matter dragged through the courts for years, he ultimately was
defeated. His troubles were exacerbated by a fondness for liquor. In
reduced circumstances, he traveled to Washington, D. C. in 1880 to
petition Congress for reimbursement for his losses. After Congress
adjourned without acting on his request, Sutter retreated to his
hotel where, shortly after, he suffered an apparent fatal heart attack.

Bayard Taylor (1825–1878)

Intrepid reporter Bayard Taylor left San Francisco on January 1, 1850 to return to New York. Rather than go via the traditional route through Panama, he went instead across Mexico. He purchased a horse and a Spanish dictionary and set off on his 1,200-mile overland journey, only to be robbed by bandits. Fortunately they let him keep his papers and the notes that he had made during his eventful year in California. From those he wrote his best selling book *Eldorado*, which is still in print. It remains one of the best portraits we have of San Francisco as it was in 1849.

Taylor married in 1850 shortly after *Eldorado* was published, but his wife died only two months later of tuberculosis. He never remarried. Always peripatetic, he spent most of the rest of his life traveling, covering Europe, Asia, and Africa, all the while writing books and articles about his experiences. Bayard Taylor died in 1878 at age 53 while serving as U. S. Minister to Germany, having been appointed to the post by President Rutherford B. Hayes.

Reverend William Taylor (1821–1902)

Methodist street preacher William Taylor stayed in California for seven years after his arrival in 1849 before taking his ministry to Canada and the eastern United States. Just as peripatetic as his namesake, Bayard Taylor, the Reverend Taylor went on to do evangelic work in Britain, the Holy Land, Australia, New Zealand, South Africa, the West Indies, India, and Central and South America, including stays in Brazil, Chile, and Peru. He is said to have crossed the Equator 37 times. In 1884 he was named Missionary Bishop to Africa and served there for 12 years. In 1896 he retired to southern California, where he died in 1902 at age 81.

John Townsend (c.1805–1850)

Dr. John Townsend, the only American alcalde who did not grant any lots, sold his house on California Street in 1849. He and his wife and baby boy, who had been born the previous November, moved to San Jose where he established a medical practice. Cholera arrived in San Francisco in October 1850 and quickly appeared in the South Bay. Dr. Townsend caught the disease and died in December 1850. His wife succumbed not long after. Their little boy was found playing quietly by his mother's body.

Townsend Street, south of Market, is named for Dr. John W. Townsend.

Chronology

1846

May 13. The United States declares war on Mexico.

July. Yerba Buena's (San Francisco's) population estimated at fewer than 100 people, with about 40 dwellings.

July 9. Captain Robert B. Montgomery of the U. S. Navy ship *Portsmouth* raises the American flag at the Plaza. U. S. troops take control of Yerba Buena.

July 31. Sam Brannan and his 200 Mormons arrive by sea in the *Brooklyn*.

August 10. George Hyde arrives in town.

August 17. Commodore Robert F. Stockton decrees that local officials should "administer the laws according to the former usages of the territory."

August 26. Captain Montgomery appoints Lieutenant Washington A. Bartlett as alcalde for the District of San Francisco.

September 15. Bartlett elected alcalde by a vote of the residents.

1847

January. Jasper O'Farrell starts his survey of the town.

January 9. Sam Brannan's *California Star* newspaper first published.

January 23. Yerba Buena's name officially changed to San Francisco.

February 22. Edwin Bryant appointed alcalde.

March 6 Colonel Jonathan D. Stevenson and the first group of his New York Volunteers arrive by sea.

March 26. Thaddeus Leavenworth arrives in San Francisco.

May 31. Colonel Richard B. Mason takes over as Governor of California from departing General Stephen W. Kearny.

May 31. George Hyde appointed alcalde.

June. San Francisco's population: 459.

July 20 to 23. Auction sale of the first beach- and water-lots.

July 28. First ayuntamiento, or city council, appointed by George Hyde.

August. Jasper O'Farrell completes his survey and publishes a map of it.

September 14. The Mexican War ends for all practical purposes when the U. S. Army takes Mexico City.

September 27. The ayuntamiento removes restriction on having to fence in and build on city lots within one year of purchase.

October 28. The ayuntamiento orders that all lots, on land or water, must be sold at auction.

1848

January 24. James Marshall discovers gold at Coloma.

February 2. The Treaty of Guadalupe Hidalgo is signed, ending the Mexican War.

February 2. The first Chinese, three servants, arrive in San Francisco.

March. San Francisco's population: 900 (est.)

March 15. The *Californian* newspaper first publishes the news of the gold discovery.

March 25. The *California Star* does its first story on the same subject.

March 31. George Hyde resigns as alcalde.

March 31. John Townsend appointed alcalde.

April 3. A public school opens on Portsmouth Square.

May 10. Sam Brannan returns to San Francisco and trumpets the gold find.

May 29. The *Californian* suspends publication.

June 14. The *California Star* suspends publication.

June 17. Word of the gold discovery reaches Honolulu.

Early July. Governor Mason and Lieutenant Sherman visit the gold country for a first-hand look.

July 15. The *Californian* resumes publication.

August 6. News reaches Governor Mason of the signing of the Treaty of Guadalupe Hidalgo.

August 18. Chile hears of the gold strike when a ship from San Francisco docks there.

September 3. Edward H. Harrison replaces Captain Joseph Folsom as Collector of the Port of San Francisco.

September 9. The value of gold is fixed at $16 an ounce at a public meeting in Portsmouth Square.

October 3. Thaddeus Leavenworth elected alcalde after serving as such since June.

December 5. President Polk delivers his message to Congress confirming the gold discovery.

1849

January 4. The *California Star* and the *Californian* merge into a new weekly newspaper, the *Alta California*.

February. San Francisco's population: 2,000 (est.)

February 21. Fifteen members elected to the Legislative Assembly.

February 28. Arrival of the *California*, the first steamship to reach San Francisco.

March 5. Members of the Legislative Assembly swear themselves into office.

March 31. The steamship *Oregon* arrives. Among the passengers is John W. Geary.

April 3. Edward A. King appointed harbor master by the Legislative Assembly.

April 13. General Bennet Riley takes over as governor when Colonel Mason departs.

May. Construction starts on Long Wharf at the foot of Commercial Street.

May 6. Governor Riley suspends Alcalde Leavenworth from office.

May 28. The *Edith* arrives in San Francisco with the news that Congress has adjourned without establishing territorial status for California.

May 31. The Legislative Assembly seizes official records from Leavenworth.

June 1. Governor Riley reinstates Leavenworth.

June 3. Governor Riley issues a proclamation calling for a constitutional convention.

June 4. Governor Riley proclaims the Legislative Assembly an illegal body and it disbands.

June 4. Leavenworth submits his resignation as alcalde effective August 1.

June 13. William M. Eddy arrives in San Francisco aboard the Steamship *Oregon*.

July 15. The Hounds attack "Chiletown."

August. San Francisco's population: 6,000 (est.)

August 1. John W. Geary elected alcalde.

August 1. Elections are held throughout California for representatives to the Constitutional Convention.

August 13. San Francisco Police Department formed with Malachi Fallon as head of a 30-man force.

August 13. William M. Eddy appointed city surveyor.

August 20. Dr. John W. Palmer appointed city physician.

August 27. The San Francisco newspaper *Pacific News* first published.

September. The ayuntamiento imposes taxes and fees on businesses of all kinds.

September 1. The Constitutional Convention opens in Monterey.

October. San Francisco's population: 12,000 to 15,000 (est.)

October 13. The Constitutional Convention concludes.

October 9–10. The first winter storm hits.

November 11. James Collier arrives as the new collector of the port, replacing Edward Harrison.

November 13. First general election of representatives and senators. California Constitution ratified.

Fall. William Eddy completes his survey, doubling the amount of city real estate available for sale.

November 19. Auction of city lots raises $67,625.

November 28. Auction of city lots raises $53,920.

December. San Francisco's population: 20,000 to 25,000 (est.)

December 10. Auction of city lots raises $61,520.

December 17. California's newly elected legislature meets for the first time.

December 20. Peter H. Burnett takes office as first civilian governor of California.

December 21. The ayuntamiento initiates legal action against G. Q. Colton for illegally selling city lots.

December 24. A fire destroys two dozen buildings including the Parker House and the El Dorado gambling saloon.

1850

January 3. City auction of additional water lots raises $137,750 as first installment of total sales of $468,780.

January 22. The *Alta California*, San Francisco's first daily newspaper, starts publication.

February 15. Governor Peter Burnett issues a proclamation suspending lot sales in San Francisco.

February 27. Prefect Horace Hawes notifies Governor Burnett that the ayuntamiento has not submitted a financial report for the year 1849 as required by law.

Late March. Governor Burnett suspends Prefect Hawes from office.

April 1. Governor Burnett restores the ayuntamiento's power to sell lots after it submits its financial report.

April 15. San Francisco's city charter is approved by the "state" legislature.

May 1. John W. Geary elected San Francisco's first mayor.

September 9. California enters the Union as the 31st state.

Appendix A

Alcaldes of San Francisco, 1846–1850

Alcalde	From	To
Washington A. Bartlett	8–26–46	12–10–46
George Hyde	12–10–46	1–10–47[1]
Washington A. Bartlett	1–10–47	2–22–47
Edwin Bryant	2–22–47	5–31–47
George Hyde	5–31–47	3–31–48
John Townsend	3–31–48	June '48[2]
Thaddeus Leavenworth	June '48	8–1–49
John W. Geary	8–1–49	5–1–50[3]

---

1. George Hyde served as alcalde temporarily after Bartlett was briefly taken prisoner by the Mexicans.
2. Townsend deserted his post to go gold mining about June. Thaddeus Leavenworth, who was second alcalde, replaced him as first alcalde.
3. John W. Geary became San Francisco's first mayor after the city's charter was approved on May 1, 1850.

Appendix B

Military Governors of California, 1846–1849

Governor	From	To
Commodore John D. Sloat	7–7–46	7–23–46
Commodore Robert Stockton	7–23–46	1–16–47
Lt. Col. John C. Frémont	1–16–47	3–1–47[1]
General Stephen W. Kearny	3–1–47	5–31–47
Colonel Richard B. Mason	5–31–47	4–13–49
General Bennet Riley	4–13–49	12–20–49

---

1. Frémont's "governorship" was a matter of dispute among the military chieftains in California. Kearny outranked Frémont, who had claimed the mantle, and had him arrested and returned to Washington, D.C. to face court-martial for failing to yield to his authority. Kearny had assumed the role of governor when Commodore Stockton left California in January 1847.

Illustration Credits

Illustration	Source
S.F./Yerba Buena 1846–47	California State Library
O'Farrell Plan, 1847	San Francisco Public Library
S.F. in Nov. 1848	San Francisco Public Library
S.F. in Nov. 1849	San Francisco Public Library
PMSS *California*	California State Library
Port of S.F., June 1, 1849	California State Library
Eddy Plan, 1849	San Francisco Public Library
Eddy Plan (detail)	San Francisco Public Library
Portsmouth Square in 1849	San Francisco Public Library
Y.B. Cove daguerreotype, 1851	California Historical Society (FN-08429)
Custom House	Malcolm E. Barker (Annals)
Schoolhouse	Malcolm E. Barker (Annals)
Alcalde's office	Malcolm E. Barker (Annals)
Post Office	California State Library
St. Francis Hotel	Malcolm E. Barker (Annals)
City Hotel	San Francisco Public Library
Parker House	Malcolm E. Barker (Annals)
First Presbyterian Church	Malcolm E. Barker (Annals)
"Street in S.F." by Revere, 1849	Huntington Library (HM 56913 p25)
Ship's Galley café	California State Library
Portable Iron Houses	San Francisco Public Library
Gambling scenes	California State Library
The Hounds attack	Malcolm E. Barker (Annals)
Rowe & Co. poster	San Francisco Public Library

People – Military

William T. Sherman	Bancroft Library (POR brk00005884 24a)

Richard B. Mason	California State Library
Joseph L. Folsom	California State Library
Stephen W. Kearny	San Francisco Public Library
Jonathan D. Stevenson	San Francisco Public Library
Bennet Riley	California State Library
Persifor Smith	California State Library

People - Alcaldes

Washington A. Bartlett	California State Library
George Hyde	California State Library
John Townsend	California State Library
Thaddeus Leavenworth	California State Library
John W. Geary	Malcolm E. Barker (Annals)

People – Other

William Leidesdorff	California State Library
Jasper O'Farrell	San Francisco Public Library
John C. Frémont	California State Library
Jessie B. Frémont	California State Library
Group portrait of 5, Brannan, etc.	Bancroft Library (POR 2 10040633A)
David C. Broderick	California State Library
Bayard Taylor	California State Library
Rev. William Taylor	California State Library
Malachi Fallon	San Francisco Public Library
Vicente Pérez Rosales	San Francisco Public Library
Thomas L. & Mary J. Megquier	Roger W. Kaufman
George Dornin	California State Library
John W. Palmer	San Francisco Public Library
Horace Hawes	California Historical Society (FN-15637)
Stephen J. Field	California State Library

Endnotes

(Bold numbers to the left refer to page numbers in the text.)

Prologue

1 Because of this shallowness . . . land their cargoes: There was by 1847 a pier about 150 feet long that extended from Clark's Point (near today's Broadway and Battery streets) into the bay. Even at high tide, however, only shallow draft vessels could tie up directly at the pier. The Broadway Wharf, as it was known, was an inconvenient distance from the heart of the commercial district—Montgomery Street near Portsmouth Square.

6 "another glittering morsel": Paul, *The Discovery of Gold*, p. 123.

6 "It was a thin scale . . .": Ibid.

6 "Boys, by god . . .": Ibid, p. 34. There has been a number of variations of just what Marshall said and to whom in the wake of the discovery. Marshall himself told it differently in recounting the tale as time passed. I have relied on Rodman Paul's *The California Gold Discovery* for my description, since he did a thorough job of comparing all the eyewitness accounts. Most instrumental of them was the one by Henry Bigler, one of the mill's workers, who recorded the find and the date of the initial discovery in his journal.

Chapter 1 – Gold Fever

7 Sutter was thunderstruck: Sutter, like Marshall, gave differing versions of these events as time passed. The events described here correspond to an early telling of the tale. In later versions Sutter, perhaps fearing to look weak, denied reaching for his rifle. He also later claimed that he was not "thunderstruck," although he was quoted as using that very word in an early newspaper report. The book *California Gold Discovery* by Aubrey Neasham provides all the versions for comparison.

7 "extraordinarily rich": Bancroft, *History of California,* vol. 6, p. 43.

8–9 Mason replied that the men . . . sentence . . . carried out: Bancroft in his *History of California* (vol. 6, p. 64) wrote that Colton was "never guilty of spoiling a story by too strict adherence to truth. . . ." It is a little hard to believe that *two* knots would have slipped at the same time. But even if this story were apocryphal such an incident would be in keeping with Mason's character.

9 He sent a letter back to Sutter: Unbeknownst to Mason, a peace treaty officially ending the war had been signed between the United States and Mexico on February 2, 1848. Word did not reach California until August.

9 "large, alert brown eyes": Bagley, *Scoundrel's Tale,* p. 347.

10 "They could not conceive . . .": Colton, *Three Years in California,* p. 247.

11 "Gold! Gold! . . .": Bagley, *Scoundrel's Tale,* p. 266.

11 "the latter for holding . . .": Bancroft, *History of California,* vol. 6, p. 59.

11 "the blacksmith dropped . . .": Colton, *Three Years in California,* p. 247.

11–12 "The whole country . . .": The *Californian,* May 29, 1848.

12 "mills were lying idle . . .": Quoted from Mason's official report of August 17, 1848 to the adjutant-general in Washington, D.C., *House Executive Documents,* p. 529.

12 Mason estimated that overall: According to *The Annals of San Francisco* (page 209), the number of miners at this time was closer to 6,000.

12 "Even the ragged Indians . . .": Sherman, Letter to Gen. George Gibson, August 5, 1848.

12 Marshall's claim may have been . . . in the Mother Lode: The term Mother Lode arose from the miners' mistaken belief that one great vein of ore—the source of all the riches—was waiting to be found.

13 "there is more gold . . .": *House Executive Documents,* p. 529.

13 "No capital is required . . .": Ibid.

14 One man told Folsom . . . avoirdupois weight: Gold is traditionally measured in Troy ounces. In Troy there are 12 ounces to a pound. In avoirdupois it is 16 ounces to a pound. Some accounts mention gold being measured in either one or the other, but most did not specify.

14 "I see no prospect . . .": Folsom, Joseph L. Folsom papers, vol. 1, p. 23.

14 "gold in fabulous quantities . . .": Sherman, *Memoirs,* p. 83.

15 "To all such we would say . . .": Dutka, "New York Discovers Gold," p. 314.

17 With all these sources of revenue: Cross, *Early Inns of California,* p. 83.

17 "Weigh out your $500 . . .": Brown, *Reminiscences,* p. 95.

17 "The accounts of the abundance . . .": Quoted in Rohrbough, *Days of Gold,* p. 24.

18 "The gold mania rages . . .": Dutka, "New York Discovers Gold," p. 315.

18 "there is something about it . . .": Buck, *A Yankee Trader in the Gold Rush,* p. 27.

18 "I am going where . . ." and "It beats all . . .": Ibid, p. 31.

Chapter 2 - Arrival

19 Many French were only too eager: After settling in California, the French would find themselves less accepted than other Europeans mainly because they stuck to themselves, their language, and customs, and were less willing to assimilate.

19 Several hundred . . . Chinese: By the end of 1849 when San Francisco's population was perhaps 25,000, fewer than 800 were Chinese.

19 The exact numbers from all countries will never be known: These estimates are from Stillman, *Seeking the Golden Fleece*, p. 32, and Groh, *Gold Fever*, p. 293. J. S. Holliday in *The World Rushed In*, p. 297, puts the sea arrivals at approximately 41,000 and those who came overland at more than 42,000.

19 There were three major ways: Smaller numbers of emigrants crossed through Mexico and Nicaragua to get to California.

22 "Death of the Oldest Inhabitant . . .": *Alta California*, October 25, 1849. Spear wasn't quite the oldest, since there were a few men in their fifties and at least one in his sixties.

22 A fair number had college degrees: Attesting to the high degree of literacy, when California's first census was conducted in 1850 it found that "only 2.86% of California residents were illiterate compared to 10.35% of the national population." (Jackson, *Gold Dust*, p. 316.) This literacy rate was probably based just on white inhabitants. Mexican and Chinese immigrants were more likely to be illiterate.

23 "Great sand dunes . . . like snow drifts . . .": Fairchild, "Reminiscences of a Forty-Niner," p. 11.

23 "The whole country is yellow . . .": Buck, *A Yankee Trader in the Gold Rush*, p. 46.

23 "a large, luxuriant elm . . .": Helper, *The Land of Gold*, p. 84. Helper didn't arrive until 1851, but his observations hold true for San Francisco in 1849.

24 "gold belonging to the United States . . .": General Persifor Smith letter to William Nelson, U. S. Consul at Panama, January 19, 1849, *House Executive Documents*, p. 716.

24 Sherman had intended to resign: Army officers were not forbidden from having businesses on the side, and Sherman had in fact made $1,500 on a share of a store he sold in Coloma. If not for that he claimed that he wouldn't have survived the winter of 1849–50 in expensive San Francisco since his Army pay was only $70 a month.

25 "like a countryman in London . . .": Coffin, *A Pioneer Voyage*, p. 55.

25 "tattooed all over . . .": Benemann, *A Year of Mud and Gold*, p. 166.

25 "jingling their spurs . . .": Buck, *A Yankee Trader*, p. 49.

25 "Ask a question . . .": de Massey, *A Frenchman in the Gold Rush*, p. 15.

26 ". . . no one was supposed . . .": Bancroft, *Popular Tribunals*, Vol. I, p. 120.

26 "it was the gentlemen . . .": Starr, *Americans and the California Dream*, p. 61.

26 "But for a few old . . .": Taylor, *California Life*, p. 19.

26 "uneven, ungraded, . . .": Palmer, "Pioneer Days in San Francisco," p. 546.

27 "So this is your Italian climate": Williams, *A Pioneer Pastorate*, p. 79.

27 "Paradise!": Ibid.

27 "the City of dust . . .": Megquier, *Apron Full of Gold*, p. 39, (Letter of September 29, 1849).

27 "the blinding and choking dust . . .": *Alta California*, October 18, 1849.

27 "one vast garbage heap": Groh, *Gold Fever*, p. 4.

27 Some of the primary buildings . . . had outhouses: There is a charming diorama of San Francisco, depicting it at the time of the gold discovery, in a glass case in the lobby of the high-rise office building on the southwest corner of Mission and Spear streets. It shows the main buildings, with outhouses nearby. Also, several contemporary pencil sketches show what appear to be outhouses on the outskirts of town.

27–28 By 1849 . . . little was done to alleviate sanitary woes: While all this sounds appalling to modern-day sensibilities it is important to note that sanitation wasn't much better elsewhere in the U. S. New York City had only installed indoor plumbing in the mid-1840s.

28 There were huge gray . . . rats: Hans Zinsser in *Rats, Lice and History* (Pocket Books edition 1945, p. 157) says that brown rats, the dominant species today, did not arrive in California until after 1851.

28 "Wrapped in rags . . .": Beilharz, *We Were 49ers!*, p. 18. When a 22-pound nugget was discovered in the Mother Lode it was called "a California vegetable." The comparing of gold to produce may have been unintentional, but on a subconscious level the analogy holds since gold, like most produce, was harvested from the ground. Gold was the sustenance that kept many going.

28 "The goldfields could not be exhausted . . .": Monaghan, *Chile, Peru and the California Gold Rush*, p. 129.

29 When Brown admonished Flaxhead: Flaxhead was right because, at least in his case, there was plenty more gold to be had. Brown ran into him in Monterey two years later. The devil-may-care miner treated Brown to the best at a local hotel, informed him that he had bought a house, gotten married, had two children, and had 30 pounds of gold dust buried in his back yard. Brown, in his reminiscences, was a good storyteller, but he sometimes got his dates wrong. He places Flaxhead's departure in February, but that would have been a little early to return to the mines since gold-country rivers would still have been swollen from snowmelt.

29 "as Spanish as Valparaiso": Monaghan, *Chile, Peru*, p. 159.

29 Mexicans and Chileans, at nearly 1500 each: *Alta California*, July 2, 1849.

30 The unnamed man Ryan saw . . . *Brooklyn*: Ryan did not know the identity of this man, but from a journal left behind by a passenger on the *Brooklyn* Stephen Fowler (in the library of the Society of California Pioneers), Ryan's description matches that of a man named John Blauvelt. Blauvelt was a jeweler from New York who had come to California to try to earn enough to support his palsied wife and their large brood of children. This *Brooklyn* was apparently the same ship that Sam Brannan and his Mormons had chartered for their voyage to San Francisco in 1846.

31 Their diet reduced . . . passengers started developing scurvy: Symptoms of scurvy quickly dissipate if vitamin C is ingested. But after about 90 days without fruits and vegetables the first sign of scurvy, chronic fatigue, sets in. After 120 days ascorbic acid levels reach zero, leading to even more fatigue. Two weeks later, ugly skin sores break out. Shortly after, purplish red sores appear and start to hemorrhage, gums start swelling, the teeth come loose, and the legs turn black and become swollen. Death soon follows. In 1850 City Health Officer J. H. Rogers visited more than 500 arriving ships and found that 1 in 26 of the passengers, or about 4 percent, were suffering from scurvy.

31 "like bees to a swarming": Kent, "Life in California," p. 30.

32 Everything here costs 12 times . . .": Geary, Letter to his parents, April 9, 1849.

32 "The crews who took boats . . .": Frémont, *A Year of American Travel*, p. 65.

32 "and a beautiful garden . . .": Ibid, p. 66.

33 The latter were two things . . . high cost of wood: Firewood, according to one source, (Delevan, *Notes on California*, pp. 38–39) was packed in on mules by native Californians, and sold for up to $50 a cord. Because it was so expensive, it was used only for cooking and not for campfires.

33 "A furious wind . . .": Taylor, *Eldorado*, p. 44.

33 "canvas sheds, open in front . . .": Ibid, p. 44–45.

33 "a sum so immense . . .": Ibid, p. 45.

34 "this infant Hercules . . .": Quelp, "Chinese Letters," p. 162.

34 "the grotesque collection of sights . . .": Ibid, p. 163.

35 "profit is the great . . .": Ibid, p. 164.

35 "These people think there is nothing . . .": Ibid, p. 166. Luchong's welcome to America was a rude one. Before he could even get ashore, thieves robbed him of his purse. The evening of that same first day he was arrested by a policeman and falsely imprisoned on a robbery charge. Luchong's letter was published in a periodical called *The Pioneer* in March 1855. His letter survives because probably it was never sent to his cousin in China. Unfortunately *The Pioneer* ceased publication shortly after the letter was published, and planned subsequent letters from Luchong never appeared in print. He stayed in San Francisco and became a successful businessman, but what happened to him after 1855 is unknown.

Chapter 3 - Necessities

36 As late as mid-1849 . . . Parker House, and the City Hotel: There had been a third hotel earlier on, the Portsmouth House, which was actually the first public house in town, but it ceased operations in mid-1848.

37 "nasal serenade": Francesca, "Reminiscences of San Francisco," p. 16.

37 "the perpetual racket . . .": "The Old El Dorado," *San Francisco Chronicle*, August 18, 1889, p. 6.

37 "experienced the peculiar . . .": Ryan, *Personal Adventures*, p. 220.

37 "more pompous than reassuring": de Rutté, *The Adventures of a Young Swiss*, p. 1.

37 "yearned for the forsaken . . .": Fairchild, "Reminiscences," p. 11.

38 "As it was customary . . .": Shaw, *Golden Dreams and Waking Realities*, p. 38.

39 "impervious to rain": Levy, *They Saw the Elephant*, p. 59.

39 "People generally slept . . .": Garniss, "Early Days of San Francisco," p. 606.

39 "five plate glass windows . . .": Peterson, "Prefabs in the California Gold Rush," p. 322.

40 "infinitely superior . . .": Ryan, *Personal Adventures*, p. 267.

41 "The fat on its back . . .": Benemann, *A Year of Mud and Gold*, p. 119.

41 "The flesh was of a bright red color . . .": Taylor, *Eldorado*, p. 245.

41 "Fried steak for breakfast . . .": Stowell, "Bound for the Land of Canaan, Ho!," p. 362. In the 19th century the noontime meal was commonly called dinner. The evening meal was called supper, or sometimes tea.

41 "very many devoured food . . .": Soulé, *Annals*, p. 641.

42 "Lucky is the man . . .": Shaw, *Golden Dreams and Waking Realities*, p. 41.

42 "It was not always easy . . .": O'Meara, "San Francisco in Early Days," p. 133.

45 After typically long waits in line for their letters: Postage to California was paid by the recipient. In 1849 it cost 40 cents per letter.

45 "and soon became oblivious . . .": Savage, Journal, *Inklings of a Voyage*.

45 "Dear Cousin . . .": Megquier, *Apron Full of Gold*, p. 40, (Letter of October 29, 1849).

Chapter 4 - Carnival of Greed

47 "many of those who have been here . . .": Geary, Letter to his parents, April 30, 1849.

47 "elegant, waterproof": Garniss, "Early Days of San Francisco," p. 600.

48 He laid boards . . . Spanish doubloons: A doubloon was valued at an ounce of gold, or $16.

49 "her long upper saloon . . .": Taylor, *Eldorado*, p. 233.

50 "daguerreotype likenesses . . .": *Alta California*, January 25, 1849. None of Carr's portraits seems to have survived. Carr left San Francisco in March for the gold fields where he had some success, accumulating $3,000 in less than a year. He bought a general store and never returned to photography.

52 "the rashest speculators . . .": Taylor, *Eldorado* p. 247.

52 "How long are you here . . .": White, *Pioneer Times in California*, pp. 84–85.

52 "a splendid looking fellow . . .": Sherman, *Memoirs*, pp. 90–91.

53 Steinberger bilked others: Speculation led to Steinberger's ruin. He went bankrupt and died a pauper in 1861.

53 "a weather-beaten man . . .": de Massey, *A Frenchman in the Gold Rush*, p. 20.

54 James Garniss, who would spend: Garniss was lax in dating his incidents. He may not have opened his store until early 1850.

54 "kept them full of sick people . . .": Garniss, "Early Days of San Francisco," p. 603.

54 "Holloa, that's just . . .": Ibid, p. 604.

55 "Satisfactory.": Dwinelle, *Diary 1849*, p. 63.

56 "It is perfectly idle . . .": Records of Macondray & Company, letter to J. M. Forbes, September 1, 1849.

56 "Two weeks ago . . .": Huse, Letter to "Dear Sir," October 31, 1849.

57 "A sailboat which carried . . .": O'Meara, "San Francisco in Early Days," p. 131.

58 "an extravagant price": Coffin, *A Pioneer Voyage*, p. 61.

59 So plentiful . . . that firearms cost: Rohrbough, *Days of Gold*, p. 167. Another observer, Horatio Blennerhassett, writing in August 1849, said that pistols worth $11 in New York were selling for from $55 to $75 in San Francisco. That probably didn't reduce demand. It likely meant that men were willing to pay more at that time.

59 "Labor is unshackled . . .": Browning, *To the Golden Shore*, p. 256.

59 "A good cook or a house steward . . .": Ibid.

59 "Meeting of Carpenters and Joiners": *Alta California*, December 6, 1849.

60 "In this country . . .": Effinger, "R. P. Effinger's Excellent Adventure," p. 62.

60 "Think of this, ye Eastern epicures . . .": *Alta California*, October 18, 1849.

60 "That is all the use lawyers are out here.": Grey, *A Picture of Pioneer Times in California*, p. 88. McGlynn told his mother that when she saw a judge they both knew to pass that bit of information on to him. His mother wrote in reply: "I saw Judge White and told him what you said, and he told me to say to you that he, as a lawyer, must say you could not have done better in the selection of a driver, and that he had no doubt your mule team would be well and *profitably* handled, for that the whole business of a lawyer is to know how to manage mules and asses, so as to make them pay."

60 "A graduate of Yale . . .": Upham, *Notes From a Voyage*," p. 266.

60 "remarkable breakdown . . .": Monaghan, *Chile, Peru*, p. 177.

61 "The very air is pregnant . . .": Taylor, *Eldorado*, p. 94.

61 "People had no time . . .": Schaeffer, *Sketches of Travels*, p. 27.

61 "time was worth fifty dollars . . .": Frémont, *A Year of American Travel*, p. 67.

61–62 "very few of the stores . . .": De Witt, Margaret De Witt letter, November 30, 1849.

62 "three quarters of the insurance . . .": Wells, "Letters of an Argonaut," p. 137.

62–63 "Gold dust is abundant . . .": Watson, "San Francisco in 1849."

63 "turned out carelessly . . .": Browning, *To The Golden Shore*, p. 298.

63 The primary problem . . . was that all states . . . banks' paper money . . . within the state of issue: Forty-niner Samuel Holladay provided an example of what a pain it was to travel from state to state under such a system when he described a journey he took in the autumn of 1847 from Cleveland to Boston. In Buffalo he had to exchange Ohio money for New York money, which, in turn, had to be exchanged for Massachusetts money in Boston. Each time he had to pay a commission on the transactions.

64 Bottle after bottle was emptied: The source of this story is "Extracts From My Diary, By An Early Californian," by James C. Ward (published in *The Argonaut*, September 28, 1878). A deed book at the San Francisco History Center at the Main Library (Transfer Deeds Book C, WPA 380, Alcalde Deeds, pp. 352–53) confirms this transaction but shows that there were two buyers, Sam Brannan and James Forbes. Brannan purchased the northern one-third of the block for $3,500 and Forbes the remainder for an unspecified amount. (Given what Brannan paid, the figure of $10,000 tallies).

Probably Brannan paid all of the $10,000 up front, and then by prior arrangement collected the rest of the amount from Forbes.

67 Early histories claim that Kohler & Company: Historian Hubert Howe Bancroft in his *History of California*, vol. 6, p. 661 states that Kohler & Company's $10 and $5 gold pieces contained only $8 and $4 respectively. Wells Fargo historian Robert Chandler in recent research (see his article "Gold as Cumbersome, Curmudgeonly Commodity, 1849–1870," p. 39) found that their coins were only on average about 3–4% short weight, not 20%.

69 "The first shipment of $40,000 . . .": Wells, "Letters of an Argonaut," p. 50.

70 "No division of profits . . .": Ibid, p. 53.

70 By the end of December Wells had accumulated $132,000: Wells's success story came to an end with the fire of May 4, 1851, the most devastating of the six major fires that ravaged San Francisco between December 1849 and June 1851. His office was destroyed and he was badly burned, never regaining the use of his hands. He returned to New Hampshire a few months later.

Chapter 5 - Gambler's Paradise

72 "the life and soul . . .": Soulé, *Annals*, p. 248.

72 "escaped fugitives . . .": *California Star*, December 25, 1847.

72 "At first you loiter . . .": Palmer, *The New and the Old*, p. 201.

72 "the incessant clink . . .": O'Meara, *San Francisco in Early Days*, p. 133

72–73 "Come gentlemen . . .": Schaeffer, *Sketches of Travels*, p. 28.

73 "a lacquered box . . .": Barker, *San Francisco Memoirs*, p. 197.

73 "in *one bet*," and "as coolly . . .": Browning, *To the Golden Shore*, p. 411.

73 "have hardly risked . . .": Ibid.

74 "put it where the devil . . .": Benemann, *A Year of Mud and Gold*, p. 90.

74 "the babel of foreign tongues . . .": de Massey, *A Frenchman in the Gold Rush*, p. 29.

74 "well-worn linsey": Schaeffer, *Sketches of Travels*, p. 27.

74 ". . . the gamblers were the aristocracy . . .": Taylor, *California Life*, p. 16.

74 "I have known dozens . . .": Barker, *San Francisco Memoirs*, p. 150.

75 "I saw one . . .": Joseph Middleton Diary, p. 213.

75 "Abandoned women . . .": Lotchin, *San Francisco, 1846–1856*, p. 303.

76 "There are several churches . . .": Henry Hiram Ellis letter, November 21, 1849. Ellis joined the San Francisco Police Department in 1855 and served as the city's Chief of Police from 1875 to 1877.

78 "A moment if you please . . .": Palmer, *The New and the Old*, pp. 182–184.

79 "Many a knife . . . ": Helms, *Pioneering in the Far East*, p. 81.

79 "When a banker . . .": Browning, *San Francisco/Yerba Buena*, p. 170.

79 "to buy his daily . . .": de Rutté, *The Adventures of a Young Swiss*, p. 10.

80 "for $20,000 in a night . . .": Browning, *San Francisco/Yerba Buena*, p. 171.

80 The dealer may have been exaggerating: We don't know if the dealer was talking about revenues or profits after payouts. The former is more likely.

81 ". . . we could see the shivered bones . . .": Helper, *The Land of Gold*, p. 126.

82 "a roly-poly little Englishman . . .": Caughey, *The California Gold Rush*, p. 278.

82 "his imitation of a German girl . . .": Margo, *Taming the Forty-Niner*, p. 90.

82 A group of "Ethiopian Serenaders" . . . at the Bella Union: The Bella Union had a reputation as a particularly dangerous and violent saloon. Dr. John W. Palmer called it "the resort of Bowie knife, revolver, and slung shot bravos." (Palmer, *The New and the Old*, p. 70.)

Chapter 6 - Goddesses and Whores

85 "Doorways filled instantly . . .": Levy, *They Saw the Elephant*, p. 178.

85 "It would have cost the wretch his life . . .": O'Meara, "San Francisco in Early Days," p. 132. Despite the veneration of women and their apparent feeling of security due to the presence of protective males, women were at risk of being raped. Records show that Alcalde Thaddeus Leavenworth was accused in the spring of 1849 of "permitting the escape of a man named Passenger (or Passanger) who was charged with the crime of rape" while he was being transferred from a jail in San Francisco to one in Sonoma. (*House Executive Documents*, p. 758.) We don't know who Passenger was accused of raping or any details of the crime. Hispanic and Indian women were more likely at greater risk of being raped than white women.

87 "more drunkenness . . .": Ryan, *Personal Adventures*, Vol. 2, p. 283.

87 "One glance of the voluptuous woman's . . .": Coffin, *A Pioneer Voyage*, p. 59. Coffin actually wrote voluptuous <u>widow's</u> eye but since she wasn't a widow I changed it to "woman's" so the sentence would make more sense.

87–88 Quotes from ". . . transients not mentioned" through "Female labor . . ." are from Merrill, Letter of March 1, 1849.

88 "If I had not the constitution . . .": Megquier, *Apron Full of Gold*, p. xviii, (Letter of June 30, 1850).

88 "The ladies have called on me . . .": Ibid, p. 41.

88 "Oh for a woman . . .": Stowell, "Bound for the Land of Canaan Ho!," p. 361.

88–89 "Wish I had a wife . . .": Ibid, p. 363.

90 "They came tumbling out . . .": Beilharz, *We Were 49ers!*, p. 86.

90 "Gentlemen, what are you willing . . .": Ibid, p. 87.

90 By one estimate the town's prostitutes: The estimate of 700 prostitutes comes from Barnhart, *The Fair But Frail*, p. 15. What percentage of San Francisco's total population in 1849 was female is a matter of conjecture, but all sources agree that prostitutes formed the bulk of the female population. If non-prostitutes totaled say 400 to 500 (a reasonable estimate), giving an overall total of 1,100 to 1,200, the latter figure divided into a total population of 25,000 gives a figure of 4 to 5 percent. So men outnumbered women by roughly a 20 to 1 ratio.

91 "Women were so scarce . . .": Garniss, "Early Days of San Francisco," p. 609.

91 "she-devils incarnate": Coffin, *A Pioneer Voyage*, p. 57.

91 "The most genteel looking house . . .": Ibid.

91 "a notorious house of ill fame": Sherman, Letter of February 28, 1850.

91–92 "most prominent men in San Francisco": Crosby, *Memoirs*, p. 107.

92 "To the best of my belief . . .": Ibid.

92 "One celebrated character . . .": Garniss, "Early Days of San Francisco," p. 609.

92 "tawny visaged": Levy, *They Saw the Elephant*, p. 151.

92 "generally the lowest . . .": Soulé, *Annals*, p. 555.

92 "stew of cheap prostitution": Palmer, *The New and the Old*, p. 70.

93 "a man named Cris Lilly . . .": Benemann, *A Year of Mud and Gold*, p. 92.

93 "she was the finest . . .": Boessenecker, *Against the Vigilantes*, p. 62.

93 "a great shout of laughter . . .": Dobie, *San Francisco's Chinatown*, p. 30. The testimony in the court case is largely based on the memoirs of "Dutch" Charley Duane. Duane didn't arrive in San Francisco until April 1850, so this court case dates from some time after that.

94 "the most flashing European . . .": *Alta California*, July 1, 1851.

94 "purposes of buggery": Johnson, "Bulls, Bears and Dancing Boys," p. 25.

94 "There we lay peacefully together . . .": Knoche, p. 12.

95 "very pretty boy": Coffin, *A Pioneer Voyage*, p. 113.

Chapter 7 - Crime Wave

96 ". . . a log cabin could hold . . .": Bancroft, *Popular Tribunals*, vol. 1, p. 62.

97 This was an age . . . government responsibility for preserving the peace: It was only in 1845 that New York had become the first American city to engage a full-time paid police force. And their officers didn't start wearing uniforms until the 1850s.

97 But surprisingly, crime was mostly confined to petty theft: The *Alta California* in its December 22, 1849 issue marveled at the mainly peaceable nature of the town: "In a populous place like San Francisco and where the inhabitants are of so mixed a character, from all quarters of the globe, it is a remarkable fact that there has been so small an amount of crime."

98–99 "Waiter!" "Waiter!" through "Left face! Forward march!": Bancroft, *Popular Tribunals*, vol. 1, p. 82

99 "several pairs of rib-bones": Ryan, *Personal Adventures*, p. 260.

99 "They were useful . . .": Bancroft, *Popular Tribunals*, vol. 1, p. 84.

100 "Death to the Chileans!": Beilharz, *We Were 49ers!*, p. 107

100 "For shame!": *Alta California*, August 2, 1849.

101 ". . . depended on Chile for her flour . . .": Bancroft, *Popular Tribunals*, vol. 1, pp. 97–98.

102 "Pale with anger . . .": Ibid, p. 98.

102 "I thought it fortunate . . .": Pomeroy, "The Trial of the Hounds," p. 162.

102 "It was very evident . . .": Cary, Memoir: "Alta California during the Mexican War/Discovery of Gold in California" (no page number).

102 It was in effect a vigilante group: It was not technically a vigilante group since it was operating with the blessing of the established government rather than opposing it. Larger and more lethal "vigilance committees" would form in 1851 and again in 1856 in response to perceived threats to public order.

102 "to commit riot . . .": *Alta California*, August 2, 1849.

103 "never to return . . .": Ibid. If Roberts was indeed deported he soon returned: In 1854 he helped organize San Francisco's Know-Nothing Party, a political party best known for its anti-Catholic, anti-immigrant stances. The Know-Nothings swept city elections that year but soon faded from prominence.

104 "influential parties . . .": Soulé, *Annals*, pp. 560–61.

104 They largely were opposed . . . some elements of a political struggle: I am indebted to author and former San Francisco Deputy Chief of Police Kevin Mullen for his pioneering research on crime and politics in early San Francisco.

104–05 "a wholesome check on roguery.": Upton, *Notes From a Voyage*, p. 222.

105 "A second offense . . .": Geming, Letter of September 29, 1849.

105 "Taken as a whole . . .": Howe, *Argonauts of '49*, p. 121.

105 Between August 12 . . . ninety-seven arrests were made: *Pacific News*, September 25, 1849.

105 "that a citizen of the United States . . .": *Pacific News*, October 2, 1849.

106 "suspicious, insane, or forlorn persons . . .": Delgado, "Gold Rush Jail," p. 135.

Chapter 8 - Scoundrel Time

107 "The government is best . . .": This was the motto of the *Democratic Review*. (From Schlesinger, "The Age of Jackson," p. 73, in Rozwenc, *The Meaning of Jacksonian Democracy*.)

108 "take care of public order . . .": *Mexico, Laws, etc.* p. 11.

109 "according to the former usages . . .": Wheeler, *Land Titles*, p. 17. (From Commodore Robert F. Stockton's proclamation of August 17, 1846.)

109 "WHAT LAWS . . .": *California Star*, January 7, 1847.

112 As an indicator of how fast . . . Bartlett's sold for $100: This was lot 82 on the Official Map of San Francisco by William M. Eddy of 1849. It's possible that a building or some other structure was erected on the property, which would have increased its value, but many of the lots, especially those farther from the center of town, were purchased with an eye toward quickly reselling them. The lot was sold on December 1 to Jasper O'Farrell. The buyer was George Hyde, meaning that Bartlett had turned it over even before this sale. (Transfer Deeds, Liber A, p. 285, WPA Alcalde 380, San Francisco History Center.)

113 On March 19, 1847 . . . Bryant granted a 100-vara lot to John C. Buchanan: (Transfer Deeds, Liber A, p. 63, WPA Alcalde 380, San Francisco History Center.) No dollar amount was given for the initial grant, but it must have been for the standard price of $25 for a 100-vara lot. Since the resale price of $28 plus one *real* equaled the amount of the lot plus recording fees, that means Buchanan sold it back to Bryant for the same price he paid for it. Buchanan Street is named for John C. Buchanan, not President Buchanan.

113 On April 14 Bryant granted . . . to a John M. Stanley: (Wheeler, *Land Titles*, p. 43 and Transfer Deeds, Liber A, p. 77, WPA Alcalde 380, San Francisco History Center). I couldn't find a dollar amount for the grant but it must have been for the standard $12.50 for 50-vara lots.

114 The highest price paid was $610, which is what William Leidesdorff: Beach and Water lots 197, 198, and 201. (Alcalde Deeds, Water Lots, "B & C" Original, pp. 167–72, WPA 379, San Francisco History Center.)

114 A couple of submerged lots on . . . Beale Street . . . five dollars each: Beach and Water lots 303 and 304, which were sold in early August 1847 to Dr. John Townsend. (Alcalde Deeds, Water Lots "B," Original, 1847, pp. 46-49, WPA 379, San Francisco History Center.) These lots today, long filled in, make up part of the Bechtel Corporation's headquarters.

115 "did not believe the titles . . . ": Sherman, *Memoirs*, p. 87.

117 "high treason,": Bagley, *Scoundrel's Tale*, p. 175.

118 Two months later he sold . . . to a Rowland Gilston: Lot 19½. (Alcalde Transfer Deeds, Liber A, pp. 134 and 187, WPA 380, San Francisco History Center.)

118 Other deals didn't produce . . . but Hyde appears: A random check of sales recorded in the Transfer Deeds books from mid-1847 to March 1849 shows five purchases and seven sales by Hyde of lots he personally owned during this period. There likely were many more.

118 As an example . . . Hyde . . . to Henry Harris: No sale price was given. Lot 1. (Alcalde Transfer Deeds, Book B, pp. 41-42, WPA 380, San Francisco History Center). Sale prices were not always given when the original grants were recorded.

119 The next day Ackerman sold . . . to Hyde: Lot 319. (Alcalde Transfer Deeds, Liber A, p. 167, WPA 380, San Francisco History Center.)

119 Hyde, hungry for more real estate . . . his second in command: Leavenworth was appointed second alcalde by Governor Mason on October 2, 1847, four months into George Hyde's term. Just days later Leavenworth started granting lots to Hyde. Governor Mason had decreed in July that the second alcalde, in the absence of the first alcalde, could "take his place and preside at the council, and then perform all the functions of the first alcalde." (*House Executive Documents*, p. 378.) This phrasing makes it clear that granting lots was beyond the scope of the second alcalde's duties, which were limited only to those being carried out while presiding at council meetings.

119 One has to wonder . . . transactions between Hyde and Leavenworth: The numbers of all the lots so granted can be found in Wheeler's *Land Titles*. In checking the Certified Grants deed books at the San Francisco History Center (WPA 375) I found no sale prices listed. On six of the 27 lots, numbers 331–36 of the water lots, I found prices of $35 or $40 recorded in folder SF MSS 23/1 at the San Francisco History Center. On the certified grants no prices were shown—unusual in that Leavenworth, as alcalde, usually listed prices for deeds he signed. And on other certified grants, notably for lots 765–69, the pages where they would be are blank, raising suspicions that maybe these were sham transactions, at least where money changing hands was concerned.

119 "official extortion,": Folsom, Papers, Box 1. Letter to Alcalde George Hyde, September 28, 1847.

121 Hyde appears to have kept no individual records: Making it even more difficult to calculate the total proceeds from the water-lots auction is that they were to be paid in four equal installments over a period of nine months.

121 "A large amount of funds . . .": *California Star*, March 25, 1848.

122 "At one time he owned . . .": *San Francisco Chronicle*, January 31, 1893.

123 The next day he bought them from Cobb for $30: Lots 706, 707, 708 and 753. (Wheeler, *Land Titles*, pp. 54–55 and Alcalde Transfer Deeds, Book C, p. 261, WPA 380, San Francisco History Center.) I couldn't find a subsequent sale by Leavenworth for these lots.

123 Leavenworth reaped a huge gain when he sold . . . for $3,800: Lot 127. (Wheeler, *Land Titles*, p. 41 and Alcalde Transfer Deeds, Book C, p. 363, WPA 380, San Francisco History Center.) The copy deed in the Alcalde Transfer Deeds, Book C, p. 363 says the property was transferred to Leavenworth by Callender on February 23, 1848 but that date must be in error since Leavenworth only first granted the property on September 1, 1848.

123 Within a day or two Clark sold it back: Lot 151. Wheeler's *Land Titles* shows the lot being granted on September 24, 1848, but the Transfer Deeds show Leavenworth buying it two days earlier. One or both of these dates is wrong. (Not the only instance in which Wheeler and the deeds differ.) This lot, on the southwest corner of California and Powell streets, was later purchased by Leland Stanford. In 1876 Stanford built his Nob Hill mansion on it.

123–24 The answer seems to be . . . Leavenworth paid Hoeppner $9,000: Lot 151. (Wheeler, *Land Titles*, p. 42 and Alcalde Transfer Deeds, Book C, pp. 243–45, 263, WPA 380, San Francisco History Center.)

124 "He made me several interesting . . .": Easterby, "Memoirs," p. 66.

124 The deliberate three-dot ellipsis Easterby: Easterby did put a more benign human face on Leavenworth when he related how the "old gentleman," whom he stayed with for a few days, taught him how to make flapjacks. Easterby said that when he finished cooking them he would peek his head through the curtain and give Leavenworth a wink, who would then adjourn court to eat them.

124 "The office of Alcalde . . .": Fourgeaud, "Letters," p.121.

124 "It was well known that . . .": *Alta California*, March 29, 1849.

125 "strictly forbidden to pay . . .": Ibid, February 8, 1849.

126 "usurped powers which are vested . . .": General Riley proclamation of June 4, 1849, *House Executive Documents*, p. 773.

129 "Welcome to the land . . .": Monaghan, *Chile, Peru*, p. 72.

129–30 Whether Harrison . . . dipped into the money sacks: James Collier was paid a salary of $1,500 a year plus 3% in fees and commissions on duties collected. It is not known if Edward Harrison received a similar percentage above his salary. The fact that he was receiving $500 more a year than his successor suggests not, but if he did it would have nicely provided a major source of income.

130 "an unforgiving personality": Blair, *A Politician Goes to War*, p. vii. Blair, in his introduction to Geary's Civil War letters, provides penetrating insight into Geary's character and personality.

131 "At this time we are without . . .": *Alta California*, August 16, 1849.

132 Jasper O'Farrell in his 1847 survey: Mawn, "Framework for Destiny," pp. 170–73.

132 "Went to office . . ." Hoadley, Diary, p. 17.

133 The three auctions brought in: The $183,065 figure comes from the *Reports of the Alcalde, Comptroller and Treasurer, 1850*, which reported a total of 551 lots sold giving an average price per lot of $332. The $400 figure was taken from an original auction catalog in the Bancroft Library, which had prices for some of the 100-vara lots penciled in. The 18 lots that had figures next to them produced an average of $436 per lot.

133 "A nice building lot,": Grey, *Pioneer Times*, p. 145.

134 "no outsiders bid . . .": Ibid, p. 146.

135 ". . . the gentleman has made good use . . .": Geary, *Col. John W. Geary*, p. 193.

135 This probably sarcastic description . . . how he managed, with no salary: While serving as alcalde, Geary appears not to have been paid a salary but rather seems to have relied, like his predecessors, on fees received for performing the various duties of his office. According to one source those fees added up to as much as $100 a day. After his election as mayor in May 1850 Geary was paid a salary of $10,000 a year.

135 So how did Geary get his hands on . . . as being the purchaser of only one lot: That was 50-vara lot 152, which was granted to him by Thaddeus Leavenworth on April 15, 1849, shortly after Geary arrived in town. Geary paid $12.50 for the lot, which was located off the northwest corner of California and Powell streets. Part of the Fairmont Hotel occupies the site today.

135 Over three-quarters of the lots . . . granted by Geary himself: A catalogue of the sale in the Bancroft Library ("Catalog of second great sale, F869.S3.9.S16) shows that more than 29 parcels were offered for sale, and a greater percentage of those not advertised had originally been granted to others than David Logan. Although it's impossible to reconcile exactly the advertised lots to the ones actually sold, it appears that the lots owned by Geary reduced the total percentage granted to Logan to about 60%.

135–36 Raising suspicions that Logan didn't pay: Geary's grants to Logan, including the number of installments, are documented in the *Reports of the Alcalde, Comptroller, and Treasurer of San Francisco, 1850*. The Bancroft Library appears to have the only complete copy of this report. Of the 12 lots Logan purchased on January 3, he is recorded as paying all four installments for 11 of them at the conclusion of the auction.

136 "When I get rich . . .": Geary, Letter to his parents, April 30, 1849.

137 Secondary sources, most notably Bancroft, claim that Geary amassed at least $200,000: Bancroft only mentioned this in a footnote (*History of California*, vol. 6, p. 220) and provided no details as to how Geary may have accumulated that sum.

137 The first day's sales fetched $105,000: A secondary source (Tinkcom, *John White Geary*, p. 57) says: "On one day's sales of lots he (Geary) realized $125,000. He probably was referring to the August 13 auction. Tinkcom also claims that Geary was reputed to be worth half a million dollars before he left San Francisco.

138 "a sovereign contempt . . .": Soulé, *Annals*, p. 238.

138 "employ a lawyer . . .": Coffin, *A Pioneer Voyage*, p. 59.

139 San Franciscans were not laughing . . . as "the Colton grants" led to . . . competing claims: Copies of existing Colton grants are all couched in the language that the grants were being made "subject to the establishment of any prior claim." This qualifier seems not to have prevented Colton grantees from pursuing claims of title against earlier grantees. Interestingly, the Colton deeds don't show any sale prices. A newspaper report (*Alta California*, August 15, 1850) indicates that Colton received $100 per lot. Some Colton deeds are found in "Almond's Records," WPA Alcalde 386, at the San Francisco History Center.

140 "one of the Alcaldes": Dwinelle, *Colonial History*, Addenda, No. CX, p. 212.

142 The real amount was only $468,780: The $635,130 reported in the *Alta California* of January 4, 1850 for 434 lots (erroneous also since the number was 344 lots) has been taken as gospel and passed down from the *Annals*, historians Bancroft, Hittell, and every author since. The true totals are found in Alcalde Deeds, Water Lots, volumes 1 and 2, WPA 379, seldom used deed books at the San Francisco History Center. These deeds, on printed forms, provide the selling price for each individual lot sold on

January 3. The Bancroft Library copy of the *Reports of the Alcalde, Comptroller, and Treasurer* provides confirmation of those numbers.

142 From September through November . . . should have . . . brought in $107, 602: (City Treasurer Cashbook, October 16, 1849 to May 18, 1851, AR 33, San Francisco History Center). Geary calculated the fourth installment as being $107,602 not $117,195 (one-fourth of $468,780) because a few of the buyers—David Logan most notable among them—paid all four installments up front. The $107,602 figure comes from a financial report from Geary that appeared in the *Alta California* on May 11, 1850.

142 Did Geary simply pocket the money: The deed books for the January 3, 1850 water lots sales have coupons attached for the three installments that were due April 3, July 3, and October 3. Most of them are blank, indicating either that the buyers didn't make the payments, or that the clerk failed to record them (more likely the latter). The first payment, a quarter of the total amount, was due with signing. John W. Geary signed each one of these, indicating that the initial purchase money had been "paid to me in hand." The *Reports of the Alcalde, Comptroller, and Treasurer* (from the copy in the Bancroft Library, F869.S3A42.X) that was presented to Horace Hawes in March 1850 also raises questions as to whether Geary turned in all monies handed to him. That document ends with Geary signing off with the statement that $320,815 had been raised in the three lot sales of late 1849, combined with the first installment (of four) of the January water-lots auction, and that he had turned over that same amount to the treasurer. Totaling up the actual line items in the treasurer's and comptroller's reports for this period shows that Geary only turned in $232,061 however, for a shortfall of $88,754.

Chapter 9 - Glimmers of Civilization

144 "We are not burdened . . .": Taylor, *California Life*, p. 183.

144 "Is this the line . . .": Taylor, *Seven Years Street Preaching*, p. 289.

145 "Protestant chaplain . . .": Coit, *Digging for Gold*, p. 17.

145 "an unbearable windbag": Ibid, p. 18.

146 "undisturbed leisure,": Williams, *A Pioneer Pastorate*, p. 31.

Chapter 10 - Ethnic Stew

149–50 "The Digger eats very little . . .": Upham, *Notes From a Voyage*, p. 240.

150 "We fear things in proportion . . .": quoting Titus Livius from Hurtado, *Indian Survival*, p. 108.

151 "forced Indian labor . . .": Ibid, p. 93.

151 "an idle, intemperate race . . .": *California Star*, August 28, 1847.

151 "Sammy, a Digger Indian boy . . .": Williams, *A Pioneer Pastorate*, p. 26.

152 Fluent in Spanish, Valentin might have been a vaquero: Indians had been employed as vaqueros on local ranchos since the late 18th century. They became skilled riders and cattle drovers.

154 "only fit for niggers . . .": Ryan, *Personal Adventures*, p. 238.

155 "but the proof resting . . .": *Daily Alta*, August 14, 1850.

155 "take off his hat . . .": Sherman, *Memoirs*, p. 89.

155 "Do you think I'll lug . . .": Lapp, *Blacks in Gold Rush California*, p. 12.

156 "a negro named George Washington . . .": Forbes, "San Francisco in 1849," p. 6.

156 "a sober and industrious people . . .": Gillespie letter of March 3, 1848, Larkin Documents, Vol. 6.

157 "to work as a coolee": Leese, Scrapbook, August 3, 1849.

157 "The saw and the hatchet . . .": Tyson, *Diary of a Physician*, p. 78.

157–58 "Search the city through . . .": *Pacific News*, September 27, 1849.

158 "The Chinese got a pretty good 'hammering' . . .": *Pacific News*, December 6, 1849.

Chapter 11 - Quagmire

159 "an immense forest . . .": Davis, *Seventy Five Years in California*, p. 178.

159 "a living mass . . .": Ibid.

160 "Two swallows of the water . . .": Perkins, Letter to his friend Len, October 8, 1849.

160 "served for tables . . .": Geming, Letter to "My dear Woodward," September 30, 1849.

162 "Don't cry, don't cry," and "I did not want . . .": Ver Mehr, "One of the Argonauts of 1849," p. 552.

162 "twittered up like a fish": Pierce, *A Forty-Niner Speaks*, p. 44.

162 "Boom, sounded just under me . . .": Ver Mehr, "One of the Argonauts of 1849," p. 554.

162 "He walks over an open lot . . .": Taylor, *Eldorado*, p. 89.

162 ". . . it is a mighty busy place . . .": Megquier, *Apron Full of Gold*, p. 48, (Letter of November 30, 1849).

163 "I wish San Francisco . . .": Williams, *A Pioneer Pastorate*, p. 91.

163 The winter of 1849–50 . . . rainiest on record: Over 33 inches of rain fell that winter, about 50 percent more than normal, placing that year in the top 20 percent for the period 1850 to 1900. (Spring Valley Water Co. records.)

163 "miserable, suicidal . . .": *Alta California*, November 15, 1849.

163 "They went out of sight . . .": Sutton, "Statement," p. 8.

164 "This street is impassable . . .": Bancroft, *History of California*, vol. 6, p. 198.

164 "with mud above . . . he had been . . .": Levy, *Unsettling the West*, p. 41.

164 "It is reported that . . .": Shaw, *Golden Dreams and Waking Realities*, pp. 47–48.

164–65 "often proves a dangerous snare . . .": Anthony, Letter of December 1, 1849.

165 "darker than the mud hole . . .": Howe, "Reminiscences of 1849."

166 He was sitting alone . . .": Taylor, *Eldorado*, p. 167.

166 "men, who in the States . . .": Browning, *To the Golden Shore*, p. 411.

166 "from which the sounds . . .": Lyman, *Around the Horn*, p. 205.

167 "sold all his clothes . . .": Benemann, *A Year of Mud and Gold*, p. 103.

167 "A sister's prayer's . . .": Stillman, *Seeking the Golden Fleece*, p. 146.

168 "blodey disentary . . . discharging nothing . . .": Benemann, *A Year of Mud and Gold*, p.70.

169 "So and so, Physician and Surgeon,": Beilharz, *We Were 49ers!*, p. 67.

169 "A man cannot afford . . .": Adams, Journal, December 15, 1849.

170 "and one got but a clumsy . . .": Palmer, *The New and the Old*, p. 241.

170 Coffins were placed in graves: Those buried at the North Beach cemetery didn't stay there for long. In 1853 the City had the bodies exhumed and moved to the new Yerba Buena Cemetery, the site of today's Civic Center. With the construction of the Civic Center complex in the 1870s the remains were moved again, this time to where the Lincoln Park Golf Course is today. Some skeletons likely remain there under the fairways.

170 "some will get into business . . .": Megquier, *Apron Full of Gold*, pp. 41–42, (Letter of November 11, 1849).

170 "to assist poor and needy . . .": Luckingham, "Religion in Early San Francisco," p. 61.

171 "A man's life here . . .": Browning, *To the Golden Shore*, p. 263.

171 "Nobody feels any interest . . .": Coffin, *A Pioneer Voyage*, p. 64.

172 Faced with all of these strains . . . men took their own lives: There is no record of any woman killing herself.

172 "There were no less . . .": Browning, *To the Golden Shore*, p. 405.

173 "The wall behind the head . . .": Palmer, *The New and the Old*, pp. 236–37. In the Bio File at the California State Library in Sacramento there is an undated and unattributed newspaper clipping which claims that Karl Joseph Krafft was a fictional creation of John W. Palmer's. The writer, possibly Palmer's widow, was attempting to make the case that Dr. Palmer was the first writer of "California fiction," ahead of Bret Harte. In his later years Palmer did write and publish a lot of fiction and poetry. Even if there wasn't a man named Krafft (he may have been a composite of several different men) the essential truth of this disturbing suicide, as depicted, remains. Palmer, as city physician in 1849, would surely have witnessed the aftermath of any number of messy suicides. In support of the accuracy of the Krafft suicide is that Palmer's depiction of other aspects of San Francisco as it was in 1849 tallies with those of other observers.

174 "The canvas town of last spring . . .": Ellis, Letter to his mother, November 21, 1849.

Chapter 12 - Fire!

175 "all these lights in the city . . .": de Massey, *A Frenchman in the Gold Rush*, p. 13.

175 "Isn't it a glorious . . .": Field, *Early Days in California*, p. 13.

176 "I have made two hundred thousand . . .": Ibid, p. 17.

176 "If it had not been . . .": Ibid.

176 "gongs, bells, and trumpets": Taylor, *Eldorado*, p. 253.

177 "Canvas partitions of rooms . . .": Ibid, p. 255.

177 "stentorian voice, shrill as . . .": Upham, *Notes From a Voyage*, p. 265–66.

177 Alcalde John W. Geary ordered . . . structures . . . blown up: Geary was sued by the property owners whose establishments were destroyed by his order. Initially they won their suits but those judgments were later overturned by the California Supreme Court.

177 There were . . . two small fire engines in town: Amazingly, one of those fire engines still exists today. Called the "Protection," the lovingly restored 1810 hand pumper is on display at the San Francisco Fire Department Museum on Presidio Avenue.

178 "paid as high rent probably . . .": *Pacific News*, December 25, 1849.

178 "a heap of potatoes . . .": Shaw, *Golden Dreams*, p. 181.

179–80 "One calamity more or less . . .": de Massey, *A Frenchman in the Gold Rush*, p. 30.

180 "Within 10 days . . .": de Massey, Ibid, p. 31.

180 "December 25th . . .": Effinger, "Excellent Adventures," p. 64.

180 "What an eventful year . . .": Adams, Journal and Papers, December 31, 1849.

Epilogue

185 The fires . . . so thoroughly remade . . . that by 1852 only one structure remained: That pre-gold rush structure was an adobe built in 1847 that stood on the northeast corner of Broadway and Powell Street. The building was there at least until 1867.

188 "a kind of huckster's shop": *Senate Reports*, p. 8.

188 True or not . . . the navy . . . drummed him out of the service: Bartlett appealed his dismissal. Lengthy hearings, along with testimony from supporters and detractors, were held by a U.S. Senate committee in 1856. After testimony concluded the matter was referred to the Committee on Naval Affairs, where it seems to have died. I could find no subsequent mention of it.

190 According to a secondary source, Bryant . . . lots . . . worth $100,000: Bryant, *What I Saw in California*, p. xviii.

191 "Hello Hall . . .": Watson, "The San Francisco McAllisters," p. 126. Larkin Street formed the western boundary of the city at that time. McAllister Street was subsequently extended through the Western Addition to Arguello Street.

191 Harriet Eddy became a widow: "Mania [a] potu," or "madness from drinking," was listed as Eddy's cause of death in the N. Gray Funeral records book 1850–1854. A photo of Eddy published in the *Chronicle* on June 18, 1905 in conjunction with an article about the laying out of the streets in the early days, shows him looking like a man of 65, not 35; it depicts him with a receding hairline and a beard that is turning gray.

196 "When the damned vampires . . .": Millie's Column, *San Francisco Chronicle*, May 27, 1960, p. 14.

200 "The very air I breathe . . .": Megquier, *Apron Full of Gold*, p. xv, (Letter of November 29, 1855).

203 He (Ryan) died there in 1852: Guy Giffen's *California Expedition*, his thoroughly researched book on Stevenson's Regiment, which details what happened to all of its members (as far as could be known), gives no birth date for Ryan but states that he died in New Orleans in 1852. Library listings for Ryan's book, *Personal Adventures*, show his dates as 1791–1855. If Ryan was really born in 1791 that would have made him about 56 years old when he arrived in San Francisco, very old in those days for a man to be a soldier and to go adventuring on the other side of the world.

205 "Poor child! . . .": *San Francisco Call*, February 15, 1894, p. 7, col. 3.

Bibliography

Primary Sources: Books, Memoirs, Letters, Diaries, Newspapers, Manuscripts, Official Documents and Records

I have included in Primary Sources books that consist of letters, diaries, etc. where an editor has compiled and arranged contemporary material, and in some cases has supplied commentary, but where the main focus is on the documents themselves. In the case of one-of-a-kind manuscripts, I have noted the call number after the citation as an aid to identifying the source. Those abbreviated citations represent the following:

BANC = The Bancroft Library, University of California, Berkeley, CA.
Beinecke WA MSS = Beinecke Library, Yale University, New Haven, CT.
CHS = California Historical Society, San Francisco, CA.
Pioneers = Society of California Pioneers, San Francisco, CA.
SFHC and SF MSS = San Francisco History Center, San Francisco Public (Main) Library, San Francisco, CA.

Unless otherwise noted all letters cited were written from San Francisco to recipients elsewhere.

Adams, Samuel. Journal and Papers (1849). CHS Vault MS 1.

Anthony, Edward G. H. Letters, 1848–1853. CHS MS 61, Folder 2.

Barker, Malcolm E., ed. *San Francisco Memoirs, 1835–1851: Eyewitness accounts of the birth of a city*. San Francisco: Londonborn Publications, 1994.

Bartlett, Washington A. Map of San Francisco, February 22, 1847. Beinecke WA MSS S-1882.

———. "Statement." c. 1878. BANC MSS C-D 39.

Beach, George Holton. "My Reminiscences." *Quarterly of the Society of California Pioneers*, December 1932, pp. 235–36.

Beilharz, Edwin A. and Carlos U. Lopez, editors and translators. *We Were 49ers!: Chilean Accounts of the California Gold Rush*. Pasadena, CA: Ward Ritchie Press, 1976.

Benemann, William, ed. *A Year of Mud and Gold: San Francisco in Letters and Diaries, 1849–1850*. Lincoln, NE: University of Nebraska Press, 1999.

Blennerhassett, Horatio N. Letter to Samuel Lyon, August 28, 1849. Beinecke WA MSS S-678 B617.

Borthwick, J. D. *Three Years in California*. Oakland: Biobooks, 1948.

Brodie, S. H. "Statement." 1878. BANC MSS C-D 52.

Brown, James Stephens. *California Gold: An Authentic History of the First Find*. Oakland: Pacific Press Publishing Co., 1894.

Brown, John Henry. *Reminiscences and Incidents of Early Days of San Francisco (1845–1850)*. 1886. Reprint. San Francisco: The Grabhorn Press, 1933.

Browning, Peter, ed. *San Francisco/Yerba Buena: From the Beginning to the Gold Rush, 1769–1849*. Lafayette, CA: Great West Books, 1998.

———. *To the Golden Shore: America Goes to California—1849*. Lafayette, CA: Great West Books, 1995.

Bryant, Edwin. *What I Saw in California*. 1848. Reprint. Lincoln, NE: University of Nebraska Press, 1985.

Buck, Franklin Augustus. *A Yankee Trader in the Gold Rush: the Letters of Franklin A. Buck*. Compiled by Katherine A. White. Boston: Houghton-Mifflin, 1930.

Buffum, Edward Gould. *Six Months in the Gold Mines*. 1850. Reprint. Taken from: *From Mexican Days to the Gold Rush: Memoirs of James Wilson Marshall and Edward Gould Buffum*. Edited by Doyce B. Nunis, Jr. Chicago: The Lakeside Press ®. R. Donnelley & Sons Company), 1993.

Burnett, Peter H. *Recollections of an Old Pioneer*. New York: D. Appleton & Co., 1880.

California Pacific Title and Trust Co., Title abstract, Beach and Water lots #317, 318, 331–36. 1913. SF MSS 23/1.

Carlton, Henry Putnam. "The Old Graveyard at San Francisco in 1849." *The Pioneer*, July 1855, pp. 42–44.

Cary, Thomas Greaves, Jr. Memoir. "Alta California during the Mexican War / Discovery of Gold in California." [1885]. SF MSS 21/36.

Christman, Enos. *One Man's Gold, The Letters and Journal of a Forty-Niner*. New York: Whittlesey House, 1930.

City Abstract and Title Insurance Company title abstract, South Half Fifty Vara Lot No. 92, San Francisco (A. J. Bowie). 1916. SF MSS 23/2.

City Treasurer Cashbook, No. 1, October 16, 1849 to May 18, 1851. SFHC AR 33.

Coffin, George. *A Pioneer Voyage and Round the World, 1849 to 1852, Ship Alhambra*. Chicago: Privately printed by his son, Gorham B. Coffin, 1908.

Cogswell, Moses. "San Francisco in August, 1849." *The Pacific Historian*, Summer 1966, pp. 12–18.

Coit, Daniel Wadsworth. *Digging for Gold without a Shovel; the letters of Daniel Wadsworth Coit from Mexico City to San Francisco 1848–1851*. Edited with an introduction by George P. Hammond. Denver: Old West Publishing Co., 1967.

Colton, Walter. *Three Years in California*. New York: A. S. Barnes & Co., 1850.

Cory, Thomas Greaves, Jr. Memoir. "Alta California during the Mexican War / Discovery of Gold in California." c.1885. SF MSS 21/36.

Crosby, Elisha Oscar. *Memoirs of Elisha Oscar Crosby*. San Marino, CA: The Huntington Library, 1945.

Dalton, Henry and Henry W. Halleck and William Carey Jones. Supreme Court of the United States. *United States vs. Henry Dalton. Jones' report on the subject of land titles in California; Halleck's report on the laws and regulations relative to grants or sales of public lands in California*. 1850. Appendix to appellant's brief.

Davis, William Heath. *Seventy-Five Years in California: Recollections and remarks by one who was a resident from 1838 until the end of a long life in 1909*. Harold A. Small, editor. San Francisco: John Howell Books, 1967.

Delavan, James. *Notes on California and the Placers*. 1850. Reprint. Oakland: Biobooks, 1960.

De Massey, Ernest. *A Frenchman in the Gold Rush: The Journal of Ernest de Massey, Argonaut of 1849*. Translated by Marguerite Eyer Wilbur. San Francisco: California Historical Society, 1927.

de Rutté, Théophile. *The Adventures of a Young Swiss in California: The Gold Rush Account of Théophile de Rutté*. Translated and edited by Mary Grace Paquette. Sacramento: Sacramento Book Collectors Club, 1992.

De Witt, Alfred. Letters to his father, September 24 and October 9, 1848, and November 30, 1849; and letter to his brother, August 28, 1849. De Witt Family Papers, Bancroft Library, BANC MSS 73 / 163 C.

Dornin, George. *Thirty Years Ago, Gold Rush Memories of a Daguerreotype Artist, 1849–1879*. 1873. Reprint. Nevada City, CA: Carl Mautz Publishing, 1995.

Dougal, William H. "Letters of an Artist in the Gold Rush." *California Historical Society Quarterly*, September 1943, pp. 235–52.

Dutka, Barry L. "New York Discovers Gold! In California: How the press fanned the flames of the gold mania." *California History*, Fall 1984, pp. 313–19.

Dwinelle, John Whipple. *The Colonial History of San Francisco*. 1867. Reprint. Berkeley, CA: Ross Valley Book Co., 1978.

———. Diary. 1849. BANC MSS C-F 85.

Easterby, Captain Anthony Y. "Memoirs Dictated by himself to his family in August 1885." Edited by Helen Putnam Van Sicklen. *Quarterly of the Society of California Pioneers*, Vol. X, 1933, pp. 57–84.

Effinger, R. P. "R. P. Effinger's Excellent Adventure: The Unknown Letters of a Young Ohio Lawyer." *California History*, Vol. 82, No. 1, 2004, pp. 2–75.

Ellis, Henry Hiram. Letter to his mother, November 21, 1849. SF MSS 5/14.

Fairchild, Mahlon D. "Reminiscences of a Forty-Niner." *CHS Quarterly*, March 1934, pp. 3–33.

Field, Stephen J. *Personal Reminiscences of Early Days in California with Other Sketches*. San Francisco: Privately printed, 1880.

Folsom, Joseph Libbey. Catalogue of Executor's Sale of Parts of the Folsom Estate of January 10, 1856. San Francisco: W. W. Barnes, printer, (1856).

———. Joseph L. Folsom Papers, 1846–1855. BANC MSS C-B 630, Box 1.

———. Letter to Thomas J. Jesup, Quartermaster in Washington, D.C., September 18, 1848. San Francisco: Grabhorn Press, 1944.

Forbes, Alexander Bell. "San Francisco in 1849." 1886. BANC MSS C-D 318.

Fowler, Stephen L. and James F. "Journal of Stephen L. and James E. Fowler of East Hampton, Long Island, 1849–1852." BANC MSS CF-144.

Francesca [pseud.]. "Reminiscences of San Francisco in 1850." *The Pioneer*, January 1854, pp. 15–17.

Fremont, Jessie Benton. *A Year of American Travel*. 1878. Reprint. San Francisco: The Book Club of California, 1960.

Gardiner, Howard C. *In Pursuit of the Golden Dream: Reminiscences of San Francisco and the Northern and Southern Mines, 1849–1857*. Dale L. Morgan, editor. Stoughton, MA: Western Hemisphere, Inc., 1970.

Garniss, James R. "Early Days of San Francisco." 1877. BANC MSS C-D 189.

Geary, John White. John W. Geary business papers, 1834–1873. Beinecke WA MSS S-209.

———. Letters to his parents, April 9 and April 30, 1849. Letter [undated – 1849] to his superiors in Washington, D.C. Part of John W. Geary Papers, 1849–1851. SF MSS 7/5.

Geary, John W. and S. C. Simmons and Gilmor Meredith. *Reports of the Alcalde, Comptroller, and Treasurer of San Francisco*. San Francisco: Alta California, 1850.

Gerstacker, Friedrich. *Scenes of Life in California.* Translated from the French by George Cosgrove. San Francisco: John Howell, 1942.

Geming, A. W. Letter to "My Dear Woodward," September 30, 1849. SF MSS 7/6.

Green, Alfred A. "Life of a 47er." 1878. BANC MSS C-D 94.

Green, John. Letter to his father, brother, and sisters, December 29, 1849. SF MSS 7/27.

Grey, William, pseud. William F. White. *A Picture of Pioneer Times in California. Illustrated with Anecdotes and Stories Taken From Real Life.* San Francisco: W. M. Hinton, Printer, 1881.

Hawley, David N. "Observations." c.1878. BANC MSS C-D 98.

Helms, Ludvig Verner. *Pioneering in the Far East and Journeys to California in 1849.* London: W. H. Allen & Co., 1882.

Helper, Hinton. *The Land of Gold: Reality vs. Fiction.* Baltimore: published by the author, 1855.

Hoadley, Milo. Diary and related papers. 1848 to c.1856. BANC MSS C-F 201.

Huse, Charles E. Letter to "Dear Sir," October 31, 1849. SF MSS 7/53.

Hyde, George. "Statement of Historical Facts on California." 1878. BANC MSS C-D 107.

————. Alcalde deed to Dr. John Townsend, 1847. SF MSS 20/19.

Jones, Elbert P. Elbert P. Jones real estate papers: San Francisco, California, 1847–1851. Beinecke WA MSS S-1944.

————. Real Estate bond, 1847. SF MSS 19/2.

Kent, George F. "Life in California in 1849." *California Historical Society Quarterly*, March 1941, pp. 26–46.

Keyes, Erasmus Darwin. *Fifty Years Observation of Men and Events.* New York: Charles Scribner's Sons, 1884.

Knight, John M. Letter to his brother Samuel, August 28, 1849. SF MSS 7/71.

Knower, Daniel. *The Adventures of a Forty-Niner: An Historic Description of California, With Events and Ideas of San Francisco and Its People in Those Early Days.* Albany, NY: Weed Parsons Printing Co., 1894.

Larkin, Thomas. Larkin Documents, vol. 6. BANC C-B 42.

Leese, Jacob P. "Scrap Book of Jacob P. Leese." Contract between Jacob P. Leese and Ansung, a Chinaman, 1849. Pioneers, Document #32.

Logan, David. Undated letter [1849] from David Logan in Stockton, California to John W. Geary in San Francisco. Part of John W. Geary papers, 1849-1851. SF MSS 7/5.

Lyman, Chester S. *Around the Horn to the Sandwich Islands and California 1845–1850: Being a Personal Record Kept by Chester S. Lyman.* Edited by Frederick J. Teggart. New Haven, CT: Yale University Press, 1924.

Lynch, James and Francis Clark. *The New York Volunteers in California 1846–1848.* Glorieta, New Mexico: The Rio Grande Press, 1970. Reprint of *With Stevenson to California 1846–1848* by James Lynch, 1882, and *Stevenson's Regiment in California 1847–1848* by Francis D. Clark, 1896.

Marye, George Thomas Jr. *From '49 to '83 In California and Nevada: Chapters From the Life of George Thomas Marye, A Pioneer of '49.* San Francisco: A. M. Robertson, 1923.

Macondray & Company. *Records of Macondray & Company, San Francisco, California, 1849–1852.* BANC MSS 83 / 142c.

McDermott, John Francis. "Two Fourgeaud Letters." *California Historical Society Quarterly,* June 1941, pp. 117–25.

Megquier. Mary Jane. *Apron Full of Gold: The Letters of Mary Jane Megquier from San Francisco, 1849–1856.* 1949. Reprint. Edited by Robert Glass Cleland. Introduction with new material by Polly Welts Kaufman. Albuquerque: University of New Mexico Press, 1994.

Merrill, Jerusha Deming. Letter to her sister, March 1, 1849. Beinecke, WA MSS 789 M552.

Mexico. Laws, etc. (Halleck and Hartnell). *Translation and digest of such portions of the Mexican laws of March 20 and May 23, 1837: as are supposed to be still in force and adapted to the present condition of California.* With an introduction and notes, by H. Halleck and W. E. P. Hartnell. San Francisco: Alta California, 1849. Beinecke Zc72 +849mfk.

Middleton, Dr. Joseph. Diary, 1849–1850. Beinecke WA MSS S-39.

Minutes of proceedings of the San Francisco Council, September 16, 1847 to April 10, 1848. BANC MSS 82/83c.

N. Gray Funeral Records, 1850–1854. SFHC.

Nasatir, Abraham P., ed. "The French Consulate in California 1843–1856, The Moerenhaut Documents." *California Historical Society Quarterly,* December 1934, pp. 355–85.

Oehler, Helen Irving, ed. "Nantucket to the Golden Gate." Letters in the Winslow Collection. *California Historical Society Quarterly,* June 1950, pp. 167–72.

Official Documents relating to early San Francisco, 1835–1857. BANC MSS C-A 370, Box 2.

O'Meara, James. "San Francisco in Early Days." *Overland Monthly,* February 1883, pp. 129–36.

Osgood, J. K. Letter to George Strang, August 23, 1849. BANC MSS C-B 547, Box 6.

Palmer, John Williamson. *The New and the Old, or California and India in romantic aspects.* New York: Rudd & Carleton, 1859.

———. "Pioneer Days in San Francisco." *Century Magazine,* vol. 21, 1891–1892, pp. 541–60.

Parrott, Enoch G. Letters to his sister, Mrs. Lyman D. Spaulding, June 27, 1847 and July 21, 1847. SF MSS 9/31.

Pierce, Hiram Dwight. *A Forty-Niner Speaks.* Oakland: Privately printed by his granddaughter, Sarah Wisnall Meyer, 1930.

Proceedings of the Town council of San Francisco Upper California. San Francisco: Alta California Press, 1849 and 1850.

Quelp [pseud.], trans. "Chinese Letters." *The Pioneer*, March 1855, pp. 162–66.

Report on the condition of the real estate within the limits of the city of San Francisco: and the property beyond, within the bounds of the Old Mission Dolores, made in pursuance of an ordinance of the Common Council of said City, creating a Commission to Enquire into City Property, 1851. BANC F869.S376 S163:\x1.

Rogers, Fred B. intro. *The California Star: Vol. I, 1847–1848*. Berkeley, CA: Howell-North Books, 1965.

Ryan, William Redmond. *Personal Adventures in Upper and Lower California in 1848–9. Vol. II*. London: William Shoberl, Publisher, 1851.

San Francisco Municipal Reports. 1859–1860.

San Francisco Town Journal 1847–1848, William Leidesdorff, Treasurer. San Francisco: H. S. Crocker, 1926. (Facsimile of the original.)

Sargent, Lorenzo. Journal: Voyage to California, a stay in the mines, and return voyage by Lorenzo D. Sargent, 1849–1850. Beinecke WA MSS S-790.

Schaeffer, Luther Melanchthon. Private Journal of L. M. Schaeffer. Beinecke WA MSS S-416.

———. *Sketches of Travels in South America, Mexico and California*. New York: James Egbert, Printer, 1860.

Shaw, William. *Golden Dreams and Waking Realities: Being the Adventures of a Gold-Seeker in California and the Pacific Islands*. London: Smith, Elder & Co., 1851.

Sherman, William. Letter "To My Dear Tripp," February 28, 1850. Beinecke, WA MSS S-1625 SH 561.

Sherman, William Tecumseh. Letter from Monterey to Gen. George Gibson, Commanding General Subsistence in Washington, D.C., August 5, 1848. San Francisco: Grabhorn Press, 1947.

———. *Memoirs of General William T. Sherman*. 1885. Reprint. New York: The Library of America, 1990.

Stillman, J. B. D. *Seeking the Golden Fleece: a record of pioneer life in California, San Francisco, and New York.* San Francisco: A. Roman & Co., 1877.

Stowell, Levi. "Bound for the Land of Canaan, Ho!: The Diary of Levi Stowell, 1849." *California Historical Society Quarterly*, December 1948, pp. 361–70; March 1949, pp. 57–68.

Sutton, O. P. "Statement." 1878. BANC MSS C-D 160.

Taylor, Bayard. *Eldorado: Adventures in the Path of Empire.* 1949. Reprint and revised edition. Berkeley, CA: Heyday Books, 2000.

Taylor, Rinaldo R. *Seeing the Elephant: Letters of R. R. Taylor forty-niner.* Edited by John Walton Caughey. Los Angeles: Ward Ritchie Press, 1951.

Taylor, William. *California Life, Illustrated.* New York: Carlton & Porter, 1858.

————. *Seven Years Street Preaching in San Francisco.* New York: Published for the author by Carlton & Porter, 1856.

Tyson, James L. *Diary of a Physician in California.* New York: D. Appleton & Co., 1850.

United States. Dept. of Justice. *The United States vs. Henry Dalton, Appendix to appellant's brief.* Washington, D.C., ©.1852).

Upham, Samuel C. *Notes of a Voyage to California via Cape Horn, together with Scenes in El Dorado, in the years 1849-50.* Philadelphia: published by the author, 1878.

U.S. Congress. House. *House Executive Documents,* 31st Congress, 1st Session, 1849–1850, Vol. 5, No. 17. SFHC UC 573.

U.S. Congress. Senate. *Senate Reports,* 34th Congress, 1st Session, 1855–1856, vol. 2, nos. 198–290, Miscellaneous. SFHC UC 837.

Ver Mehr, J. "One of the Argonauts of 1849." *Overland Monthly,* June 1873, pp. 546–54.

Ward, James C. "Extracts From My Diary, By An Early Californian." *The Argonaut,* September 21 and 28, 1878.

Watson, Robert Sedgwick. "San Francisco in 1849: Stray Leaves by a Pioneer." 1877. BANC MSS C-D 5149.

Wells, Thomas Goodwin. "Letters of an Argonaut. From August 1849 to October 1851." *Out West*, January – June 1905, pp. 48–54, 136–42, 221–28.

Wheeler, Alfred. *Land Titles in San Francisco and Laws Affecting Same.* San Francisco: Alta California Steam Printing Establishment, 1852.

Wierzbicki, Felix Paul. *California as It Is and as It May Be, or a Guide to the Gold Regions.* 1849. Reprint of Second Edition. Tarrytown, NY: William Abbott, 1927.

Williams, Albert. *A Pioneer Pastorate and Times embodying contemporary local transactions and events.* San Francisco: Wallace and Haskett, Printers, 1879.

Williams, Henry F. "Statement of Recollections on Early Days of California By The Pioneer of 1849 Henry F. Williams." 1878. Henry F. Williams Papers 1849–1911, Bancroft Library, BANC MSS C-D 212.

———. "The Port of San Francisco, June 1, 1849." (Memoir dated March 5, 1910) Henry F. Williams Papers 1849–1911, Bancroft Library, BANC MSS C-D 212.

Woods, Daniel B. *Sixteen Months at the Gold Diggings.* New York: Harper & Brothers, 1851.

Wyman, Walker D., ed. *California Emigrant Letters: The Forty-Niners Write Home.* New York: Bookman Associates, 1952.

Deed books at the San Francisco History Center (SFHC) which were of particular use included the following:

Alcalde "Blotter B," 1847–1849. WPA 377.
Alcalde Certified Grants, 1847–1850. WPA 375.
Alcalde Deeds, 1847, 1849–1850. WPA 379.
Alcalde District records, 1847–1849. WPA 376.
Alcalde Transfer Deeds, 1846–1849. WPA 380.
"Almonds Records." WPA 386.
Miscellaneous, 1847–1851. WPA 392.

Newspapers used as resources (select issues):

California Star, 1847–1848.
Alta California, 1849–1850.
The Californian, 1848.
The Pacific News, 1849–1850.
Daily Alta California, early 1850s.
San Francisco Call (select issues 19th century)
San Francisco Chronicle (select issues 19th and 20th centuries)

Secondary Sources: Books, Periodicals, and Theses

N.B.: For scholarly journals and periodicals, for the sake of brevity I have just used the month and year of publication and have not included volume and issue numbers unless they were necessary for identifying a particular article.

Adams, Edgar H. *Private Gold Coinage in California, 1849–1855: Its History and Issues*. Brooklyn, NY: Edgar H. Adams, 1913.

Avella, Stephen M. "Phelan's Cemetery: Religion in the Urbanizing West, 1850–1869, in Los Angeles, San Francisco, and Sacramento." *California History*, Summer 2000, pp. 250–79.

Bagley, Will. *Scoundrel's Tale: The Samuel Brannan Papers*. Logan, UT: Utah State University Press, 1999.

Bailey, Paul. *Sam Brannan and the California Mormons*. Los Angeles: Westernlore Publishers, 1953.

Baird, Joseph A. Jr. and Edwin C. Evans. *Historic Lithographs of San Francisco*. San Francisco: Burger & Evans, 1972.

Baker, Hugh Sanford Cheney. "A History of the Book Trade in California, 1849–1859." *California Historical Society Quarterly*, June 1951, pp. 97–115.

Bakken, Gordon Morris. "The Courts, the Legal Profession, and the Development of Law in Early California." *California History*, Vol. 81, No. ¾, 2003, pp. 74–95.

Bancroft, Hubert Howe. *History of California,* vol. 5, *1846-1848.* 1886. Reprint. Santa Barbara, CA: Wallace Hebberd, 1970.

———. *History of California,* vol. 6, *1848-1859.* 1886. Reprint. Santa Barbara, CA: Wallace Hebberd, 1970.

———. *Popular Tribunals,* vol. 1. San Francisco: The History Company, 1887.

Barnhart, Jacqueline Baker. *The Fair But Frail: Prostitution in San Francisco 1849–1900.* Reno, NV: University of Nevada Press, 1986.

Barry, T. A., and B. A. Patten. *Men and Memories of San Francisco in the "Spring of '50."* San Francisco: A. L. Bancroft & Co., 1873.

Barth, Gunther. *Instant Cities: Urbanization and the Rise of San Francisco and Denver.* Albuquerque: University of New Mexico Press, 1988.

Bartlett, Irving H. *The American Mind in the Mid-Nineteenth Century.* New York: Thomas Y. Crowell, 1967.

Bash, Col. L. H. Manuscript. Notes on the Life of Brevet Major General Persifor Frazer Smith, U.S.A. Compiled from Official Reports, etc. by Colonel Bash at Fort Mason, San Francisco, August 25, 1927. (California State Library.)

Bastian, Beverly E. "I Heartily Regret That I Ever Touched a Title in California: Henry Wager Halleck, The *Californios,* and the Clash of Legal Cultures." *California History,* Winter 1993/94, pp. 310–21.

Baur, John E. "The Health Factor in the Gold Rush Era." *Pacific Historical Review,* February 1949, pp. 97–108.

Berry, Thomas Senior. "Gold! But How Much?" *California Historical Society Quarterly,* Fall 1976, pp. 247–55.

Blair, William Alan, ed. *A Politician Goes to War: The Civil War Letters of John White Geary.* University Park, PA: Penn State University Press, 1995.

Blaisdell, William F., and Moses Grossman. *Catastrophes, epidemics, and neglected disasters: San Francisco General Hospital and the evolution of public care.* San Francisco: San Francisco General Hospital Foundation, 1999.

Blodgett, Peter J. *Land of Golden Dreams: California in the Gold Rush Decade, 1848–1858*. San Marino, CA: Huntington Library, 1999.

Boden, Charles P. "San Francisco's Cisterns." *California Historical Society Quarterly*, December 1936, pp. 311–23.

Brands, H. W. *The Age of Gold: The California Gold Rush and the New American Dream*. New York: Doubleday, 2002.

Brooks, B. S. "Alcalde Grants in the City of San Francisco." *The Pioneer*, March 1854, pp. 129–44.

Burns, Thomas P. "The History of a Montgomery Street Lot in Yerba Buena From November 4, 1837 to June 15, 1850." *California Historical Society Quarterly*, March 1932, pp. 69–72.

Cartwright, David T. "Violence in America: What Human Nature and the California Gold Rush Tell Us about Crime in the Inner City." *American Heritage*, September 1996, pp. 36–51.

Chan, Sucheng. "A People of Exceptional Character: Ethnic Diversity, Nativism, and Racism in the California Gold Rush." *California History*, Summer 2000, pp. 44–85.

Chandler, Robert J. "Gold as a Cumbersome, Curmudgeonly Commodity, 1849–1870." *The Argonaut* (Journal of the San Francisco Museum and Historical Society), Winter 2002, pp. 28–69.

Cornford, Daniel. "We all live more like brutes than humans: Labor and Capital in the Gold Rush." *California History*, Winter 1998/99, pp. 78–104.

Cowan, Robert Ernest. "The Leidesdorff-Folsom Estate: A Forgotten Chapter in the Romantic History of Early San Francisco." *California Historical Society Quarterly*, June 1928, pp. 105–11.

Cross, Ira B. *Early Inns of California, 1844–1869*. San Francisco: Cross and Brandt, 1954.

———. *Financing an Empire: History of Banking in California*. vol. 1. San Francisco: S. J. Clarke Publishing Co., 1927.

Daniels, Douglas Henry. *Pioneer Urbanites: A Social and Cultural History of Black San Francisco*. Berkeley, CA: University of California Press, 1990.

DeArment, Robert K. *Knights of the Green Cloth: The Saga of Frontier Gamblers.* Norman, OK: University of Oklahoma Press, 1982.

Deitcher, David. *Dear Friends: American Photographs of Men Together, 1840–1918.* New York: Harry N. Abrams, 2001.

Delgado, James P. "Gold Rush Jail: The Prison Ship Euphemia." *California History,* Summer 1981, pp. 134–41.

Dow, Gerald Robert. "Bay Fill in San Francisco: A History of Change." Master's thesis, California State University, San Francisco, 1973.

Dobie, Charles Caldwell. *San Francisco's Chinatown.* New York: D. Appleton-Century Co., 1936.

Dressler, Albert, ed. *California's Pioneer Circus: Memoirs and Personal Correspondence of Joseph Andrew Rowe.* San Francisco: H. S. Crocker, Printers, 1926.

Drury, Clifford M. "John W. Geary and his Brother Edward." *California Historical Society Quarterly,* March 1941, pp. 12–25.

Editors of Time-Life Books. *The Gamblers.* Alexandria, VA: Time-Life Books, 1980.

Eldridge, Zoeth. *The Beginnings of San Francisco,* vol. 2, 1774–1850. San Francisco: Zoeth S. Eldridge, 1912.

Ellison, Joseph. "The Struggle for Civil Government in California, 1846–1850." *California Historical Society Quarterly,* March and June 1931, pp. 3–26, 129–64.

Ferrier, William W. *Ninety Years of Education in California, 1846–1936.* Berkeley, CA: Sather Gate Book Shop, 1937.

Foreman, Grant. *The Adventures of James Collier, First Collector of the Port of San Francisco.* Chicago: Black Cat Press, 1937.

Fracchia, Charles A. "Gold Dust and Banking: Banking in Gold Rush San Francisco." *The Argonaut* (Journal of the San Francisco Museum and Historical Society), Winter 2002, pp. 4–26.

Franklin, William E. "Peter H. Burnett and the Provisional Government Movement." *California Historical Society Quarterly*, June 1961, pp. 122–36.

Fritzsche, Bruno. "San Francisco 1846–1848: The Coming of the Real Estate Speculator." *California Historical Society Quarterly*, Spring 1972, pp. 17–34.

Gardner, Frances Tomlinson. "The Gold Rush and a Hospital." *Reprints From Medical Journals*, pp. 371–88. Reprinted from *The Bulletin of the History of Medicine*, April 1942.

————. "John Townsend—The Peripatetic Pioneer." *Reprints From Medical Journals*, pp. 1–14. Reprinted from *California and Western Medicine*, September 1939.

Gates, Paul W. "Carpetbaggers Join the Rush for California Land." *California History*, Summer 1977, pp. 98–127.

Geary, Paul McClellan. *Colonel John W. Geary in the Mexican War and California in '49*. Pacifica, CA: Shade Tree Press, 2000.

Gentry, Curt. *The Madams of San Francisco: A hundred years of the city's secret history*. 1964. Reprint. Sausalito, CA: Comstock Editions, 1977

Giffen, Guy. *California Expedition: Stevenson's Regiment of New York Volunteers*. Oakland, CA: Biobooks, 1951.

Grivas, Theodore. *Military Governments in California, 1846–1850*. Glendale, CA: Arthur H. Clark Co., 1963.

Grivas, Theodore. "Alcalde Rule: The Nature of Local Governments in Spanish and Mexican California." *California Historical Society Quarterly*, March 1961, pp. 11–32.

Groh, George W. *Gold Fever: Being a True Account, Both Horrifying and Hilarious, of the Art of Healing (so-called) During the California Gold Rush!* New York: William Morrow & Co., 1966.

Gudde, Erwin G. "Mutiny on the Ewing." *California Historical Society Quarterly*, March 1981, pp. 39–47.

Hansen, Gladys, comp. *Behind the Silver Star: An Account of the San Francisco Police Department*. San Francisco: Archives Publication No. 3, San Francisco Archives, Main Library, 1981.

Hansen, Woodrow James. *The Search for Authority in California*. Oakland, CA: Biobooks, 1960.

Hendrick, Irving G. *The Education of Non-Whites in California, 1849–1870*. San Francisco: R & E Research Associates, 1977.

―――. "From Indifference to Imperative Duty: Educating Children in Early California." *California History*, Summer 2000, pp. 226–49.

Hittell, John S. *A History of San Francisco and Incidentally of the State of California*. 1878. Reprint. Berkeley, CA: Berkeley Hills Books, 2000.

Hittell, Theodore. *History of California*, vols. 2 and 3. San Francisco: N. J. Stone & Co., 1897.

Holliday, J. S. *Rush for Riches: Gold Fever and the Making of California*. Berkeley, CA: University of California Press, 1999.

―――. *The World Rushed In: The California Gold Rush Experience; An Eyewitness Account of a Nation Heading West*. New York: Simon & Schuster, 1981.

Howe, Octavius Thorndike. *Argonauts of '49: History and Adventures of the Emigrant Companies from Massachusetts, 1849–1850*. Cambridge, MA: Harvard University Press, 1923.

Hubbard, Anita Day. "Water One Dollar the Pailfull." *San Francisco Bulletin Magazine*, December 4, 1924, p. 3.

Hunt, Rockwell D. *California's Stately Hall of Fame*. Stockton, CA: College of the Pacific, 1950.

Hurst, James Willard. *A Legal History of Money in the U. S., 1774–1970*. Lincoln, NE: University of Nebraska Press, 1973.

Hurtado, Albert L. *Indian Survival on the California Frontier*. New Haven, CT: Yale University Press, 1988.

―――. "Sex, Gender, Culture, and a Great Event: The California Gold Rush." *Pacific Historical Review*, February 1999, pp. 1–19.

Ignoffo, Mary Jo. *Gold Rush Politics: California's First Legislature*. Sacramento, CA: California State Senate and California History Center and Foundation, and Cupertino, CA: De Anza College, 1999.

Jackson, Donald Dale. *Gold Dust*. 1980. Reprint. Lincoln, NE: University of Nebraska Press, 1982.

Jellinek, Lawrence James. "'Property of Every Kind': Ranching and Farming during the Gold-Rush Era." *California History*, Winter 1998/99, pp. 233–49.

Johnson, David A. "Vigilance and the Law: The Moral Authority of Popular Justice in the Far West." *American Quarterly*, 1981, 33 (5): pp. 558–86.

Johnson, Kenneth M. "The Judges Colton." *Southern California Quarterly*, Winter 1975, 57 (4): pp. 349–60.

Johnson, Susan Lee. "Bulls, Bears, and Dancing Boys: Race, Gender, and Leisure in the California Gold Rush." *Radical History Review*, Fall 1994, pp. 4–37.

Johnson, William Weber. *The Forty-Niners*. New York: Time-Life Books, 1976.

Kagin, Donald H. *Private Gold Coins and Patterns of the U. S.* New York: Arco Publishing, Inc., 1981.

Kazin, Alfred. "Fear of the City." *A Sense of History: The Best Writing from the Pages of American Heritage*. New York: Smithmark Publishers, 1996, pp. 351–60.

Kemble, John Haskell. "The 'Senator': The Biography of a Pioneer Steamship." *California Historical Society Quarterly*, March 1937, pp. 61–78.

Kent, George F. "Life in California." *California Historical Society Quarterly*, March 1941, pp. 26–46.

Kirk, Anthony. "'As jolly as a clam at high water': The Rise of Art in Gold Rush California." *California History*, Summer 2000, pp. 169–203.

Knowles, Barton Harvey. "The Early History of San Francisco's Water Supply, 1776–1858." Master's thesis, U. C. Berkeley, 1948.

Kooiman, William. "*S.S. California:* First Steamer Through the Golden Gate." *Sea Classics,* September 1990, pp. 18-21.

Kowaleski, Michael. "Romancing the Gold Rush: The Literature of the California Frontier." *California History,* Summer 2000, pp. 204–25.

Kurutz, Gary F. *The California Gold Rush: A Descriptive Bibliography of Books and Pamphlets Covering the Years 1848–1853.* San Francisco: The Book Club of California, 1997.

———. "Popular Culture on the Golden Shore." *California History,* Summer 2000, pp. 280–315.

Lapp, Rudolph M. *Blacks in Gold Rush California.* New Haven, CT: Yale University Press, 1977.

Leonard, J. P. "Medical Observations of J. P. Leonard, M.D." *California Historical Society Quarterly,* September 1950, pp. 213–16.

Levy, JoAnn. *They Saw the Elephant: Women in the California Gold Rush.* Norman, OK: University of Oklahoma Press, 1992.

———. *Unsettling the West: Eliza Farnham and Georgiana Bruce Kirby.* Santa Clara, CA: Santa Clara University, and Berkeley, CA: Heyday Books, 2004.

Lockwood, Charles. *Suddenly San Francisco: The Early Years of an Instant City.* San Francisco: San Francisco Examiner Special Projects, 1978.

———. "Tourists in Gold Rush San Francisco." *California History,* Winter 1980, pp. 314–33.

Lorenz, Anthony. "Scurvy in the Gold Rush." *Journal of the History of Medicine,* October 1957, pp. 473–510.

Lotchin, Roger W. *San Francisco 1846–1856: From Hamlet to City.* 1974. Reprint. Lincoln, NE: University of Nebraska Press, 1979.

Luckingham, Bradford. "Religion in Early San Francisco." *Pacific Historian,* Winter 1973, pp. 56–74.

Lyman, Edward Lee. "The Beginnings of Anglo-American Local Government in California." *California History,* vol. 81, No. ¾, 2003, pp. 199–223.

Lyman, George D. "The Scalpel Under Three Flags." *California Historical Society Quarterly*, June 1925, pp. 142–206.

———. "Victor H. Fourgeaud, M.D." *California Historical Society Quarterly*, June 1932, pp. 138–49.

Mawn, Geoffrey P. "Framework for Destiny: San Francisco, 1847." *California Historical Society Quarterly*, Summer 1972, pp. 165–72.

McCutcheon, Mark. *Everyday Life in the 1800s: A Guide for Writer's, Students and Historians*. Cincinnati: Writer's Digest Books, 1993.

Melendy, H. Brett and Benjamin F. Gilbert. *The Governors of California: Peter H. Burnett to Edmund G. Brown*. Georgetown, CA: The Talisman Press, 1965.

Monaghan, Jay. *Australians and the Gold Rush: California and Down Under, 1849–1854*. Berkeley, CA: University of California Press, 1966.

———. *Chile, Peru and the California Gold Rush of 1849*. Berkeley, CA: University of California Press, 1973.

Moore, Shirley Ann Wilson. "We Feel the Want of Protection: The Politics of Law and Race in California, 1848–1878." *California History*, No. ¾, 2003, pp. 96–125.

Morefield, Richard Henry. "Mexicans in the California Mines, 1848–1853." *California Historical Society Quarterly*, March 1956, pp. 37–46.

Moses, Bernard. *The Establishment of Municipal Government in San Francisco*. Baltimore: Johns Hopkins University Press, 1889.

Mullen, Kevin J. "Founding the San Francisco Police Department." *The Pacific Historian*, Fall 1983, pp. 36–49.

———. *Let Justice Be Done: Crime and Politics in Early San Francisco*. Reno, NV: University of Nevada Press, 1989.

———. "Malachi Fallon: San Francisco's First Chief of Police." *California History*, Summer 1983, pp. 100–105.

Mumford, Lewis. *The City in History: Its Origins, Its Transformations, And Its Prospects*. New York: Harcourt, Brace & World, Inc., 1961.

Muscatine, Doris. *Old San Francisco: The Biography of a City From the Old Days to the Earthquake.* New York: G. P. Putnam & Sons, 1975.

Neasham, Aubrey. *California Gold Discovery: Centennial Papers on the Time, The Site and Artifacts.* San Francisco: California Historical Society, 1947.

Nussbaum, Arthur. *A History of the Dollar.* New York: Columbia University Press, 1957.

Palmquist, Peter E., ed. *The Daguerreian Annual: Official Yearbook of the Daguerreian Society.* Eureka, CA: Eureka Printing Co., 1990.

Paul, Rodman. *The California Gold Discovery: Sources, Documents, Accounts and Memoirs Relating to the Discovery of Gold at Sutter's Mill.* Georgetown, CA: The Talisman Press, 1966.

Peterson, Charles E. "Prefabs in the California Gold Rush, 1849." *Journal of the Society of Architectural Historians,* December 1965, pp. 318–23.

Phelps, Robert. "'All hands have gone downtown': Urban Places in Gold Rush California." *California History,* Summer 2000, pp. 113–40.

Phillips, Catherine Coffin. *Portsmouth Plaza: The Cradle of San Francisco.* San Francisco: John Henry Nash, 1932.

Pitt, Leonard. "The Beginnings of Nativism in California." *Pacific Historical Review,* February 1961, pp. 23–38.

Rawls, James J. "Gold Diggers: California Indians in the Gold Rush." *California Historical Society Quarterly,* Spring 1976, pp. 28–45.

———. "A Golden State: An Introduction." *California History,* Winter 1998/99, pp. 1–23.

Richards, Leonard L. *The California Gold Rush and the Coming of the Civil War.* New York: Alfred A. Knopf, 2007.

Rochlin, Fred and Harriet. *Pioneer Jews: A New Life in the Far West.* Boston: Houghton Mifflin, 1984.

Pomeroy, Earl S. "The Trial of the Hounds, 1849: A Witness's Account." *California Historical Society Quarterly,* June 1950, pp. 161–65.

Rohrbough, Malcolm J. *Days of Gold: The California Gold Rush and the American Nation.* Berkeley, CA: University of California Press, 1997.

———. "The California Gold Rush as a National Experience." *California History*, Spring 1998, pp. 16–29.

———. "No Boy's Play: Migration and Settlement in Early Gold Rush California." *California History*, Summer 2000, pp. 25–43.

Royce, Josiah. *California From the Conquest in 1846 to the Second Vigilance Committee in San Francisco: A Study of American Character.* 1886. Reprint. New York: Alfred A. Knopf, 1948.

Rozwenc, Edwin C., ed. *The Meaning of Jacksonian Democracy.* Boston: D. C. Heath & Co., 1963.

Sandos, James A. "Because he is a liar and a thief: Conquering the Residents of 'Old' California, 1850–1880." *California History*, Summer 2000, pp. 86–112.

Schultz, Charles R. "Methodists to the California Gold Fields In 1849." *The American Neptune*, April-June 2000, pp. 149–68.

Schweikart, Larry and Lynne Pierson Doti. "From Hard Money to Branch Banking: California Banking in the Gold Rush Economy." *California History*, Winter 1998/99, pp. 209–32.

Soulé, Frank, John Gihon and James Nisbet. *The Annals of San Francisco.* 1855. Reprint. Berkeley, CA: Berkeley Hills Books, 1998.

Starr, Kevin. *Americans and the California Dream, 1850–1915.* New York: Oxford University Press, 1973.

———. "The Gold Rush and the California Dream." *California History*, Spring 1998, pp. 57–67.

———. "Rooted in Barbarous Soil: An Introduction to Gold Rush Society and Culture." *California History*, Summer 2000, pp. 1–24.

Storer, Tracy I. and Lloyd P. Tevis, Jr. *California Grizzly.* Berkeley, CA: University of California Press, 1996.

Sullivan, G. W. *Early Days in California: The Growth of the Commonwealth Under American Rule, With Biographical Sketches of the Pioneers.* San Francisco: Enterprise Publishing Co., 1888.

Swasey, W. F. *The Early Days of Men of California.* Oakland, CA: Pacific Press Publishing Co., 1891.

Tinkcom, Harry Martin. *John White Geary, soldier-statesman, 1819–1873.* Philadelphia: University of Pennsylvania Press, 1940.

Tong, Benson. *Unsubmissive Women: Chinese Prostitutes in Nineteenth Century San Francisco.* Norman, OK: University of Oklahoma Press, 1994.

Trafzer, Clifford E. *California's Indians and the Gold Rush.* Sacramento, CA: Sierra Oaks Publishing, 1989.

Van Sicklen, Helen Putnam. "Jasper O'Farrell: His Survey of San Francisco." *Quarterly of the Society of California Pioneers,* vol. 10, 1933, pp. 5–100.

Watson, Douglas S. "The Flea in California History and Literature." *California Historical Society Quarterly,* December 1936, pp. 329–37.

———. "The San Francisco McAllisters." *California Historical Society Quarterly,* June 1932, pp. 124–28.

Wiltsee, Ernest A. *Gold Rush Steamers of the Pacific.* San Francisco: The Grabhorn Press, 1938.

Wright, Doris Marion. "The Making of Cosmopolitan California." *California Historical Society Quarterly,* December 1940, pp. 323–43.

Wright, Flora Alice. "Governor Richard B. Mason and the Civil Fund." *Quarterly of the Society of California Pioneers,* December 1929, pp. 187–206.

———. "Richard Barnes Mason, Governor of California." Master's thesis, U. C. Berkeley, 1919.

Index

N.B.: Numbers in parentheses, e.g. (30n), are Endnote numbers. The numbers preceding them are the pages in the text where they can be found.